MW00719162

Introduction to Financial Products

2nd Edition

Dearborn
Financial Services
A **Kaplan Professional** Company

This publication is designed to provide accurate and authoritative information in regard to the subject matter covered. It is sold with the understanding that the publisher is not engaged in rendering legal, accounting or other professional service. If legal advice or other expert assistance is required, the services of a competent professional person should be sought.

This text is updated periodically to reflect changes in laws and regulations. To verify that you have the most recent update, you may call Dearborn at 1-800-423-4723.

©1994, 2000, 2001 by Dearborn Financial Publishing, Inc.®
Published by Dearborn Financial Institute, Inc.®

All rights reserved. The text of this publication, or any part thereof, may not be reproduced in any manner whatsoever without written permission from the publisher.

Printed in the United States of America.

Second printing, September 2002

Library of Congress Cataloging-in-Publication Data

Introduction to financial products / Dearborn Financial Publishing.
    p. cm.
    ISBN 0–7931–3819-1 (alk. paper)
    1. Investments.   2. Financial instruments.   I. Dearborn Financial Publishing.

HG4521 .I3855 2000
332.63—dc21   99-088410

..... Table of Contents

..... Acknowledgments

T he publisher wishes to acknowledge the efforts of the following individuals for their perceptive reviews, comments and suggestions, which were invaluable in the development and revision of this text:

Ron Atkins, Continuing Education Instructor
The Institute of Financial Education

William F. Doy, FICF, CLU, ChFC, Manager of Field Education
Modern Woodmen of America

William H. Hewitt, Regional Marketing Director
Nationwide

Philip B. Rosen, CIC, Vice President
Insurance Service Center, Inc.

Terry Simmons, LUTCF, FIC, Field Development Consultant
Aid Association of Lutherans

••••• Introduction

W elcome to *Introduction to Financial Products*. This course is for anyone who wants to know more about financial resources and financial planning—whether for personal or professional reasons. For example, it will give an individual a better understanding of various financial resources, as well as how to evaluate and manage them, so that he or she can do a better job of investing and handling his or her own financial affairs.

Introduction to Financial Products is also for life insurance professionals who:

- want to know how to evaluate a moderate to very wealthy client's financial resources, objectives and risk tolerance;

- are considering expanding their product lines;

- want to discuss investment and savings vehicles intelligently—even those vehicles that may compete for their sales or service dollars; or

- want to help clients reach their financial objectives.

This course surveys a broad range of basic information and concepts that you may apply as appropriate in specific client situations. Its purpose is not to create expertise in the uses of specific investments. *Introduction to Financial Products* is designed to help you attain a sound, thorough understanding of each of the contemporary financial resources employed by individuals to accumulate, conserve or distribute their wealth. Those objectives pertain to people's needs and desires to save or invest successfully, to build estates, to reduce or defer taxes, to avoid financial losses and so on. Client objectives also may include the desire to experience the challenges and thrills of great risks or sheer speculation.

One of the beneficial by-products of this course is the breadth you will acquire as a business and professional person. The information in this course provides ways to measure an investment's potential risk and rewards, as well as its advantages and disadvantages. As a current or potential investor, you will become more knowledgeable about the investments open to you.

Although *Introduction to Financial Products* will provide you with a broad spectrum of information, this course (or any other) *alone* cannot make you a financial planner. It will give you a working knowledge of financial products. It will not instruct you on how to do anything in the way of making specific application of the information and concepts provided. At a minimum, as a financial planner you would be expected to have completed advanced studies in the areas of estate, business and pension planning. If you are interested in becoming a certified financial planner, several organizations and associations grant credentials that signify a financial planner's level of education, including the *Certified Financial Planner (CFP)* and *Chartered Financial Consultant (ChFC)* designations.

It is our sincere hope that you will enjoy your study of *Introduction to Financial Products* and that, because of that study, you will grow both personally and professionally.

Bob Redman
Editor

1
The Role of Investments

T here are many types of financial resources available to individuals wishing to satisfy any financial objective. These financial resources range from simple savings accounts to highly sophisticated investments—and vary substantially in nature, characteristics, utility, return, risk, liquidity, distribution alternatives, tax treatment, legal complexities, government regulation and so on. Because of these variations, one product frequently can do a more effective job than any other of satisfying an individual's specific objective, whereas other products may better serve in other situations.

Accordingly, as a financial professional, it is imperative that you have a sound understanding not only of the available financial resources but also of how to evaluate those resources in terms of their ability to satisfy the specific financial objectives of your clients. These objectives usually involve the accumulation, conservation and distribution of wealth. In everyday language, those objectives pertain to people's needs and desires—to save or invest successfully; to build estates; to reduce or defer taxes; to avoid financial losses; to be able to obtain or distribute earnings or principal when and to whom desired; and so on. Client objectives also may include the desire to experience the challenges of great risks or speculation in some investments.

In this first chapter, we set the stage for what follows in this text. We begin by looking at basic concepts of investment, investment objectives and net worth. A discussion of the investment process leads to possible effects on investments of the government's fiscal and monetary policies, inflation, spending and the business cycle. We list the steps involved in evaluating whether a particular financial resource is appropriate for an individual and, finally, we outline your role as a financial professional.

■ ■ ■ ■ ■

■ THE CONCEPT OF INVESTMENT

As a financial professional, you know that money does more than just buy the goods and services people need and want. It influences how individuals feel about themselves and other people. It has a great deal to do with a person's standard of living and his or her ambitions for the future. The ability to manage money and to invest it wisely has an immense bearing on the degree of satisfaction a person will gain from life.

Many people have problems managing money effectively. Some people have great difficulty getting along on what they earn, even though they earn enough to provide a good standard of living. These individuals have never considered what they most want in life and how best to achieve it, so they're inclined to spend on impulse. Others, with the same income or even less, live well all their lives. They are the ones who, with careful planning, have learned how to make their dollars work for them by *investing*.

In the past, individuals who put money into passbook accounts and government savings bonds were considered *savers* and those who purchased stocks, bonds and mutual funds were considered *investors*. Saving was considered risk free; investing was regarded as speculative. However, with today's variety of financial products and competitive interest rates, such clear distinctions between savers and investors are beginning to fade. In fact, the terms "saving" and "investing" can be used almost interchangeably.

An *investment* is any vehicle into which funds can be placed with the expectation that they will increase in value and/or generate some return, with preservation of the funds as a secondary objective. Cash stored in a mattress is not an investment, since it fails to earn any interest and its value will be eroded by inflation. The same cash in a savings account, however, becomes an investment because it is earning interest.

Most investments yield some sort of cash flow or return on investment. The *return on investment* is defined as the pretax profit on an investment, expressed as an annual percentage of the investor's original capital. For example, if a $1,000 investment earned $100 over a period of one year, its return is 10 percent. There is a *trade-off* between the return an investor can expect on an investment and the amount of risk or illiquidity he or she must accept to earn that return. To reap larger returns, the investor must take larger risks or give up short-term access to his or her original principal. Briefly, *risk* is the potential that actual returns could differ from those expected or that principal could be lost. In general, the greater the variation in actual returns versus expected returns, the greater the investment's risk. Conversely, the smaller the range, the smaller the risk. Therefore, low-risk investments usually mean lower expected returns and high-risk investments have the potential for much higher returns. We'll discuss risk and return in more detail in Chapter 2, but for now, keep in mind that such trade-offs are part of the investment process.

Investor's Objectives

The key to successful investing is to understand why one is investing, so whether individuals are looking for long-term capital growth or immediate cash flow, they must begin by defining their investment objectives and planning how to reach them. These objectives typically include both short-term and long-term financial goals. Short-term goals might include paying off a small debt or saving for a vacation; long-term goals might include buying a home or saving for retirement.

To achieve their goals, investors tend to divide their investment dollars among various investment options that can provide one or more of the following four results:

1. *Long-term capital growth*—for investors seeking capital appreciation over a period of time to provide funds at some future date for retirement, educational expenses, a higher standard of living or the purchase of a home;

2. *Income*—for those looking for immediate cash flow with emphasis on safety of principal and liquidity should the funds be needed on short notice;

3. *Short-term profits*—for speculators willing to take above-average risks to obtain a high return in the shortest time possible; and/or

4. *Tax savings*—for investors looking for tax-free income, a shelter to ease their current tax burden or tax-deferred capital appreciation.

The investor's objectives, available funds and risk tolerance should determine which investments are selected. For example, young investors should be concerned with saving for a house, providing a college fund for their children and building an estate. Any investment plan for this group should begin with traditional life insurance products, such as whole life, which offers a safe investment with a guaranteed return. Another financial product well-suited to this group's current and future financial needs is an annuity. Its somewhat compulsory savings features and the lifetime guarantee of benefits are appealing. Young investors may also be interested in purchasing mutual funds—an investment alternative available to individuals who pool their money to buy stocks, bonds and other securities based on the expertise of professional money managers who work for an investment company. Finally, these investors may be willing to take some investment risk in the form of stocks, bonds and real estate investments to generate larger returns to fund their long-term goals.

Although mature consumers may have the means to purchase many financial products to supplement personal income, those close to retirement are often conservative and risk averse. It's likely that their goal will be to *preserve* the money they have and to make it grow and last throughout their retirement years by investing. Safety of principal will probably be very important to them. In addition, near-retirees and retired persons on fixed incomes are especially affected by *inflation*, a general rise in prices, because their financial resources are limited. Thus, each year as inflation rises, a larger percentage of their income is spent for necessities such as food, shelter and medical care. Although Social Security and some employer-sponsored retirement plans make periodic adjustments to retirement and other benefits based on changes in the *Consumer Price Index (CPI)*, inflation can quickly erode a retiree's *purchasing power*—the amount of goods or services that can be bought with a given amount of currency, such as one dollar.

Although life insurance remains important to the mature consumer, intergenerational wealth protection may become a higher priority, replacing dependent income needs as the primary reason for acquiring and maintaining life insurance. Consumers may also choose from a wide variety of what are perceived to be low-risk investments—savings accounts, certificates of deposit (CDs), money-market accounts and annuities—and moderate-risk investments—stocks, bonds and mutual funds. Speculative investments—commodities, precious metals and collectibles—are usually not recommended for retirement planning. In later chapters, we'll look at each of these investment options in more detail.

ILL. 1.1 ■ *Achieving Financial Goals*

People must take charge of their own financial security if they hope to have financial independence at any stage of life. To achieve their financial goals, investors should:

- establish an emergency fund;
- set short-term goals (for the next few months or within one year);
- set middle-range goals (for the next two to five years); and
- set long-term goals (for longer than five years).

Age Group: 20s and 30s—Building Wealth

- Establish and maintain good credit
- Begin a savings program
- Buy life, health and disability insurance
- Invest in growth-oriented financial products (growth stocks, recession-resistant companies with steadily increasing earnings, AAA-rated bonds, mutual funds)
- Establish a plan for retirement

Age Group: 40s and 50s—Increasing Wealth

- Make a will or establish a trust
- Make ongoing contributions to retirement plans
- If a home is not owned already, invest in real estate for a tax deduction on interest and property tax payments
- Invest in tax-free municipal bonds, growth stocks, tax-deferred annuities, real estate

Age Group: 60 and Beyond—Preserving Wealth

- Review and understand retirement plan
- Shift some growth investments into income-producing investments, such as high-yielding common stock, tax-free municipal bonds and Treasury securities

Source: Judy Lawrence, *The Budget Kit: The Common Cent$ Money Management Workbook*, Dearborn Financial Publishing, Inc.

Making a Wise Investment Decision

Some financial objectives are conflicting. For example, the individual who wants to maximize safety of principal with a higher-than-average current yield will have a hard time finding a suitable investment. Such conflicts may be impossible to resolve fully and, in these cases, good financial management requires making trade-offs to satisfy the individual's priorities.

Then, too, there will be uncertainties as to what the future holds with respect to the individual's own objectives and needs, as well as the future economy and the future performance of various financial products. Here, sound financial management calls for selecting products that provide the flexibility required to make needed or desired adjustments or changes in the future, while satisfying current objectives to the maximum extent possible.

Moreover, careful consideration should be given to the *opportunity costs* of each selection—that is, what other assets and opportunities (including all they have to offer) must be given up to acquire each asset selected.

Suggested Evaluation Procedure

It is important to note that financial products do not operate in isolation. A single product may not meet an investor's overall objectives, but a *portfolio* of two or more products working together may be the answer. In essence, there is no "perfect" product, but an investor may build a customized portfolio of a variety of products that, when combined, meet his or her safety, liquidity, income, short-term income and long-term growth needs.

Here is the basic outline of an effective four-step evaluation procedure that your prospects or clients might use to answer the question, "Should I own this particular financial resource?" Using this outline and answering this question can help your prospects or clients decide whether a financial product should be purchased, held or sold.

1. *Clearly establish the individual's financial objectives and overall portfolio priorities.* The vital first step in evaluating a financial product is determining exactly what the person wants to accomplish with that product.

2. *Carefully and critically examine the particular financial product being considered in terms of its ability to satisfy the specific objectives established in Step 1.* Throughout this text, you will find guidelines that clients might use for developing a portfolio that consists of investments that can produce capital growth, income or short-term profits.

3. *Compare the ability of this financial product with that of other financial products to satisfy the objectives in Step 1.* Risk is inherent in almost all investments so the same consideration indicated in Step 2 must be given to every product being compared.

4. *Evaluate the financial product as an investment or as an estate asset to satisfy the objectives of this individual only, based on the results of Steps 2 and 3.* From a practical standpoint, keep in mind that the expected satisfactions should always be in line with acceptable cost and risk, as well as with the particular circumstances and temperament of the individual.

Use of the four-step evaluation procedure, combined with the understanding of financial resources and analysis that the remaining chapters of this course provide, should prove helpful to individuals in making the right decisions whenever a question arises as to the advisability of buying, holding or disposing of a particular financial product.

■ BASIC CONCEPTS OF WEALTH

As stated earlier, the investment process involves making a trade-off between expected returns and the risk of not achieving those returns or not having funds available when needed. In a broader sense, the investment process is concerned with preserving and increasing purchasing power and wealth. What is *wealth*? This commonly used term can mean many things to many people. For the purposes of this course, *wealth* is whatever constitutes a valuable and exchangeable resource in the mind of an individual—whatever is included in that person's concept of wealth.

How does one determine an individual's wealth or net worth? It's a good practice to begin by looking at a person's personal *balance sheet*—a financial statement that provides a picture of a person's assets, liabilities and net worth as of a particular date. The difference between a person's assets (what is *owned*) and liabilities (what is *owed*) is his or her *net worth* or *wealth*. Let's briefly look at the three components of the balance sheet: assets, liabilities and net worth.

Personal Assets

Assets may be defined as the entire property (of all sorts) of a person, association, corporation or estate applicable or subject to the payment of his, her or its debts. Since this course pertains solely to individuals, the discussion here will be limited to the kinds of property (assets) commonly owned by individuals—that is, to *personal assets*. Such assets fall into three major categories: (1) cash and cash equivalents, (2) tangibles and (3) intangibles.

Cash and Cash Equivalents

This category of personal assets includes money and any assets that can be used as money or that can be almost instantly converted to money. Checking and NOW accounts, traveler's checks, money orders, certified and cashier's checks, bank passbook savings accounts, credit union savings accounts and daily cash money-market drafts are all examples of cash equivalents.

Tangible Assets

Tangible assets are possessions that have physical substance and are themselves objects of value, such as real estate; oil, meat, grain and other commodities; gold, silver and other precious metals; and gems, works of art and other collectibles.

Intangible Assets

Intangible assets are possessions that represent ownership of (or ownership interests in) things of value, but have little, if any, intrinsic value themselves. They include such assets as stocks, bonds, Treasury bills, CDs, mortgages, mutual fund shares, real estate investment trust (REIT) shares, money-market fund shares, patents, copyrights and life insurance and annuity contracts.

Liabilities

An individual's *liabilities* are simply his or her debts and other financial obligations. They include such payable or repayable items as personal or commercial loans, mortgage loans, financed-purchase loans, home improvement loans, taxes due, legal judgments and so on.

People often feel they are morally obligated to provide financially for the education of their children or the medical care of elderly parents, if needy. But as important as such moral obligations may be to an individual, they are not liabilities in the legal sense unless the individual is legally obligated to pay them.

Current Liabilities

Any debt that must be paid within one year is called a *current liability*. There are two sources of current liabilities: unpaid bills (rent, utility bills and so on) and portions of installment loans (car payments, home equity loans and so on) that are due within one year.

Long-Term Liabilities

All debt obligations that are due beyond one year are called *long-term liabilities*. There are two types of long-term liabilities. The first type represents the noncurrent portion of installment loans on automobiles, furniture, major appliances or credit card balances. These debts have specific schedules for repayment. The second type of long-term liability consists of loans that do not have a repayment schedule, such as a loan on a life insurance policy.

Net Worth

The *net worth* of any owner of financial resources is the value of the owner's total *assets* (everything owned) *less* the value of the owner's total *liabilities* (everything owed). Knowing one's net worth is important for a number of reasons other than the personal satisfaction (or dissatisfaction) of knowing one's current financial status. For example, it is a major factor in a person's current or potential buying power; in the availability of credit to the individual, as well as the amount available and the rate charged; in the person's investment earning power; in the analysis and planning of the individual's estate; and so forth.

Net worth is the best measurement of a person's wealth, even though it may be difficult to put market values on some assets. Simple as that determination would seem from the above definition (net worth = assets – liabilities), there are some complexities, particularly in the evaluation of assets and liabilities.

Market Value Changes in Net Worth

The usual definition of *market value* is the price at which both buyers and sellers, dealing at arm's length, are willing to do business. This value is determined chiefly by (and tends to rise and fall with) supply and demand barring artificial controls (laws, taxes and so forth). Changes in net worth may occur when the market values that one owns at the beginning of a period increase or decrease during the period.

Solvency, Bankruptcy and Insolvency

Three additional terms, broadly used with reference to net worth, that should be mentioned here are *solvency, bankruptcy* and *insolvency.*

Solvency is the state of having sufficient assets to cover all legal liabilities. *Bankruptcy* is just the opposite—that is, the state of not having sufficient assets to cover all legal liabilities. Both terms are used in a general, nonlegal way to indicate whether more is owned than owed, or vice versa, with respect to either individuals or businesses.

These terms may also be used in a legal sense (e.g., individuals and businesses may be declared to be legally solvent or bankrupt). When a person or business is legally bankrupt, all assets are subject to being administered under the bankruptcy laws for the benefit of creditors. Those same laws do, however, provide some protection for the bankrupt.

Incidentally, it should be mentioned here that *insolvency,* as generally used, refers to the state of having too little liquidity (cash) to meet current debts or liabilities—not necessarily insufficient assets to cover them. Sometimes it is used erroneously to mean bankruptcy.

For example, assume a person has everything tied up in a nonliquid asset, such as developmental real estate valued at $1,000,000. Assume a note comes due for $10,000, but the person doesn't have enough cash or liquid assets to pay it. The person is *not bankrupt* in this situation because his or her assets exceed this liability 10 times over; but, because the assets cannot be converted immediately to cash sufficient to pay the note, the person is technically *insolvent.*

Long-term financial success is usually accomplished by achieving short-term goals. Budgets and financial statements can help individuals to determine their existing net worth so that they can plan effectively for the future. Careful financial planning also helps individuals manage future income, thereby increasing their net worth.

■ THE INVESTMENT PROCESS

What an individual perceives as spendable wealth is that which remains, in real purchasing power, after inflation and after what the federal, state, county and city governments take in taxes. As a financial professional, you can assist your prospects and clients in meeting their financial objectives. In general, this means increasing net income by accessing current assets, considering alternative and future investments and taking into account all forms of tax and current, as well as future, economic conditions.

The economic strength of the United States is partially the result of strong and efficient financial markets. In a broad sense, a *financial market* includes all financial transactions between those who have money to invest (suppliers of funds) and those who need money (demanders of funds). For example, when a person places funds in a bank savings account, he or she engages in a financial market transaction in the broadest meaning of the term. Most commonly, the term *financial intermediaries* refers to *financial institutions*—banks, savings banks, credit unions, insurance companies and pension funds—or *financial markets*—stock markets, bond markets and options markets—that bring suppliers and demanders of funds together to make transactions.

Suppliers and demanders of funds may be of two types—individuals or institutions. *Individual investors* usually place their additional funds in specific investment vehicles with the expectation of increasing their value and/or earning a positive return to provide current income or retirement income or to reach some other financial goals. Unlike individual investors, *institutional investors*, such as banks or insurance companies, tend to invest large sums to earn significant returns for their customers.

Flow of Funds Through the Economy

In the United States, the three key participants in the investment process are households, businesses and government. Each participant acts as both a supplier and demander of funds. As shown in Ill. 1.2, investment funds flow from one sector of the economy to another in an efficient and competitive manner. This flow of funds enables available capital from investors to be put to use by other sectors of the economy. Let's look more closely at how each of these participants supplies and uses funds.

Households

Households (individuals or families) are the major supplier of investment funds. Households receive wages from their employers (business) and/or *transfer payments* (such as direct welfare payments, food stamps, Social Security benefits and unemployment compensation) from government and usually save some portion of their income in financial intermediaries (commercial banks, savings banks, mutual savings banks and credit unions).

These various financial intermediaries, in turn, make *indirect investments* in the capital markets. *Capital markets*, a broad descriptive term for the institutions and financial instruments comprising intermediate and long-term funding, are competitive markets for equity securities or debt securities with maturities of more than one year. Common examples of capital market securities include common stocks, preferred stocks and bonds.

However, the economy cannot survive on long-term capital alone. Although an advantage of long-term capital is that it can be raised in large amounts at competitive rates, raising that capital is often a long, complex process. The U.S. economy requires a constant availability of short-term funds, both cash and credit. Households often purchase *money market instruments*, such as Treasury bills or commercial paper, forms of debt that mature in less than a year. Money market instruments are very liquid and provide ways for businesses, financial institutions and governments to meet their short-term obligations and cash requirements yet avoid the time and expense of SEC registration of securities (required for those with maturities of 270 days and greater).

ILL. 1.2 ■ *Flow of Funds Through the Economy*

Financial institutions—commercial banks, savings and loans, mutual savings banks and credit unions—act as intermediaries to help funds flow more efficiently from one sector of the economy to another. The use of intermediaries permits the best allocation of funds from suppliers to demanders at the lowest cost.

GOVERNMENT

Taxes

Taxes

Deficit

Wages, pensions and interest

Purchases of goods and services

Investment funds

BANK
$

Loans

Savings

INVESTMENT AND SAVING

Net savings

BUSINESS

HOUSEHOLDS

Wages, pensions, interest and dividends

Purchases of goods and services

In addition to placing funds in savings accounts and purchasing money market securities, households may purchase debt or equity instruments, buy insurance, participate in private pension plans or profit sharing and/or purchase various types of property. As stated earlier, households are the primary suppliers of investment funds, putting more funds into the investment process than any other group, so their role in providing the funds needed to supply economic growth is significant.

Businesses

Businesses provide funds to other businesses and government units, particularly the U.S. Treasury, through taxes. They also provide wages, pensions, interest and dividends to their employees. Typically, businesses invest their excess funds in safe, liquid investment vehicles that have short maturities, such as Treasury securities.

Businesses issue both debt and equity securities. *Debt securities*—bonds, notes, commercial paper and others—are issued when the business needs to borrow money. *Equity securities*—common and preferred stock of the business itself—are issued to provide investors partial ownership interest in the business. For example, if investors buy a company's bonds, they are its creditors; if they purchase its stock, they are part owners of the company.

Government

Various government units purchase goods and services from businesses and pay wages, pensions and interest to households. To continue their operations, all levels of government—federal, state and local—require vast quantities of funds.

Many government units issue *debt instruments*—Treasury bills, municipal bonds, government agency issues—to finance their operations. These instruments appeal to investors for various reasons. For example, Treasury issues are considered the safest of all investments and local government debt issues are free of federal income tax.

In summary, investing is necessary to the economy because it supplies funds required to finance the needs of government, business and individuals. If funds are not available, economic activity slows down. The rewards from investing—interest, dividends, increased net worth—provide an incentive to savers to provide funds to borrowers.

■ ECONOMIC CONDITIONS

Understanding fiscal and monetary policies, inflationary expectations, consumer and business spending and the state of the business cycle may help investors avoid some unprofitable moves. The stock market is the most closely watched investment market in the country and its cycles are closely related to underlying economic cycles. For example, an expanding economy causes sales to rise, inventory levels to decline, working hours to expand, income to increase and corporate profits and dividends to rise. In times of rising stock prices (*bull market*), many corporations see an opportunity to raise capital by selling part interest in their companies to the public in the form of stock. A weak economy, in contrast, generally affects the stock market (and business) adversely, and stock prices fall (*bear market*).

The general health of the economy is measured in many ways. Economists have developed *economic indicators*, key economic statistics that provide clues about the state of the future economy. Economic indicators come in three varieties: (1) leading economic indicators that anticipate a business cycle; (2) lagging indicators that follow changes in a business cycle; and (3) coincident indicators that run in step with the business cycle. Of these three, the most attention is paid to *leading economic indicators*.

Leading Economic Indicators

As shown in Ill. 1.3, there are 12 commonly used leading indicators that serve as a barometer of future economic activity. Data on these statistics are published quarterly by the Department of Commerce, and the trend of leading indicators is usually reported in the press. The leading indicators create an index, expressed in percentages, that includes a variety of factors, from stock prices to the average number of hours worked each week. The resulting percentage is measured against 100 percent, representing the calculation first made in 1967. For example, an index of 180 percent in June, 1994, means that particular index was 80 percent higher than the 1967 base. The higher the index, the more the economy has grown since 1967.

Consumer Price Index

Another measurement of the economy's health is the *Consumer Price Index (CPI)*, a price index that uses the prices of goods and services consumers generally buy to calculate the price level and the rate of inflation. To measure price changes, the *Bureau of Labor Statistics* at the Department of Labor collects data every month from a variety of retail stores and service establishments. In essence, the government "shops" for a specific *basket of goods and services* that is typical of the average consumer's lifestyle—food and beverage, housing (including rental costs), clothing, transportation, health care, recreation, education and communications, and other goods and services. The total cost of these goods and services, issued monthly, is compared against its base year of 1967 to determine whether costs have risen or fallen.

Producer Price Index

The Bureau of Labor Statistics also publishes the *Producer Price Index (PPI)*, a price index that calculates the general level of prices and the rate of inflation of

---

ILL. 1.3 ■ *Leading Economic Indicators*

Common stock prices	Orders for new plants and equipment
Length of the average workweek	Consumer goods orders
Net business formation	Producer price changes
New building permits	Real money balances
Unemployment	Changes in the holding of financial assets
Vendor performance	Changes in business inventories

Source: Department of Commerce, *Survey of Current Business*, various editions.

goods that businesses purchase. This index excludes consumer prices and instead covers about 2,800 industrial commodities, from raw materials to finished goods.

The government also measures increases or decreases in corporations' purchase of *durable goods*—expensive items such as heavy machinery and large computers. When inflation is high, corporations tend to put off buying durable goods, but quickly purchase such goods when they believe prices will rise.

Gross Domestic Product

The *Gross Domestic Product (GDP)*, the most comprehensive measure of the total output of the nation's economy, measures the value of all the goods and services produced by workers and capital located in the United States, regardless of ownership. A *good* is a tangible object, such as an automobile, that has economic value; a *service*, such as an airline flight, is an intangible object. The GDP is an estimate based on a wide variety of data from all sectors of the economy. These estimates, which are announced quarterly, are compared to other years' estimates and the comparison is a highly useful measure of economic health.

Measures of the gross domestic product have some limitations. Only finished products and services that have been bought by their ultimate users are included in the GDP. Products in the intermediate stages of production are *not* included. In addition, the selection of items to be included is somewhat arbitrary and not all goods and services are measured. Further, some economic activity cannot be measured because it is illegal or not reported to the government. These activities range from illegal transactions in drugs to legal cash payments to contractors who do not report the income to avoid taxes.

To help investors understand how economic conditions affect investments, let's begin by looking at the government's fiscal and monetary policies.

■ GOVERNMENTAL FISCAL ACTIVITIES

Fiscal and monetary policies often are used to balance, encourage or discourage foreign trade. For example, tariffs and import duties directly increase the consumer cost of foreign products so that domestically produced goods have a price advantage. These trade barriers generally fuel inflation because inefficient, less productive methods of production are sheltered from competition.

Another common objective of most governments today is regulation of the economy to assure long-term growth and maximum total production of goods and services. Idle workers or plants and equipment are "costs" that the economy essentially never recovers. Using the monetary and fiscal techniques attributed to the English economist John Maynard Keynes, governments can strategically affect the country's financial resources by:

1. *Stimulating current consumption.* The main tool for manipulating consumer spending is the personal income tax. Each $1 of tax reduction will lead to about 90 to 95 cents of additional spending eventually. Consumer spending reduces excess inventories, which in turn generally increases or slows falling prices and increases plant production, reducing unemployment.

ILL. 1.4 ■ *CPI's Market Basket of Goods*

The components of the Consumer Price Index (CPI)—and their relative importance
—are reconsidered every few years to reflect changes in American lifestyles. The
current components of the CPI are illustrated here.

5.5%
Education and
Communications

4.6%
Other Goods
and Services

16.4%
Food and
Beverage

6.2%
Recreation

MILK

5.2%
Medical
Care

17.0%
Transportation

39.8%
Housing

4.8%
Clothing

2. *Encouraging investment.* This applies to resources committed to the purchase
   of plant and equipment or other inputs to production that add capacity for
   future output. Used by economists, this term differs from normal usage. For
   example, the purchase of existing shares of common stock is economic "saving" to the purchaser, but is only a transfer of existing "investment" to the corporation.

3. *Encouraging allocations to or from certain uses.* The government helps to determine how *scarce resources* (natural resources, labor and capital) are used. This reduces dislocations within the economy and "structural unemployment"; it also assures an adequate industrial, technical base for world economic competitiveness, future growth and self-defense.

4. *Discouraging current consumption.* The government can establish price controls that result in a shortage of items whose prices are controlled. For example, the government can impose rent controls to protect consumers from high rents. Unfortunately, some property owners, discouraged by the low rents, convert their apartment buildings into office spaces or other uses. When the number of dwellings supplied are less than the number demanded by renters, a housing shortage is created.

5. *Encouraging future consumption.* The government encourages population growth, acquisition of natural resources and raises consumers' expectation of living standards to encourage consumption.

The mechanisms government uses to implement these strategies are complex. Using the tools and policies at its disposal, the government can:

- reduce the rate of inflation by reducing aggregate demand for goods and services if price levels are excessive; or

- increase the rate of inflation by increasing aggregate demand if low inflation or deflation is contributing to unemployment and economic stagnation.

Fiscal and monetary policy and theory center on *money* as the tool for change.

The Money Supply

The *money supply* is a measure of the amount of money in circulation as reported weekly by the Federal Reserve. There are actually three categories that measure the money supply: M1, M2 and M3.

- M1 is the narrowest measure of money supply. It measures all money in immediately spendable forms: currency, demand deposits and NOW accounts.

- M2 is a broader measure that includes M1 but adds savings accounts, money market deposit accounts and money market mutual funds.

- M3, the broadest of the money supply measures, includes M1 and M2 plus big deposits. Big deposits include institutional money-market funds and agreements among banks.

Many economists have found a direct link between how fast the money supply is expanding or shrinking and how fast the economy as a whole is expanding or shrinking. A reasonable growth in the money supply is necessary if the economy is to expand. However, a rapid rate of growth in the money supply is considered inflationary, while a sharp slow-down in the growth rate is recessionary.

Government Role as Creator and Provider of Money

The *Federal Reserve System* (the *"Fed"*) is the central bank of the United States, which regulates the U.S. banking system and money supply. It helps to control just how much money, or purchasing power, is created. Basically, banks create money by making loans to their customers. Banks can make loans whenever their reserves—cash in bank vaults and noninterest-bearing deposits of the Federal Reserve System—exceed the minimum required reserves set by the Fed. The Fed requires banks to keep a certain amount of money in the Fed's own account. If the *reserve requirement* (which the Fed can raise or lower) is 10 percent, a bank must keep $100 on reserve in the Fed's vaults for every $1,000 of its customers' deposits. Once this requirement is met, the bank may create $9 for every additional $1 on reserve by providing loans to its customers.

When a bank makes a loan, it credits the proceeds to the borrower's transaction account. When the borrower spends this "newly created" money, the recipient deposits it in another bank, which in turn can use its excess reserves to make another loan. In this way, each dollar of new reserves that the banking system receives becomes the basis for a multiple expansion of deposits.

The Fed attempts to maintain just the right balance of money in the economy by controlling the amount of money in circulation. If there is too much money available, people spend too much. If there is too little, people don't spend enough. The Fed influences the creation of money by regulating how much money banks may borrow from the Fed when they need additional funds to conduct business or when unexpected withdrawals have left them with less than the required amount of reserves. If the Fed wants to encourage more borrowing, it lowers the *discount rate*—the interest rate the Fed charges member banks for funds it provides—and lending is further stimulated. To "tighten" money, the Fed does the reverse. When the discount rate is high, banks are discouraged from borrowing from the Fed and, therefore, from lending money to consumers.

The Fed, through the 12 Reserve Banks, acts as the U.S. Treasury's bank. The Treasury deposits and withdraws funds like any other customer. The Fed directs the Treasury to deposit federal unemployment taxes, withholding taxes, corporate income taxes and certain excise taxes. The Reserve Banks issue savings bonds and Treasury securities for the government and release funds to pay the government's obligations, such as foreign aid and payments to defense contractors and welfare recipients. These dollars (whether printed as currency or checks) are recycled through banks, thereby becoming new money within the M1 category. In this way, the Federal Reserve System expands the money supply.

The foregoing discussion is a very simplified explanation of money and its regulation. Often the system seems to defy simplistic analysis. For example, the Fed might tighten money by not purchasing Treasury debt. Instead of the supply declining or stabilizing, M1 and M2 keep rising. Why? Basically, Fed policies provide incentives for results, not ironclad controls. For instance, banks may keep on loaning money at increasing interest rates if businesses are so troubled they must have the money at any cost.

ILL. 1.5 ■ *The Federal Reserve*

Unlike the central banks of most countries, the Fed is not 1, but 12 banks, with 25 regional branches spread across the nation.

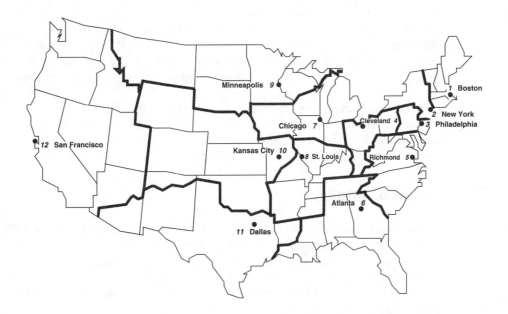

Each Federal Reserve branch issues money according to the needs of its region. The following letters and numbers on our bills stand for the different banks:

A	1	Boston	G	7	Chicago
B	2	New York	H	8	St. Louis
C	3	Philadelphia	I	9	Minneapolis
D	4	Cleveland	J	10	Kansas City
E	5	Richmond	K	11	Dallas
F	6	Atlanta	L	12	San Francisco

■ EFFECTS OF INFLATION AND DEFLATION

Consumer trends in spending, borrowing, saving and investment reflect changes in the economy. Two important economic influences on measures of net worth and investment return are *inflation* and *deflation*. Although the terms are commonly used and most people have at least a general idea of what they mean, a complete understanding of their meanings is vital for any investor.

Inflation

It is probably no surprise to learn prices rise each year. *Inflation*, a general increase in prices, means the purchasing power of a dollar decreases and buys less over time. Even a low rate of inflation can significantly affect the price of things. If prices rise only 5 percent a year, an item that costs $100 today will cost $105 a year from now. Over a 10-year period, that same item will cost almost $163. Due to inflation, the cost of that product will have risen almost 63 percent during that 10-year period.

When inflation is high, consumers tend to spend less on nonessential items and shop for greater value and better quality. Many save less and increase their use of credit during inflationary periods. They tend to invest in money market funds as a hedge against inflation. Since tangible items tend to increase in value during inflationary times, many speculative investors invest in gold, silver and other precious metals.

During periods of low inflation and stable prices, consumers tend to become more prudent shoppers who watch for sales and look for discounts. In addition, investors tend to switch their assets out of money market funds, which pay lower yields during inflation, into stocks and bonds, which have a greater potential for appreciation.

Causes of Inflation

Although all economists do not agree on how and why inflation occurs, one common explanation is that inflation is caused by a rapid expansion of the money supply. As explained earlier, the Fed can increase the money supply by lowering the discount rate to encourage lending. However, if the Fed creates *too much* spending money and there are not enough goods and services on which to spend that money, prices will escalate as consumers compete for limited goods.

Theories about the causes of inflation can be broadly divided into two categories: *demand-pull* and *cost-push*. Briefly, *demand-pull inflation* is a rise in prices owing to increases in expenditures on goods and services. Too much spendable money competes for the limited supply of goods and services available at full employment, and thus *pulls* prices and wages up. Economists are in general agreement that the demand-pull cause of inflation can be controlled by application of proper doses of monetary and fiscal policy:

- holding down unemployment by enough expansion to lead the economic system to the brink of full employment, but not so much expansion that purchasing power goes over the edge and causes price inflation; and

- curbing an inflationary gap by cutting back by just enough to return the system reasonably close to full employment, without going so far as to cause recession or depression unemployment.

Cost-push inflation results when prices and wages rise before the system reaches a reasonable degree of full employment (i.e., before tight labor markets and full-capacity utilization cause them to rise). What happens seems to be that employers are pressed to pay higher labor costs (wages) and other costs (regardless of levels of employment and supply) versus demand. This results in higher production costs which, in turn, *push up* prices and this *cost-push* of prices triggers yet another round of inflation at still higher levels.

Because cost-push inflation seems to continue, virtually unrelated to levels of employment and supply versus demand, there is little agreement among economists as to how to solve the problem. Nothing tried to date has produced a satisfactory result. When monetary and fiscal brakes are applied, the rate of cost-push inflation is limited but, at the same time, prosperity declines accordingly, tending to bring recession and higher rates of unemployment, which causes some to feel that the cure is worse than the ailment. Clearly, a new approach is needed to satisfactorily solve this modern cause of inflation.

Deflation

The opposite of inflation, *deflation* is defined by *Webster's* as "a contraction in the volume of available money or credit that results in a decline of the general price level." Deflation (also called *disinflation*) tends to favor creditors and fixed-income receivers at the expense of debtors and profit receivers—the opposite is true with inflation. The effects of inflation and deflation are obvious: If a person owes, say, $10,000 payable at the end of six years and prices double due to inflation in that period, the debtor will pay off the debt with half the purchasing power—certainly good for the debtor and unfavorable for the creditor. If prices, instead, drop to half because of deflation, the debtor will pay off the debt with twice as much purchasing power—good for the creditor and bad for the debtor.

■ THE TIME VALUE OF MONEY

As mentioned earlier, your clients will need to set aside a certain amount of money in savings accounts and investments that will grow over the years to partially offset the effects of inflation. As you know, an amount of money invested today will increase as a result of earned interest. This concept, called the *time value of money*, is based on the fact that a dollar received today is worth more than a dollar received a year from now. The dollar received today can be invested immediately and, when combined with the interest earned, will be worth more a year from now. Conversely, a dollar received a year from now is worth less than a dollar received today because the investment income will have been lost.

The time value of money consists of two factors: present value and future value. The *present value* of a sum of money is simply the amount invested today. The *future value* is the amount to which a current sum will increase based on a certain interest rate and period of time. To determine how much a client's money will grow if he or she invests it today and leaves it for a specified period, assuming it earns a specified rate of return for that period, you need to find the future value (FV) of that sum of money. You may refer to a future value or compound interest table that shows the future value of $1 for various investment periods and interest rates, or use the FV formula:

$$FV = PV \times (1 + i)^n$$

where FV = the future value,
PV = the present value (amount invested today),
i = the interest rate and
n = the number of periods the money is to be invested at the interest rate.

For example, $1,000 invested for three years and earning 10 percent per year grows to $1,331 [$1,000 × (1 + .10)^3] = ($1,000 × 1.331).

Present value is the current value of a future sum based on a certain interest rate and period of time. To find the present value (PV) of a single payment, tables or a formula reversing the process of finding the future value may be used:

$$PV = \frac{1}{(1+i)^n}$$

After you have reviewed your client's investment objectives, you can use future value tables or these formulas to illustrate how investments made today can grow over time to accomplish those objectives.

■ THE ROLE OF THE FINANCIAL PROFESSIONAL

As a life agent, you are already aware of the vital role you play in your community. You know that life and health insurance provide a practical solution to the economic losses associated with sickness, accidents and death. But, did you know that as a life insurance agent, you are uniquely qualified to assist your clients with setting and achieving their financial objectives?

A life insurance agent is in a good position to help prospects and clients identify their goals and develop financial plans to meet those goals. First of all, the agent understands how to recognize and communicate about needs. This ability is vital for the financial products market. Second, the products and services the agent represents, from insurance to annuities, are the core of any investment plan. Third, agents can assist their clients in creating a comprehensive financial plan and follow-up with periodic reviews and service. Finally, agents know how to motivate a complacent client—one who is not aware of the potential financial shortfalls he or she may be facing without an investment plan—and can propel that individual to take action.

Expertise Needed

Even the most knowledgeable and successful life insurance agents may not be in a position to formulate a complete financial plan for their clients with life insurance. You will need additional credentials and licensing to sell a wider variety of financial products. If you wish to sell variable life insurance, for example, you must be registered with the *National Association of Securities Dealers (NASD)*. Life insurance agents generally must obtain a Series 6 or Series 7 NASD license to sell variable life insurance or variable annuities. A Series 6 license allows the sale of variable contracts, mutual funds and investment company products. A Series 7 license allows the sale of variable contracts, stocks, bonds, mutual funds, municipal securities and other securities.

Life agents should also be aware that complicated financial plans require the coordinated efforts of a number of professionals. For example, only *attorneys* can draft legal documents such as wills, contracts and trusts. Those who attempt to complete these documents without a law degree may be guilty of a crime, the unauthorized practice of law.

In addition to a life agent and an attorney, investors will need a *property-casualty insurance agent* to provide coverage for their property and liability needs, as well as for risk management expertise. Many people will also need an *accountant* to prepare tax returns.

Many people feel that sound, professional management of financial resources requires the continuous effort of *investment advisers* or *financial planners*. These professionals maximize the individual's investment objectives by establishing and managing their investment plan. This means assistance at the time the asset is acquired, throughout the holding period and when each asset is sold or traded. This also means continuous evaluations of, and comparisons with, alternative financial products that might do a better job of maximizing objectives. Because most states do not restrict the term *financial planner*, people with varying degrees of knowledge and expertise use the term.

Financial Planner Designations

Several associations and organizations grant credentials that signify a financial planner's level of education. Some of the most commonly recognized designations include:

- *Certified Financial Planner.* The International Board of Standards and Practices for Certified Financial Planners, Inc. (IBCFP) licenses people who have taken a rigorous self-study program and then passed certification exams in financial planning, insurance, investing, taxes, retirement planning, employee benefits and estate planning. In addition to passing these tests, a CFP must have experience in the financial services industry, have a certain amount of college education, participate in ongoing continuing education and abide by a strict code of ethics.

- *Chartered Financial Analyst (CFA).* The Financial Analysts Federation grants this designation after a candidate passes a test that demonstrates expertise in investing in stocks, bonds and mutual funds.

- *Chartered Financial Consultant (ChFC).* The American College confers the ChFC after the candidate passes 10 college-level courses dealing with personal finance and life insurance topics. The ChFC must possess industry experience and adhere to a code of strict ethical standards.

Rationale for Learning About Financial Products

As a life agent, you can serve as the catalyst who brings order out of chaos in personal financial plans and estates. You should have a clear, unbiased understanding of the various concepts, methods and resources that are appropriate to meet your clients' needs. By understanding how your products and services fit within an individual's total financial picture, you become a more complete analyst, a more competent adviser and a more professional salesperson.

By understanding the basics of a variety of financial products, you will become more aware of what makes the money markets and other financial markets "go." Perhaps as a current or potential investor, you will become more knowledgeable about the avenues of investment that beckon to you. The information this course provides will help any person who seeks to learn more of the world of finance and other investment sources with their potential for safety versus high risk, gain versus loss, hedging against inflation and protection against deflation.

The single greatest skill you should develop as a financial professional is the ability to understand people and how to communicate. Communication is complicated by the fact that people are complex and often don't want to reveal attitudes, values and characteristics they feel are personal. People are threatened when someone knows too much about them. Money matters are very *personal*. However, most investors have limited financial resources that must be allocated in such a manner as to maximize total satisfaction. An investor is "satisfied" when his or her objectives or goals are met with the aid of a financial professional.

■ SUMMARY

Your primary role as a life insurance agent is to identify your clients' personal, financial and business needs, and whenever possible, to satisfy those needs with insurance products. Most commonly, your clients will need funds to protect their families in the event of a premature death, a disability or other financial contingency. However, your clients may also ask your assistance in choosing investments to protect their wealth, increase their income and/or fund their retirement.

Saving and investing are the most important means of achieving the financial goals many people have for their future financial security. As a life agent, you are able to offer insurance products with certain unique features, and you can serve your clients by assisting them in identifying their goals and developing investment strategies to meet their goals.

In Chapter 2, we will discuss the concept of investment *risk and return*. Failure to understand this concept is the primary reason many investors choose the wrong investments with unfortunate results. As part of that discussion, we'll look at the *investment pyramid*, a visual representation of the risk and return concept that many investors use when they are diversifying their portfolio. Investments at the base of the pyramid (such as life insurance and annuities) entail the least amount of risk to the investor's principal. We'll outline ways your clients can use additional types of investments to build on their solid base of life insurance and annuities.

■ CHAPTER 1 QUESTIONS FOR REVIEW

1. All of the following should determine which financial products are selected, EXCEPT

    A. the investor's goals and objectives

    B. the investor's moral obligations

    C. the amount of funds available for investment

    D. the type of risk the investor is willing to accept

2. Some risk is inherent in most investments. In general, the greater the risk, the

    A. more expensive the financial product
    B. smaller the potential return
    C. greater the potential return
    D. most likely the investment is to fail

3. All of the following are debt securities EXCEPT

    A. commercial notes
    B. commercial paper
    C. bonds
    D. preferred stocks

4. Cost-push inflation occurs when

    A. the cost of goods is pushed up because of higher wages
    B. the cost of goods is pushed down because of lower wages
    C. too much money in circulation causes prices to fall
    D. too little money in circulation causes prices to fall

5. The life insurance agent's primary role in financial planning is to identify a client's needs and, when possible, satisfy those needs with

    A. a portfolio of investment products
    B. tangible or intangible assets
    C. life insurance products
    D. debt and equity securities

2

Risk and Return

W hether an individual follows a conservative, speculative or middle-of-the-road investment path depends, in part, on his or her perceptions about the future. If the person is apprehensive about economic conditions, a conservative investment plan may be undertaken. In times of relative prosperity, a person might maintain a more aggressive investment position. To a certain extent, all people tailor their investments to meet their own risk-taking desires. However, simply taking risks is not a virtue—prisons are full of risk takers. The important idea is to *match an acceptable return in a given period of time with the desired level of risk*.

In this chapter, you will be introduced to various investment options and several factors that affect investment alternatives. By placing money into investments with the potential to grow and/or produce income, people are better able to accumulate large sums of money that may be needed to live comfortably today and to provide a secure retirement. We'll also take a preliminary look at some of the factors that go into developing an overall plan for the management and evaluation of an individual's financial resources to fit with his or her investment objectives.

■ ■ ■ ■ ■

■ UNDERSTANDING RISK

There are a number of ways to define the term *risk*, but, in this text, *risk* is defined as the potential that actual returns will differ from those expected. Generally speaking, the greater the variation in potential gains or losses, the greater the investment's risk. The smaller the range, the smaller the risk. Therefore, low-risk investments, such as savings and money market deposit accounts, usually mean lower expected returns than high-risk investments such as commodities and financial futures.

It is important that investors understand that the risk associated with any investment is directly related to its expected return and its expected holding period. Investors should also understand the relationship between the return they can expect on an investment and the amount of risk that they must take to earn that return. In general, investors seeking higher returns must be prepared to assume higher risks or reduced

ILL. 2.1 ■ *Relationship Between Risk and Return*

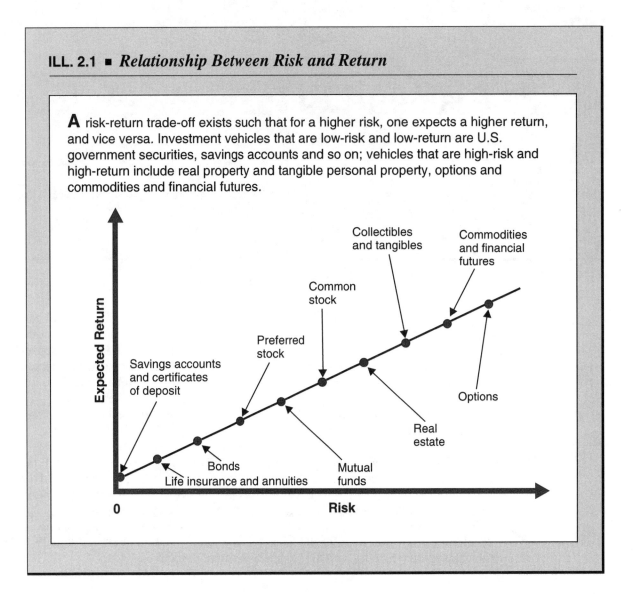

A risk-return trade-off exists such that for a higher risk, one expects a higher return, and vice versa. Investment vehicles that are low-risk and low-return are U.S. government securities, savings accounts and so on; vehicles that are high-risk and high-return include real property and tangible personal property, options and commodities and financial futures.

liquidity. Failure to understand this *risk-return trade-off* is the primary reason many investors choose the wrong investments and face catastrophic results.

Opportunity Cost

Economists frequently say, "There is no such thing as a free lunch." A fundamental principle of life—and investing—is that most things come at an *opportunity cost*. If the investor uses money or other resources in a particular way, those resources cannot be used for anything else at the same time. Every investment choice must be made at some cost. For example, if an investor uses available capital to purchase a mutual fund, that capital cannot be used at the same time to purchase commodities.

Many investors purchase stocks and bonds because they provide current income in the form of dividends or interest. Other investments, such as gold, gemstones and collectibles, provide no current income but often *appreciate in value*, providing investors with *capital gains*. If such investments do not appreciate rapidly in value, investors may face substantial lost opportunity costs in the form of lost income that could have been earned on capital invested in other ways.

The Risk Factor

Various types of risk, even when objectively measured, may exist for a single asset. It is helpful to itemize some of these forms of risk, because to a large degree these are criteria by which the investment choices will be made. As noted in Ill. 2.2, there are a number of risks that an individual must weigh when selecting an investment. The most important of these risks that widen an investment's range of possible return are:

- purchasing power risk

- interest rate risk

- liquidity risk

- market risk

- financial risk

- business risk

Let's briefly look at these major areas of investment risk so that you can assess your own and your clients' attitudes about each type of risk.

Purchasing Power Risk

Changes in price levels in the economy result in risk. As we discussed, inflation— the general rise in prices over a period of time—tends to reduce purchasing power. As prices increase, the purchasing power of a fixed amount of principal declines. In other words, if investments don't grow faster than the rate of inflation, the investor is losing money. Therefore, investors must seek investments that produce a rate of return that compensates for lost purchasing power. Although there are no guarantees, in times of low or moderate inflation, a long-term investment in a portfolio of equity investments can provide some hedge against inflation. However, the value of stocks tends to fall in times of rapid inflation if the government uses monetary policy to fight inflation.

Interest Rate Risk

The *interest rate risk* associated with investments in stocks and bonds is a result of changes in the overall interest rates in the economy caused by a fluctuation in the supply of or demand for money. Interest rates seldom remain stationary for long periods. As they rise and fall, they affect the value of fixed value investments, such as bonds. For example, as interest rates increase, the value of bonds falls; when interest rates decline, the value of bonds increases.

ILL. 2.2 ■ *Types of Risk*

- *Business risk*—Degree of uncertainty associated with an investment's earnings and its ability to pay investors the returns owed them

- *Death risk*—Risk of nonrealization of financial objectives due to the investor's premature death

- *Disability risk*—Risk that the investor's illness or disability will terminate income and expose the individual (or family members) to an indeterminable future of continued medical, living and other expenses

- *Expense risk*—Investments have an element of expense connected with their acquisition, maintenance and distribution

- *Financial risk*—Degree of uncertainty associated with the mix of debt and equity used to finance a firm or property

- *Interest rate risk*—Used to measure opportunity cost, it in turn becomes a risk

- *Investment risk*—Risk that the value of an asset will rise and fall in the interim between its purchase date and the time it is needed

- *Liquidity risk*—The possibility that when the seller needs or wants to sell an asset there will not be a ready, willing and able buyer for the asset at an acceptable price

- *Management risk*—Risk that guidance provided by others will be inadequate or inappropriate

- *Market risk*—Risk or changes in investment returns that result from political, economic, social or investor changes

- *Misinformation risk*—Risk that forecasts of future events and conditions may be inaccurate

- *Opportunity risk*—Risk that investment in one specific asset means that money is no longer available for purchase of another asset or for consumption

- *Physical risk or loss*—Risk of deterioration of a tangible asset or damage to tangible property by fire, flood, theft, accident or violent acts of nature

- *Political risk*—Risk of expropriation, legislation, zoning, etc., impacting an investment

- *Purchasing power risk*—Risk of inflation or deflation

- *Risk of loss to creditors/divorce settlement*—Risk of loss due to foreclosure or property settlements as a result of divorce

- *Security of principal*—Risk that an asset will later turn out to be worth less than its initial value

- *Tax risk*—Risk of loss of income to tax collector

- *Yield risk*—The probability that the payments or percentage yield will be less than expected

For example, assume that a $1,000 corporate bond matures in 20 years and pays 9 percent interest ($90) each year. If bond interest rates increase to 12 percent on comparable bonds, the value of the 9 percent bond falls because people can purchase bonds paying a higher return. As a result, the original bond must be sold for less than $1,000 or held until maturity.

Liquidity Risk

Some investments may be difficult to sell after they are purchased. An individual's investment strategies should include an estimate of the time period over which the asset will be held. *Liquidity risk* is the possibility that a seller will not find a ready, willing and able buyer for an asset or that, if a buyer exists, he or she will not be willing to offer an acceptable price for the investment. For example, there may always be a buyer for the Andy Warhol print the investor just purchased, but perhaps only at a price the buyer sets and at a commission of 20 percent of the sale.

The expression "for every buyer there must be a seller" expresses a fundamental principle of any transaction. Even long-term investments are eventually sold, unless the objective is to transfer the actual property at death to heirs or to a charity. When the asset is put up for sale, the buyer not only must be located but also must be *willing* and *have the resources* to consummate the exchange to the satisfaction of the seller.

The asset's selling price is determined by the law of supply and demand. The supply is a function of how *little* utility the potential seller has in continuing to hold the asset. The demand is a function of how *much* utility the potential buyer can derive from acquiring the asset. These utilities are price sensitive. The lower the price, the less the seller wants to quit holding the asset, but the more eager the buyer is to acquire it. If the buyer has no use for the asset, the price would have to be zero (or less if the "seller" had to pay the "buyer" to take the worthless possession away).

Market Risk

The price of real estate, mutual funds and other investments may fluctuate because of economic, social or political conditions. For example, investors who are interested in purchasing stocks in multinational corporations, such as IBM or Nestlé, should carefully consider the political climate in various countries in which the corporations do business. Unstable governments or civil war can create volatile investment environments. As a result, the value of stocks can change overnight.

As a result of market risk, market growth is not as predictable and systematic as most investors would like to believe. As you will recall from Chapter 1, trends in the stock market are summarized as either *bull* (rising) or *bear* (falling) markets. In a bull market, economic and political influences are favorable to market growth and investors purchase stocks because they are optimistic about the overall economy. In a bear market, prices of securities are falling and investors tend to sell stocks because they believe that the condition will continue for a few weeks, months or years.

Financial Risk

The amount of risk investors experience is also influenced by how a business firm finances its operations. Many firms borrow large amounts of capital, usually with property as collateral, to continue their operations. The use of debt, or *leverage*, often increases a company's earnings per share of common stock if the company can earn more on its investments than it must pay to finance those investments. However, if either sales or operating income fall, earnings per share will fall.

The larger the amount of leverage used to finance a firm, the greater is its *financial risk*. Leverage increases potential profits, but it also increases risk since debt service (the cost related to repaying the debt) must be allowed for, which can weaken the company's cash flow and make it difficult to operate the business. In the event of liquidation, creditors would be paid before stockholders.

Business Risk

Successful investment in common stock, preferred stock and bonds depends on the proper management of the business that underwrites the investment. For example, if the company issuing stock is well-managed and its product line is flourishing, it should pay dividends and its stock should become more valuable. However, if the business operates at a loss, it may eventually file for bankruptcy and the stock becomes worthless. The best way to protect against business risk is to carefully research the company before investing in its stock.

The risks listed above are not cumulative. By exposing an individual investor to one risk by choosing a strategy that is compatible with stated objectives, another type of risk exposure actually may be reduced. How much risk, and the types of risk an individual assumes, depend on a number of factors, including the investor's temperament or psychological adaptability to risk.

Some individuals cannot live with risk because they "know that they are destined to lose" and seek to minimize risk at all costs. *Risk* to the untrained individual simply means the possibility that loss may result from a decline in the market value of the asset. The *risk avoider* fails to realize that by such strategies, other risks may be increasing. For example, reluctance to invest in financial products that can earn a positive rate of return can actually cost an individual money. Even a relatively low rate of inflation can significantly affect the price of things. With an inflation rate of 4 percent, actual purchasing power has declined by 4 percent. The individual who seeks to avoid risk either has not been informed of these risks (and opportunities), has blocked them out mentally to avoid stress or has assigned them very low priorities in his or her financial plan.

■ RISK MANAGEMENT

Why expose anyone to these risks? Risk is unavoidable. By doing nothing, one has *unconsciously chosen* a strategy—one that, in and of itself, entails risk. By doing nothing (e.g., spending everything) opportunity cost risk is elevated. By failing to put money to work, the effects of inflation are increased. For example, if a dollar buys a certain amount of food today, but only half as much 10 years from now, individuals have lost real purchasing power. Additionally, by spending everything one is exposed to the risks of disability, death or excess longevity.

Just as there are many ways to define risk, there are many ways to deal effectively with it. There are three basic methods for handling risk.

1. *Avoid it.* For the same reason some people don't play cards for money, others avoid various risks by choice. By choosing not to purchase stocks, one could eliminate the risk of losing capital if the price of stocks falls. It is, however, impossible to avoid simultaneously all forms of risk.

2. *Accept it.* Before any investment is made, an individual can estimate what the risks might be in relation to the potential return. Conservative investors may prefer almost risk-free Treasury bonds, but, if the potential reward of a more speculative real estate investment justifies the assumption of risk, even a conservative investor may be willing to assume the additional risk.

3. *Minimize it.* Risk can be reduced or eliminated by transferring it to another party. Insurance, for example, is a business tool for handling risk by spreading it among a sufficiently large number of similar exposures to predict the individual chance of loss. *Hedging*, used by commodity futures traders, is an investment strategy to offset or minimize potential damage caused by adverse price changes. Another way to minimize or offset risk is *diversification*, which is the inclusion of a variety of investment products in one's portfolio.

■ THE RISK PYRAMID

Investors must study the overall economy and the performance of particular investments to determine where to invest their funds. Most financial planners recommend that investors find a comfortable balance of security and risk that works for them. Investors can achieve this balance by building a *portfolio*, a collection of assets, to spread risk. Adequate *diversification* reduces the amount of risk associated with individual investments. By holding a number of different investments, the effect of one or more securities failing or suffering a temporary decline is minimized and the possibility of successful investing is enhanced.

Most of your clients will invest in low-risk/low-return to moderate-risk/moderate-return investments such as stocks, bonds and/or mutual funds. You should be familiar with these investment vehicles—as well as alternative investment vehicles—that your clients may choose as a means to preserve or enhance income. We'll cover each investment in more detail in later chapters, but let's briefly look at investment choices in the following sections.

■ LOW RISK/LOW TO MODERATE RETURN

At the base of the pyramid are conservative investments whose features include low risk, low to moderate return and high liquidity. All investment plans should begin with a solid base consisting of cash, insurance and other low-risk investments.

ILL. 2.3 ■ *Risk Pyramid*

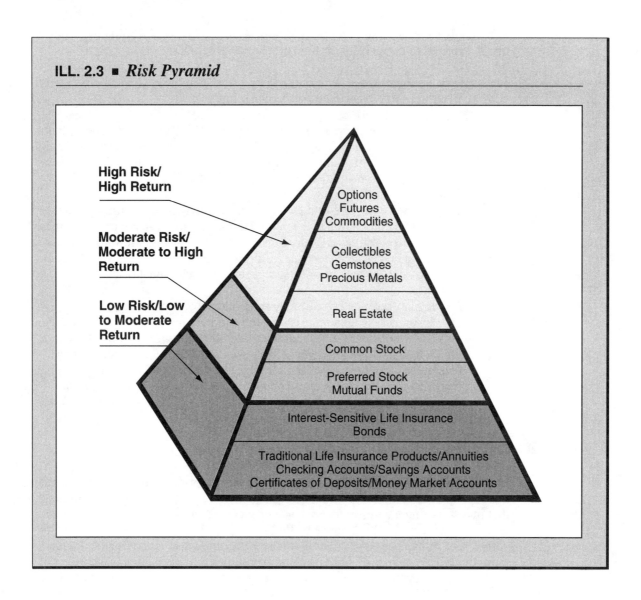

Traditional Life Insurance

The primary purpose of insurance is to protect policyholders and their dependents from financial loss in the event of property damage, illness, accident, disability or death. Individuals should purchase a base amount of life, health, disability, property and liability insurance before investing in other financial products, because protection against financial hardships takes precedence over efforts to increase income.

The core of any investment plan is *traditional life insurance products*, notably term and whole life. Some insurance products stress protection while others offer savings and accumulation potential, but many combinations are available. Overall, the growth potential of life insurance is relatively small but the available options are almost risk free and relatively liquid.

Annuities

In addition to life insurance, individuals may use *annuities* as a type of savings plan in which the investor pays a predetermined sum to a company and at a specified age receives the money with interest in either a lump sum or monthly payments. These payments can be arranged to cover a certain number of years, a lifetime or a combination of both. Annuities can be purchased for a lump sum (single-premium) or in installments.

One of the benefits of investing in annuities is the tax treatment. During the accumulation period, taxes on the investment buildup of earnings are deferred. Although not particularly liquid during the early years, an annuity is completely liquid after its surrender charge period expires. This investment offers safety and a moderate return.

Checking and Savings Accounts

Traditional savings vehicles—*checking* and *savings accounts*—are highly liquid and almost risk free on a short-term basis because they are often insured by the federal government. Because of the low risk, the return is also low. Most financial planners recommend that some money should be set aside in these accounts for monthly expenses and an emergency fund. After such a fund is established, additional funds can be made available for other investments.

Money Market Deposit Accounts

Banks and other financial institutions also offer *money market deposit accounts*, a combination of savings and checking accounts. A sound savings base can be built with these accounts. They offer unregulated money market rates, require a minimum deposit and permit limited withdrawals so funds in the account cannot easily be depleted. Funds are federally insured (within certain limits) and may be accessed through automated teller machines (ATMs).

Certificates of Deposit

The *certificate of deposit (CD)* was designed with safety of principal in mind. They are federally insured, redeemable debt obligations issued by banks and other depository institutions. Certificates of deposit are time deposits that mature at a specific time, such as 31 days, 90 days, 6 months and so on. They pay a fixed rate of interest for the term the principal is invested. In return for this longer commitment, higher rates of interest are available. Although funds may be withdrawn prior to maturity, there is a penalty for early withdrawal.

Money Market Mutual Funds

Money market mutual funds, sponsored by nonbank financial institutions, offer small investors attractive yields on short-term, highly liquid securities. These funds pool the resources of many investors to purchase short-term securities issued by the U.S. Treasury, large commercial banks and financially strong corporations. Although not federally insured, these investments are usually safe.

Bonds

A *bond* is a certificate of debt or a negotiable promissory note of a corporation or public body that promises to repay on a maturity date some years distant and to pay periodic interest until then. Most commonly, bonds are issued in denominations of $1,000 and $5,000. Bond issuers (borrowers) pay interest to the investor until the bond matures, at which time the bond is redeemed and principal is repaid. These investments include corporate bonds, U.S. Savings bonds, Treasury bonds and so on. Bonds are fairly liquid and are normally purchased for moderate interest income.

■ MODERATE RISK/MODERATE TO HIGH RETURN

The middle section of the risk pyramid consists of investments that are purchased for growth, income or speculation. Depending on the investment selected, there is modest risk/moderate return to high risk and potentially high return. For example, an investor may choose *blue-chip stock* (safe and conservative), *income stock* (usually utility stock that pays higher than average dividends) or *speculative stock* (higher risk stocks).

Common Stock

Common stock is a unit representing partial ownership in a corporation. Stockholders share the possibility of both a company's gain and its loss. Dividends are paid only after preferred stock dividends have been satisfied. In case of dissolution of the business, common stock investors have last claim on the assets of the corporation, after bondholders, creditors and preferred stockholders.

Preferred Stock

Any stock represents a share of partial ownership of a corporation's equity resulting from contributed capital. *Preferred stock* is a form of equity security that has specific features distinguishing it from common stock. Preferred stock has a set *dividend* and priority of claim on the assets of the corporation over common stock in the case of dissolution. Priority is also granted over common stock in the payment of dividends. Finally, the holders of preferred stock have no voting rights.

Pooled Investment Vehicles

Investment companies sometimes offer investors the opportunity to own shares in an *investment pool*—a portfolio of diversified assets that are professionally selected, managed and held for the collective benefit of the individual investors. Investment pools include face-amount certificate plans, unit investment trusts and, by far the most popular pooled investment, mutual funds.

Mutual funds are open-ended management companies (or investment companies) that pool money from thousands of shareholders and invest it with specific goals or objectives in mind. Popular objectives of mutual funds include current income, long-term growth and preservation of capital.

There are several different kinds of mutual funds from which to choose. *Growth funds* usually hold stocks of companies that are still in an expansion stage. *Income funds* generally include common stock, preferred stock or bonds with higher current yields. *Balanced funds*, with safety of principal and stability of income being the main objectives, distribute investments among conservative stocks and bonds. The best known funds are *money market mutual funds*, which invest in U.S. Treasury bills and commercial paper. These funds offer a high degree of safety because the funds are managed to maintain a net asset value of $1 per share regardless of market or interest changes.

■ HIGH RISK/HIGH RETURN

The top of the risk pyramid includes speculative investments that might return large profits in short periods of time. However, there are no guarantees a profit will be made and, in fact, there is a real danger that there will be no gain and even the principal may be lost. Although some investors enjoy the risk associated with speculation, high-risk investments are usually not appropriate for most investors and should remain a small portion of the overall portfolio since the risk of losing everything usually outweighs the potential high return.

Real Estate

The term *real estate* includes land and structures that are purchased for growth in value for capital gains, potential high returns from leverage of equity and positive cash flow from rental income. Although it can be profitable for seasoned investors, investment property can create problems for the beginner. In addition, the original capital must remain committed for several years. The value of the property may decrease because of changing economic conditions and mortgage interest may or may not be tax deductible. Because managing rental property is time-consuming and difficult, a professional property manager may be needed. Finally, when the investor wishes to sell, the real estate market may be soft and the selling price may be less than desired because of the economic conditions.

Tangible Investments

Assets listed in this section are tangible items that have substance and can be seen and touched. This category, near the top of the risk pyramid, includes gold, silver and other precious metals; gemstones; and such collectibles as stamps, coins, fine art and antiques. These items are acquired not only for their financial gain but for their intrinsic value. The value of these assets is relative and based, in part, on the tastes of the viewer.

Precious metals, gemstones and collectibles generally produce no income until they are sold. Such assets involve all of the risk inherent in traditional investments plus they are highly illiquid, very speculative and subject to fraud. Because of the high risk, investors interested in these speculative investments should deal only with reputable dealers and investment firms.

Futures and Options

Speculation in *commodities*—a select group of consumer goods that includes cotton, silver, corn, pork bellies and many other items—can be accomplished through commodity futures contracts. A *futures contract* is an agreement for the purchase and sale of a commodity or a *financial instrument* (such as foreign currencies or interest rate futures) at an established quantity and price at some set point in the future. The value of a futures contract varies with the supply and demand for the commodity itself.

Trading in futures is quite risky and requires substantial time, expertise and financial resources. The commodity's performance depends on weather conditions, government intervention, consumer attitudes and a variety of other factors. Generally, speculative investments are not recommended as a major part of the portfolios of most investors because the potential for loss is great, and most speculative instruments pay no interest and offer few tax advantages.

Options are a type of security that gives the holder the right to buy or sell a certain amount of an underlying financial asset at a specified price for a specified period of time. Options are highly leveraged investments—the options investor puts down a relatively small amount of money on his or her belief that a stock will go up or down and has the opportunity to walk away with large profits. As with many investments, investors also risk losing the money they invest in options.

As stated earlier, an investment portfolio should begin with a sturdy foundation of safe, liquid investments that can be relied on in case of an emergency. Most experts feel that at least six months of after-tax income should be invested in bank accounts, money market funds, Treasury bills or other short-term investments to take care of medical emergencies and to cover living expenses in case individuals lose their jobs. Only after that safety net is in place should someone move into other investment areas that are longer term and riskier in nature.

Experts agree that investors should never assume more financial risk than they feel comfortable assuming. At the same time, investors should understand that to reap larger rewards, they either have to take larger risks or give up significant liquidity. Generally, investors gain an increased return in exchange for accepting lower liquidity. Investors must find a comfortable balance between security and risk/liquidity that works for them.

■ MEASURING RETURN ON INVESTMENT

As stated earlier, most investments yield some sort of cash flow or return on investment. The return can be seen as the reward for investing. In this text, the term *return on investment (ROI)* is used in a broad sense that includes virtually all results of investment: earnings and capital growth, tangible and intangible, gross and net. Consequently, this discussion will be broken down into five segments: (1) gross return—earnings; (2) gross return—capital growth; (3) investment costs; (4) net return—earnings; and (5) net return—capital growth.

Gross Return—Earnings

These kinds of returns include interest, dividends, rents and other cash flow from investments, before any costs relative to the investments are deducted. Most commonly, earnings are referred to as *current income*, cash or an asset that can be easily converted into cash.

Interest

By far the most common kind of earnings return on investment is *interest*. It is the payment for the borrowed use of money, and thus often is described as "the rental payment" for borrowed funds. Savings accounts and certificates—bills, notes, bonds (government, commercial or personal)—and mortgages all represent borrowing by, and loans to, the issuers of those accounts or instruments. And all these issuers pay for the use of what is borrowed in one or more forms of interest, chief of which are called *simple*, *compound* and *discount* (or *accrual*). Investors are also interested in the *yield* on an investment.

Simple Interest. *Simple interest* is interest computed a single time on the original principal only. For example, assume you lend a friend $5,000 at 9 percent simple interest (annual rate) for six months. At the end of six months, the friend would owe you simple interest of $225 ($5,000 × .09 / 2), plus the principal of $5,000. Moreover, even if the interest and principal were not repaid to you on time, your friend would owe you no more than that, unless a new or extended loan was provided for originally, or was negotiated on or by the due date.

Compound Interest. *Compound interest* is interest on principal that is increased or augmented periodically by the interest paid on the previous amount of interest. It is computed periodically on the sum of original principal plus accrued interest. Periodic compounding may be continuous, daily, weekly, monthly, semiannually or annually.

For example, assume the above loan was at compound (rather than simple) interest—$5,000 for six months at 9 percent compounded monthly. At the end of six months, your friend would owe you the $5,000 principal plus compound interest of $229.26, calculated as follows. (Note that the annual interest rate is reduced to a monthly rate by multiplying the rate by $\frac{1}{12}$.)

First month	$5,000 × ($\frac{1}{12}$ × .09) = $37.50
Second month	$37.50 + $5,000 × ($\frac{1}{12}$ × .09) = $37.78
Third month	$37.78 + $5,037.50 × ($\frac{1}{12}$ × .09) = $38.06
Fourth month	$38.06 + $5,075.28 × ($\frac{1}{12}$ × .09) = $38.35
Fifth month	$38.35 + $5,113.34 × ($\frac{1}{12}$ × .09) = $38.64
Sixth month	$38.64 + $5,151.69 × ($\frac{1}{12}$ × .09) = $38.93
Total interest	$37.50 + $37.78 + $38.06 + $38.35 + $38.64 + $38.93 = $229.26

Thus, compound interest for six months at 9 percent produces $4.26 more earnings on the $5,000 principal than does simple interest. This may not seem like a great difference over a short period, but the ever-increasing amount of interest added each successive month of compounding will make it more significant over a number of years. In 93 months (7¾ years) the interest will make the total amount repayable more than double ($10,017.42). In just 55 more months (4½ years)—a total of 12¼ years—the amount due would be more than *triple* the amount of the original loan at 9 percent compounded monthly.

Discount Rate. The *discount* (or *accrual*) *rate* is the interest rate at which future sums or annuities are discounted back to the present. It is the form of interest commonly earned on short-term investments, such as bonds, Treasury bills and so on. The security is purchased at a price below its *redemption value*, the difference being the interest earned. Bonds, for example, are often bought at a discounted price. A $1,000 par value (the face value payable at maturity) bond maturing in two years might be purchased at $875 today—and the bond would be said to be purchased (or sold) at a $125 or 12.5 percent discount. Actually, this is equal to approximately 7 percent compound annual interest for two years. (Note the years are counted as 360 days for this calculation.)

$$\frac{\text{Present rate}}{\text{of return}} = \frac{(^{360}/_{720}) \times (\$1,000 - \$875)}{\$875} = \frac{.50 \times \$125}{\$875} = \begin{array}{l} .0714 \text{ or} \\ 7.14\% \end{array}$$

Yield or Internal Rate of Return. Investors are usually concerned with an investment's *yield* or the amount of profit (or return) on an investment of capital. When an investment is purchased and held for a year or less, it is easy to calculate the return on investment. For example, assume an investor has $1,000 and wishes to know its worth after one year if the capital is invested and grows at 10 percent per year. At the end of the year, the investor will have $1,000 × 1.10 or $1,100. Such an investment provides at 10 percent yield $100/$1,000 = 10 percent). If the investor is currently earning 9 percent on other similar investments, the proposed investment would be acceptable since its yield exceeds the investor's current returns. On the other hand, an investment having a yield below 9 percent would be unacceptable because it fails to provide a satisfactory rate of return, compared to what the investor is currently earning.

The simple calculation illustrated above may be used for investments held for one year or less; however, it cannot be used to calculate the yield on long-term investments. There are two factors that affect the yield that an investor may earn on investments held for more than one year: (1) the time value of money and (2) interest that will compound over time to increase the overall rate earned. The actual rate of return earned by a long-term investment, called its yield or *internal rate of return (IRR)*, takes the time value of money and compounded interest into account.

After calculating a long-term investment's IRR, investors can decide whether the anticipated future returns are sufficiently large enough to justify a current outlay of funds. To work from the future to the present, they can use a very simple formula and present value table (Ill. 2.4).

Let's illustrate how a long-term investment's yield is calculated. Assume a $2,000 investment is expected to grow to $2,800 after five years. To determine the annual yield on this investment, first divide the present value of the single sum investment by its compound sum (or future value). The result will be the *present-value interest factor*. In this case, the calculation is:

$$\frac{\text{Present value}}{\text{Future value}} = \frac{\$2,000}{\$2,800} = .714$$

The determination of the present-value interest factor does not give the final answer but, in effect, scales down the problem so that the investor can discover the answer from a present value table (Ill. 2.4). The resulting factor is then located on the table and will indicate the yield. (If a factor does not appear under a given interest rate, an approximation is usually adequate.)

For the example shown above, the resulting factor of .714 for five years is located on the present value table (the closest factor is .713) and indicates a yield of 7 percent. If the interest rate on similar investments is 5 percent, this investment's 7 percent yield would be acceptable; if the interest on similar investments is 9 percent, the 7 percent yield would probably be unacceptable.

Dividends

Just as interest is the earnings on lender investments, so *dividends* generally are the distributed earnings on *owner (equity) investments*. The word "distributed" is important because there are some earnings on owner investments that are not distributed, and those will be discussed later.

Dividends, in general, may be defined as portions of a corporation's net profits that have been officially declared by the board of directors of the corporation for distribution on its outstanding shares of stock to its stockholders. The total to be distributed is divided by the number of outstanding shares to determine the dividend per share, then each shareholder receives a distribution equal to that dividend per share times the number of shares he or she owns. Obviously, such dividends may vary in amount because the board's periodic decisions are influenced, of course, by the net income (profit) of the company—although a company prefers to pay an equal or larger dividend with each successive dividend declaration.

Dividends usually are distributed in *cash* (by check) on a regular periodic (e.g., quarterly) basis. But sometimes dividend distributions are made in *stock, bonds, property* or *promissory notes*. Sometimes stockholders are given the option of receiving cash or stock dividends. There are also *liquidation* dividends, which represent the return of capital to the owners—as distributions of funds arising from the operation of wasting assets (e.g., from depreciation allowances) or as distributions to owners of a corporation's net assets when the company is winding up its affairs (closing).

There are also *insurance policy dividends*, which are not dividends in the sense described above. They are really distributions of the excess of the premium paid for coverage at the beginning of a period (usually a year) over the actual premium needed as determined at the end of the period. This excess arises from such sources as savings in actual to expected claims (in life insurance, more favorable than expected mortality), savings in actual to expected expenses and excesses in actual over expected earnings on assets, that is, actual compared to the expected claims, expenses and earnings assumed in the original premium calculation. Since these are refunds to policyowners of excess premiums paid, insurance dividends are not considered to be income for tax purposes, although interest paid on accumulation of those dividends is considered to be taxable income.

The above, and other less typical dividends, will be discussed more fully later, notably in the chapters on stocks, annuities and life insurance.

ILL. 2.4 ■ *Present-Value Interest Factors for One Dollar (PVIF)*

Year	1%	2%	3%	4%	5%	6%	7%	8%	9%	10%
1	.990	.980	.971	.962	.952	.943	.935	.926	.917	.909
2	.980	.961	.943	.925	.907	.890	.873	.857	.842	.826
3	.971	.942	.915	.889	.864	.840	.816	.794	.772	.751
4	.961	.924	.888	.855	.823	.792	.763	.735	.708	.683
5	.951	.906	.863	.822	.784	.747	.713	.681	.650	.621
6	.942	.888	.837	.790	.746	.705	.666	.630	.596	.564
7	.933	.871	.813	.760	.711	.665	.623	.583	.547	.513
8	.923	.853	.789	.731	.677	.627	.582	.540	.502	.467
9	.914	.837	.766	.703	.645	.592	.544	.500	.460	.424
10	.905	.820	.744	.676	.614	.558	.508	.463	.422	.386
11	.896	.804	.722	.650	.585	.527	.475	.429	.388	.350
12	.887	.789	.701	.625	.557	.497	.444	.397	.356	.319
13	.879	.773	.681	.601	.530	.469	.415	.368	.326	.290
14	.870	.758	.661	.577	.505	.442	.388	.340	.299	.263
15	.861	.743	.642	.555	.481	.417	.362	.315	.275	.239
16	.853	.728	.623	.534	.458	.394	.339	.292	.252	.218
17	.844	.714	.605	.513	.436	.371	.317	.270	.231	.198
18	.836	.700	.587	.494	.416	.350	.296	.250	.212	.180
19	.828	.686	.570	.475	.396	.331	.277	.232	.194	.164
20	.820	.673	.554	.456	.377	.312	.258	.215	.178	.149
21	.811	.660	.538	.439	.359	.294	.242	.199	.164	.135
22	.803	.647	.522	.422	.342	.278	.226	.184	.150	.123
23	.795	.634	.507	.406	.326	.262	.211	.170	.138	.112
24	.788	.622	.492	.390	.310	.247	.197	.158	.126	.102
25	.780	.610	.478	.375	.295	.233	.184	.146	.116	.092
30	.742	.552	.412	.308	.231	.174	.131	.099	.075	.057
35	.706	.500	.355	.253	.181	.130	.094	.068	.049	.036
40	.672	.453	.307	.208	.142	.097	.067	.046	.032	.022
45	.639	.410	.264	.171	.111	.073	.048	.031	.021	.014
50	.608	.372	.228	.141	.087	.054	.034	.021	.013	.009

Rent

Rent is the payment or series of periodic payments that owners of property receive from others for the possession, occupancy or use of that property. It is the form of earnings return received from income-producing *real property* (such as farm, residential and business real estate), or from income-producing *personal property* (such as rental machinery, equipment, vehicles and the like).

Copyrights

Copyrights on the works of authors and composers, and *patents* on the works of inventors, are assets that often produce income. The earnings that owners receive on copyrights and patents are called *royalties*. These usually are payments based on specified amounts or percentages of price per copyrighted item or patented article sold.

A royalty also may be a share of the product or profit reserved for the owner of a valuable right that has been granted to someone for use or exploitation. Grantors of oil and mining leases, for example, would be recipients of such royalties.

Gross Return—Capital Growth

Capital growth, another return on investment, means an increase in the value of the asset itself. There are several ways that such an increase can occur. For one, the earnings can be plowed back into the asset (e.g., a business buying new equipment) to increase its capital value. Or labor and material can be added to increase the capital value of the asset. But these are actually reinvestment or additional investments that make the combined old and added values worth more than the original value.

Appreciation

The primary form of capital growth—*appreciation*—increases the value of an asset (in excess of its depreciable cost) due to economic and other conditions, and differs from value resulting from improvements or additions.

Here is an example of appreciation in asset value: 100 shares of XYZ stock are purchased at $30 per share for a total of $3,000. Two years later, the market price of XYZ stock is $40 per share, so the value of those 100 shares is up to $4,000. The $1,000 increase in value ($10 per share) is not an earnings return. It is *appreciation* in the asset's capital value and, if the stock is sold, represents a capital growth return on the asset.

Investment Costs

To this point, the discussion of "return on investment" has been limited to gross return, earnings and capital growth. Now consider the *costs of investment* that may be broken down into three major categories: (1) acquisition costs; (2) holding costs; and (3) disposition costs.

"What about taxes?" you might ask. Applicable taxes (income, capital gains, sales, gift, estate and any other taxes involved) are indeed costs and fall into the three major categories cited above. They will be included (as appropriate) in the following discussions of those categories.

Acquisition Costs

These are the costs associated with purchasing or acquiring investment property or other financial resources. In addition to the *basic purchase price*, these costs normally include some of the following:

- *Sales costs*—charges, fees, commissions and so on—frequently fall in this category. Sometimes these sales costs are obviously charged directly to the investor (buyer), but other times this is not so obvious. For example, frequently the sales charge, fee or commission is simply added onto the net value of whatever is being purchased and included in the price that the investor pays. This is often so even when, technically, the seller pays this cost.

- *Taxes*, payable by the recipient because an asset is acquired, are also costs that pertain to some investments and other financial resources. In the transfer of stocks on the New York Stock Exchange, for example, there are certain state transfer taxes and SEC fees (which are virtually the same as taxes) payable. Generally, these taxes and fees are paid by the seller.

- There are other *miscellaneous acquisition costs* applicable to various investments, such as attorney fees, appraisal fees, finder fees, title search fees or title insurance premiums, loan points, buyer's closing costs and so on. These, as well as the sales and tax acquisition costs mentioned above, will be discussed more specifically later with the specific kinds of financial resources to which they apply.

Holding Costs

While an individual holds investment property or other financial resources, there are certain costs that occur because of and during that holding. These costs commonly include the following:

- *Advisory*, or *management fees*, as well as *operating costs* are generally charged to owners of shares in managed funds, property in trusts or professionally managed rental property, and so on, throughout the period those assets are held.

- *Repairs, maintenance and needed improvements* may arise during the holding of some assets. If so, they may be considered as holding costs, although some of them may be considered as capital improvements for tax purposes. Rental properties (real estate or personal) are assets that commonly involve these kinds of holding costs.

- Various forms of *property* and *liability insurance* also may be needed (sometimes required by law), and the *premiums* on such coverages would be holding costs. So would any *losses* by fire, storm, flood, accident or the like—if not covered by insurance.

- *Taxes* are still another kind of holding cost. These include *income taxes* on interest, dividends, rents, royalties and other earnings returns (received or accrued) on properties held—except for those specifically exempted (such as interest on certain municipal bonds) and those specifically tax deferred (such as earnings on "qualified" retirement plans, pension and profit-sharing plans, IRAs and so on) until those earning actually are received. Then there may be capital gains taxes on any distributions considered by the taxing authorities to represent *increases* in principal rather than *returns* of principal.

- And, of course, there are *intangible taxes, personal property taxes, real estate taxes* and so forth that state and local taxing jurisdictions assess when a person owns and holds those various assets.

Disposition Costs

Finally, there are costs that arise because of, and at the time of, the disposition or liquidation of investment property and other financial resources. In addition to debts against the property, such costs include the following:

- *Sales costs*—charges, fees, commissions, etc.—that the seller must pay are, of course, disposition costs. In the case of stocks, for example, the seller pays a broker a commission for selling just as the buyer pays a broker a commission for buying.

- *Taxes* are another major disposition cost. Any untaxed earnings returns, including those deferred under qualified retirement or other tax-deferred plans, generally are subject to *income tax* on disposition or liquidation of the assets. Any capital growth returns are generally subject to a *capital gains tax*. Transfer of property to someone else by gift may subject those assets to a *gift tax*. Transfer at death may subject those assets to *estate tax* and usually to *inheritance tax*. Any transfers of stocks on an organized exchange are subject to a *Securities and Exchange (SEC) fee* and usually to an exchange *transfer tax*, both generally paid (at least technically) by the seller.

These and other disposition costs also will be discussed in more detail later, as will acquisition and holding costs, with the particular financial resources to which they pertain.

Net Return—Earnings

The *earnings* form of net return includes all the *gross earnings* discussed earlier (interest, dividends, rents, royalties, etc.) *less* any of the *costs applicable to the earnings* (advisory and management fees, operating costs; repairs, maintenance and needed improvements, other than capital improvements; property insurance premiums; income taxes on earnings, intangibles taxes, personal property taxes, real estate taxes).

That difference is the *net earnings return* on any asset or combination of assets to which it applies, generally expressed as a percentage of net periodic earnings return on the net capital value of the asset or assets. It may be determined periodically (monthly, quarterly or annually), or it may be totaled or averaged over an entire holding period. It may be figured currently on actual experience or it may be forecast into the future by projecting on the basis of past performance, arbitrary assumptions or fixed earnings provisions.

Net Return—Capital Growth

The *capital growth* form of net return includes the *gross value* at time of valuation (usually the gross sale price plus any capital distributions since acquisition) *less* any *indebtedness*, *less* the *cost basis* (usually the basic purchase price plus any subsequent capital investments and capital improvements but less any indebtedness), *less* any of the *costs affecting capital values* at time of acquisition or disposition, or while holding.

Those costs affecting capital values include such items as:

- sales costs whenever incurred;

- taxes and fees incurred because of acquiring, holding or disposing of assets (including taxes on capital gains but not on earnings);

- transfer taxes and fees;

- sales taxes;

- title and other fees for ownership—not for use;

- gift, estate and inheritance taxes; and

- other costs incurred with respect to acquisition or disposition, such as closing costs whenever incurred (including legal and appraisal fees; title search fees or title insurance premiums; costs of acquiring, establishing or providing clear title; loan points incurred to obtain financing; etc.).

Each financial product should be evaluated according to the various risk elements discussed earlier. This may be easier with some types of financial products than others. Some elements of risk, as applied to a specific asset, may be measured quantitatively. For example, an investment is usually acceptable if the rewards of purchasing it equal or exceed its costs.

■ INVESTMENT STRATEGIES

Some investments are best suited for short-term goals, others for long-range ones. For example, if the investor's goal is to establish an emergency fund, he or she should be concerned with safety and liquidity. On the other hand, if the objective is retirement income, potential long-term growth and safety might be the investor's top priorities.

As stated earlier, each investor has specific, individual reasons for investing. Whether they want to supplement their current income, plan for major purchases or

ILL. 2.5 ■ *Risks Involved with Typical Investment Alternatives*

Type of Investment	Factor to Be Evaluated				
	Safety	Risk	Income	Growth	Liquidity
Bank accounts	High	Low	Average	Low	High
Common stock	Average	Average	Average	High	Average
Preferred stock	Average	Average	High	Average	Average
Corporate bonds	Average	Average	High	Low	Average
Government bonds	High	Low	High	Low	High
Mutual funds	Average	Average	Average	Average	Average
Real estate	Average	Average	Average	Average	Low
Commodities	Low	High	N/A	Low	Average
Options	Low	High	N/A	Low	Average
Strategic metals, gemstones, collectibles	Low	High	N/A	Low	Low

N/A = Not applicable

provide an estate for their dependents, investors must consider a number of factors before they invest. How important each of these factors is to the individual investor will determine which investments and which investment strategies they choose.

In future chapters we'll look at specific types of financial products and the salient features of each that suggest the strategies an investor may use to reach his or her goals. Here, we'll look at investment strategies in general.

Buy-and-Hold Strategy

Many investors are concerned about an investment's *safety factor*, or its minimal risk of loss. Because the amount of risk and return on a given investment is affected by a variety of changing economic and business conditions, the investor must understand these conditions and decide how much risk he or she is willing to assume. Those investors who are concerned about safety of principal tend to select low-risk investments.

Conservative investors tend to choose a conservative *buy-and-hold* investment strategy. Their objective is usually to place money in secure investments that will grow over time. This strategy is often used to accumulate capital over time, to finance the children's college education or to plan for retirement. Very safe investments—such as Treasury bonds backed by the U.S. government—appeal to conservative investors who usually wish to preserve their original capital. Most of the income from these investments will be plowed back into the investment portfolio.

High Income Strategy

Investors who are primarily concerned with current income may use a *high income* investment strategy. These investors often include people who are trying to supplement their income and for whom safety of principal and stability of income are more important than capital gains. If dividend or interest income is a primary objective, investors often select corporate bonds or the common or preferred stock of a corporation whose overall future earnings picture and dividend policies are favorable.

Other investments that provide income potential include income mutual funds and real estate rental property—although income from rentals is not guaranteed because there is the possibility of vacancies. Speculative investments, such as commodities and collectibles, offer little potential for regular income.

Quality Long-Term Growth

Investors who are primarily concerned with how much their investments will increase in value will probably use a *quality long-term growth* strategy. When growth is a primary objective, common stocks issued by growth companies—electronics, health care and energy firms—offer the potential for substantial growth. Generally, corporate and government bonds are not purchased for growth. Both growth-oriented mutual funds and real estate offer growth possibilities, but speculative investments stress immediate returns rather than continued growth.

Aggressive Stock Management

More assertive investors seeking capital gains as their primary source of return may use an *aggressive stock management* strategy. This also uses quality stock issues for growth and as an added source of income. With this strategy, however, the investor concentrates on seeking attractive rates of return through aggressive trading. For example, blue chips and growth stocks might be traded in less than a year to quickly realize gains. This investment strategy consumes a great deal of the investor's time and skill. Although this strategy can be quite risky, the potential returns are high.

Speculation and Short-Term Trading

Unlike conservative investors who prefer relatively safe, liquid assets, highly risk-tolerant investors may hold strategic metals, gemstones and collectibles—the least liquid assets. These investors follow a *speculation and short-term trading* strategy that often requires them to move quickly in and out of the market. For example, they might buy and sell copper in a single day or hold pork bellies for less than a week. Key to this investment strategy is having the finances and risk tolerance for absorbing huge losses as well as potential capital gains.

■ CREATING AN INVESTMENT PLAN

As an insurance professional eager to assist your clients with their financial planning, it is imperative that you understand where they stand today and where they expect to be at some point in the future. To quote Yogi Berra, "If you don't know where you're going, you'll wind up someplace else." In your client's financial plan, it is critical to identify three points for reference—*objectives, development* and *current position*.

Objectives

Planning for financial success begins with setting concrete goals. These goals will be both nonfinancial—pertaining to love, family and religion—and financial—pertaining to current and future consumption. Financial goals form the basis for financial planning. Unless these goals are clearly defined, your client cannot hope to achieve financial success.

People's needs and objectives change throughout their lives. You can assist your clients in formulating financial goals that are appropriate for each phase of their lives. For example, young adults' objectives should include establishing credit and purchasing adequate insurance. Those age 65 and over might be more likely to have concerns about estate planning.

Financial planners generally agree that people's lives consist of the following three phases:

1. *Career entry phase.* The young wage earner leaves school and enters the income-earning period of life. The job must be mastered and expenses are high. Acquisition of property is a key objective. Marriage and children are huge responsibilities. If children are to go to college, a savings program often conflicts with the property acquisition objectives. Budgets are very tight.

2. *Career maturity phase.* In the mid-life cycle the wage earner(s) has (have) become established in a career (or separate careers). Equity in real property, either inherited or accumulated, is now well under way. Two-wage-earner couples with no children may start out in this phase. Budgets now have more room for saving and investing.

3. *Retirement phase.* Some people slow down as they approach retirement age. Their job responsibilities are handled with well-refined skills. They have attained the right to longer and longer vacations. Others seek to delay their retirement and may work the same (or longer) hours to prove their worth. Eventually, however, whether by mandatory means or by voluntary choice, people retire. This phase lasts until death.

Development

After the client outlines his or her financial objectives, the financial planner can review the client's past financial experiences and attitudes for perspective. The planner should identify particular strengths and weaknesses. For example, one might try to focus on such areas as:

1. *Consumption/savings ratio.* Does the individual live within his or her financial means? Do savings fluctuate widely? Has the individual's lifestyle increased as his or her income has increased?

2. *Income.* Is the source of income stable? Can it be directed or controlled?

3. *Family.* Has the family size increased? Is it now stable?

4. *Education.* How educated is the individual? What capacity to learn is exhibited?

5. *Investment/financial expertise.* Look for particularly rewarding past performance (or failures). If the individual can earn 20 to 30 percent on capital invested in a privately held business, this obviously should be reflected in the financial plan. Does the individual have insight into technical areas that can be utilized in selecting stocks or other investments? (Note: This can be measured by results. Doctors, for example, may understand medicine but fail miserably when investing in pharmaceutical stocks.)

Current Financial Position

This forms the starting point for strategy analysis in a financial plan. The family finances are a reflection of conscious or unconscious priorities. To take a snapshot look at where the starting position of the financial plan lies, it is necessary to evaluate existing financial resources. Just like any business, the family unit is a microeconomic unit. That is, it must accept the broader government, tax and economic systems as they exist and operate within these parameters. Like any economic unit, the family operates with already accumulated limited resources, revenues and expenses, fixed overhead and liabilities.

In the final analysis, each asset must be evaluated, both in quantitative (dollar amount) and subjective terms, from the perspective of the risks covered earlier. Thus, in focusing on the death risk in the financial plan, for example, the worth of real estate might be *quick sale value* (low market value minus selling expenses, minus mortgage indebtedness), while a life insurance policy might be valued at full face amount. In focusing on the risk of opportunity costs, it may be better to use the real estate's loan value (70 to 90 percent of assessed value minus any *points* or costs of processing) minus the existing loan balance.

A budget may identify potential sources of funds for future investment, without jeopardizing the individual's lifestyle. It is the connecting factor between current assets (with the earnings and gains they are expected to generate) and the future objectives identified. Most people view savings as the residual balance between income and expenses. An exception might be the Christmas Club, where a target is established first and then the weekly deposit is determined. This emphasis on current expenses is the ruination of many families' finances. Savings, as the residual, is a misapplication of perspective but reflects the pressures placed on individuals to "buy now, pay later."

This course assumes that the reader already is licensed to sell life insurance products. It further assumes that the life agent will orchestrate and coordinate the actions of other professionals who may be needed to create an investment plan for his or her client. This need not be a conflict of interest. As covered in this course, the life insurance industry offers financial products and services that fill financial needs uniquely by providing insurance protection that reduces risk. Many of the risks covered can be addressed with various insurance products.

■ SUMMARY

The total financial plan evaluates assets in terms of *risk* and *return*. Though very important, the risks of loss of principal or market value are only two of a long list of risk factors. Financial reward (or avoidance of loss) is the opposite of risk. In general, the higher the risk, the greater the potential reward. Risks may be interrelated. A risk trade-off occurs where assuming more risk in one area reduces the risk level in the other. Risk is *personal* and different individuals have different risk attitudes. Therefore, specific strategies should be employed to maximize the effectiveness of any investment plan. This is an ongoing, personal process of monitoring, refining and adapting the plan to reflect actual experience, family changes and exterior factors over time.

No matter what the investor's current age or financial situation, an investment strategy should begin with traditional savings vehicles—checking and savings accounts—that are highly liquid and almost risk free because they are generally insured by the federal government. In Chapter 3, we'll look at various savings vehicles that offer protection and liquidity along with the potential for modest return on investment.

■ CHAPTER 2 QUESTIONS FOR REVIEW

1. In general, the greater the variation in an investment's potential gains or losses, the

   A. smaller the investment's return

   B. greater the investment's return

   C. smaller the investment's risk

   D. greater the investment's risk

2. Which of the following statements best reflects the time value of money theory?

   A. It is reasonable to expect prices to rise over time.

   B. A dollar received today is worth more than a dollar received tomorrow.

   C. A dollar received today is worth less than a dollar received tomorrow.

   D. The purchasing power of money gradually increases over time.

3. An increase in the value of an asset due to economic and other business conditions is called

   A. interest

   B. dividends

   C. appreciation

   D. depreciation

4. All of the following are considered to be moderate risk/moderate to high return investments EXCEPT

 A. common stocks
 B. mutual funds
 C. money market mutual funds
 D. preferred stocks

5. The costs of investment include all of the following EXCEPT

 A. acquisition costs
 B. holding costs
 C. disposition costs
 D. sales costs

3
Savings/Liquidity Vehicles

E very investor should begin his or her savings or investment program with an emergency fund that can be obtained quickly in case of immediate need. This fund should include a nest egg of cash and cash equivalents such as savings accounts, money market funds and certificates of deposit. Only after individuals have saved between three and six months' worth of living expenses should they look at additional investments that offer higher potential returns.

In this chapter, we discuss a number of financial products in which people can store their wealth, usually on a relatively short-term basis, until they are ready to spend that wealth for purposes of consumption—or to convert it to an alternate form of savings or investment. Called *savings/liquidity vehicles* here, these financial products are of the cash and near-cash variety. They generally offer a high degree of convenience in financial transactions and provide a relatively high degree of safety. Most of these short-term investments, while held, pay interest to their owners. We will examine common characteristics of these vehicles, such as liquidity, relative safety and convenience. Then we'll look at various types of savings/liquidity vehicles, including what they are, how they work, how they are used and how they are taxed.

■ ■ ■ ■ ■

■ FINANCIAL INSTITUTIONS

In general, people meet their cash needs with currency and coins and basic deposit accounts—passbook savings, checking and NOW accounts and other deposit accounts. These assets are very *liquid*, meaning they can be easily withdrawn with little or no delay or complications. As we've stated, selecting highly liquid financial assets requires trade-offs between interest yield, on the one hand, and risk and liquidity, on the other. Typically, basic deposit accounts are stored in a number of *financial institutions* (also called *financial intermediaries*), including banks, savings and loans and credit unions. These financial institutions accept, store and use money for the benefit of customers.

Deposits in these financial institutions offer a high degree of safety because they are insured, primarily by the *Federal Deposit Insurance Company (FDIC)*.* Since it was established in 1933, no depositor with insured accounts of $100,000 or less has lost a penny of principal or interest. It is important, however, to understand what federal deposit insurance covers. Under current law, each account registered at a bank or savings and loan is insured up to $100,000. For example, a married couple may have three accounts: one in the husband's name, one in the wife's name and a joint account in both their names. Each account is insured up to $100,000, for a total, in this case, of $300,000. (Recent legislation limits insurance on Individual Retirement Accounts (IRAs) to $100,000 per financial institution, not per account.)

Before we discuss the types of financial products that these institutions offer, let's take a brief look at some of the financial institutions that offer these products.

The term *bank* is often used to describe any institution that accepts deposits and then allows checks to be written against these deposits as a means of making payments. More precisely, banks are organizations that provide services for the transaction and management of money and other assets. Banks belong to a large group of institutions that are described as *financial intermediaries*—institutions that "stand between" savers and depositors, on the one hand, and borrowers and spenders, on the other. Banks may be typified by these five characteristics:

1. charter (federal or state);

2. ownership (stock or mutual);

3. operations (commercial or savings);

4. membership (Federal Reserve member or nonmember); and

5. insurance (whether or not the organization holds federal deposit insurance).

Despite a number of changes in the banking environment over the past several years, many people prefer to make deposits in banks rather than other types of financial institutions, even though these other institutions offer similar savings accounts and services to their customers.

Commercial Banks

Commercial banks are privately owned, profit-seeking institutions that offer a wide range of financial services to their customers, such as installment loans, interest-bearing checking accounts and trust management. Commercial banks may be chartered by the states or by the federal government. Nationally chartered banks are supervised by the Federal Reserve Bank, the central bank of the United States. Commercial banks accept deposits from individuals, businesses and the govern-

---

* Although the FDIC is the primary insurer of deposits, banks are also covered by the *Bank Insurance Fund (BIF)*, savings and loans are covered by the *Savings Association Insurance Fund (SAIF)* and credit unions are covered by the *National Credit Union Share Insurance Fund*, administered by the *National Credit Union Association (NCUA)*.

ment and are the main source of commercial loans to businesses. However, almost all of them aggressively seek individual checking and savings deposits, as well as personal installment loans.

The Federal Reserve requires commercial banks to maintain *reserves* equal to some fraction of bank deposits to meet obligations to depositors. Primary reserves consist of cash on hand and in the collection process and outstanding balances due from other banks. The nation's economic activity and the stability of the banking system depend on achieving and maintaining a proper level of reserves.

Mutual Savings Banks

Mutual savings banks specialize in savings accounts for individuals, investing such savings in long-term bonds, mortgage loans and other high-quality investments for the benefit of all depositors. In terms of the services provided, they are more closely related to savings and loan associations than to commercial banks. They are operated as prescribed by law and by a self-perpetuating board of trustees for the benefit of their depositors, who really are the owners. These banks also pay, credit or accrue interest on savings vehicles either in specified percentages on balances or in percentages determined by specified formulas.

These banks are depositor-owned and mutually distribute any net returns (gross profits *less* bank expenses and reserves for guaranty funds for depositors and so on) to their depositors as dividends. They have little or no power to perform commercial functions.

Savings and Loan Associations

Many consumers deposit their savings in their local *savings and loan association (S&L)* (also commonly called *savings banks* and *savings institutions*), a financial intermediary that operates much like a commercial bank but usually offers fewer services and facilities. Savings and loan associations were originally called *building societies* because they used their savers' deposits to lend funds to home builders. Today, savings from depositors are primarily invested in mortgages, notes and other financial instruments.

Savings and loan associations may be state-chartered or federal-chartered financial intermediaries that receive the savings of their depositors (usually called *members*) and invest those savings in long-term amortized mortgage loans to their members and the general public. They may be organized and operated as either *mutual* associations or as capital *stock* corporations. *Mutual savings and loans* are owned by their depositors, who receive *dividends* on their deposits. The Internal Revenue Service (IRS) considers these dividends to be interest payments for federal income tax purposes. A *corporate savings and loan* is a profit-seeking corporation similar to a commercial bank. Depositors receive *interest*—not dividends—on their deposits.

The similarities between S&Ls and banks do not end with those noted above. In fact, although there are some *technical* differences that are of no consequence in this discussion, there are virtually no *practical* differences in the savings vehicles offered by these two types of financial institutions. For that reason, the various savings vehicles that S&Ls offer simply will be listed throughout this chapter, with only variations from bank-issued vehicles noted.

Credit Unions

Almost 70 million Americans belong to the 12,000 credit unions in the United States. The majority of these credit unions are federally chartered; the rest are state chartered.

Credit unions are nonprofit financial cooperatives organized to serve members of a particular group (e.g., people working for the same employer, people who live in the same community or those who belong to the same fraternal organization, church or labor union). The basic savings plan is the *share account*, which is the equivalent of a bank passbook savings account. Money can be deposited and withdrawn at will and interest is paid on the balance. Unlike banks and S&Ls, credit unions require that depositors first become *members* of the credit union by paying a small membership fee and purchasing at least one share in the credit union.

Credit unions may be incorporated in the United States under a federal law or under state laws in virtually all 50 states. These organizations are managed by boards of directors and committees made up of and elected or appointed by members (the depositors) of the respective credit unions. Generally, each member has one vote (regardless of the size of his or her savings) for each office or matter that comes up for a vote.

The purpose of credit unions is not to make money, but to help their members save for the future and make intelligent use of credit. Accordingly, credit unions are owned by their members who save their money together and make relatively low interest loans to each other from the resulting accumulated funds. After expenses and legal reserve requirements are met, virtually all of the earnings of credit unions are returned to their members in the form of *dividends* on shareholdings and are credited proportionately to share accounts of the members.

Many credit unions offer accounts similar to money market deposit accounts or money market mutual funds. Deposits made at credit unions are used for making consumer loans, and sometimes mortgage loans, to members. Loan rates are typically much lower than those charged by other financial institutions. In addition to savings, credit unions also offer share certificates, interest-bearing checking accounts, individual retirement accounts (IRAs), credit cards, traveler's checks, money orders and check-cashing services.

Again, there are some *technical* differences between credit unions and S&Ls or banks, but these are of little consequence in this discussion. Of greater significance is the fact that there are virtually no *practical* differences in the savings vehicles offered by these three financial institutions. In fact, they are highly competitive with one another.

With this brief discussion of financial institutions in mind, let's turn our attention to the kinds of savings/liquidity vehicles these institutions offer, beginning with the features and characteristics they share.

■ COMMON CHARACTERISTICS OF SAVINGS/LIQUIDITY VEHICLES

Many people begin their investment portfolio as children when they make their first deposit in a passbook savings account at their local bank or savings and loan. As they get older, they typically add a number of other accounts, such as checking and NOW accounts, certificates of deposit and so on, to their portfolio. But, before we look at the types of savings/liquidity vehicles that are available, it is important to understand why cash or near-cash must be held in the first place. There are at least four reasons to hold assets in this category:

1. Liquidity

2. Safety of principal

3. Convenience

4. Emergency fund

Let's look at each of the reasons individuals should establish a cash reserve.

Liquidity

Liquid assets (also called *quick assets*) are cash or any other assets that can be converted to cash with a minimum amount of inconvenience in a short period of time and without substantial loss. The most liquid of all assets are coins and currency. However, since coins and currency in a billfold or purse pay no return and can easily be lost or stolen, most people limit the amount of coins and currency held. Instead, larger amounts of money are usually held in a checking (or NOW) account to pay current bills.

ILL. 3.1 ■ *Major Financial Instruments Ranked in Approximate Order of Liquidity*

1. Cash or cash equivalents

Currency
Demand deposits
Money market mutual funds
Time deposits
Credit union shares
U.S. savings bonds

2. Money market instruments

Federal funds
U.S. Treasury bills
Commercial paper
Negotiable certificates of deposit
Bankers' acceptances

3. Capital market instruments

U.S. Treasury notes
U.S. Treasury bonds
U.S. agency securities
Municipal bonds
Corporate bonds
Mortgages

4. Corporate equities

Preferred stock
Common stock

In concept, the criteria of liquidity are chiefly *time* and *acceptance*. From a time standpoint, a liquid resource must be immediately (or almost immediately) available or usable as money. From an acceptance standpoint, it must be acceptable as money by all parties concerned. All financial assets included as savings/ liquidity vehicles in this chapter share those time and acceptance criteria of liquidity in virtually all situations.

Safety of Principal

Safety in an investment means a minimal risk of loss. In terms of dollars, all of the savings/liquidity vehicles discussed in this chapter offer virtually absolute *safety of principal* except for physical loss, theft, fire loss or the like. Some do and some don't provide return (earnings and/or growth), but whether they do or don't, they generally don't decline in *dollar value* while they are being held or owned.

From the standpoint of *purchasing power value*, on the other hand, the principal usually tends to decline with inflation, just as it tends to do with other fixed-dollar assets. The only exceptions are savings/liquidity vehicles, such as bonds, that generate variable-dollar growth returns (positive or negative) such that their principal values tend to remain fairly constant in terms of purchasing power.

Convenience

Although several vehicles in this category yield returns (sometimes quite substantial returns), the emphasis is on their *convenience*—as a means of meeting day-to-day and month-to-month money needs, such as buying goods and services and paying bills. Moreover, they are convenient to carry, handle or transfer. Those that are not already forms of money or substitutes that can be used as money (e.g., a cashier's check) are readily convertible to such forms.

Generally, savings/liquidity vehicles are used for relatively short-term needs, partly due to the convenience these vehicles offer. On the other hand, when financial objectives are relatively long-range, less liquid and consequently less convenient (although often higher yielding) resources are more often used.

Emergency Fund

Money held in a savings/liquidity vehicle makes a good *emergency fund* that can be obtained quickly in case of immediate need. In fact, any savings or investment program should begin with such a fund. The amount in this fund will vary, but most financial planners agree that it should be at least three months' salary (after taxes). In fact, many feel that six months' salary (after taxes) is a better safety cushion. This fund should be deposited in a savings account at the highest available interest rate.

Disadvantages of Savings/Liquidity Vehicles

While they do offer advantages such as great liquidity, safety of principal, convenience and so on, cash and cash equivalent financial vehicles also involve some trade-offs or *opportunity costs*. Such costs include, for example, the giving up of greater returns (earnings and/or capital growth) and hedges against inflation, either or both of which generally are available through use of other financial resources.

Opportunity Costs

With respect to greater returns as an opportunity cost, some of the cash and cash equivalent forms offer no returns, while others offer modest to relatively substantial *earnings return* (no capital growth). There are a number of financial resources in other categories, however, which generally return much higher earnings and/or capital appreciation. The resources in those other categories are discussed in later chapters.

Little Hedge Against Inflation

As hedges against inflation, cash and cash equivalent forms offer little, if any. They are cash, cash substitutes or debt-type vehicles that represent fixed-dollar values and that return, if anything, fixed-dollar earnings (no appreciation). The rate of return on savings should be compared with the inflation rate. For example, when the inflation rate is high (say 10 percent), people whose money is in savings accounts earning 5 percent or 6 percent experience a loss in the buying power of that money.

■ NO-RETURN TYPES OF VEHICLES

Most people need to safely store some funds to meet their everyday needs. Although almost everyone would like to earn some return on their savings, some types of savings/liquidity vehicles do not provide any return, earnings or capital growth. They include cash, money substitutes and regular checking accounts.

Cash

This word has several meanings and usages, but here *cash* includes *currency* (paper money) and *specie* (metal money or coins), both of which are legal tender. *Legal tender*, of course, is any money that is recognized as being lawfully used by a debtor to pay a creditor, who must accept that money in the discharge of a debt, unless a contract between the parties specifically states another type of money is to be used. Certainly, this is the ultimate example of liquidity.

Cash itself earns no income unless it is loaned at interest or invested to grow. However, cash is the most liquid of all assets. To encourage individuals to forgo some liquidity, an institution must offer to pay a reasonable interest rate in return. The less liquid the account becomes, the more interest the institution must pay. For example, a bank may pay 2.5 percent on a highly liquid passbook savings account but 5 percent on a three-year certificate of deposit (CD).

Currency

Currency is paper money printed by the government and circulated freely throughout the country at its *par* (denomination) *value*, as legal tender. It is commonly circulated in denominations of $1, $5, $10, $20, $50 and $100. Clearly, there is no return (earnings or capital gain) on currency while it is held, except as its purchasing power value may rise or fall with the economy.

Specie

Specie is metal money (coin) minted by the government and, like currency, circulated freely throughout the country at its par (denomination) value, as legal tender. Its commonly circulated denominations include 1 cent, 5 cents, 10 cents, 25 cents, 50 cents and $1. Here again, there is no investment return while cash is held in this form, except as its purchasing power rises and falls with prevailing economic conditions.

Collectible Coins and Currency

Although these certainly would be cash if so used, rare coins and currency are not so used and thus are not included here as cash. Instead, they are considered to be "collectibles" and are discussed in a subsequent chapter.

Foreign Cash and Currency

If actually being used as money—say, to pay expenses when vacationing in the country of the money's origin or to buy goods or services in that country—*foreign cash and currency* are forms of cash in the sense intended here. But if (as more often is the case) they are being (1) held as collectibles or (2) bought or sold to hedge or profit on the money exchange rate, they are not included as "cash" here, but are included in other categories that are discussed in later chapters.

Money Substitutes

Mainly for convenience and safety from theft or physical loss, several forms of *money substitutes* are in common use today. Good examples are money orders, traveler's checks, certified checks, cashier's checks and credit cards. Traditional checks or checking accounts will be discussed separately below.

Money Orders

A *money order* is a directive issued by a post office, bank or telegraph office for payment of a specified sum of money, usually at another office. Money orders are instruments commonly purchased for a fee by people who don't have checking accounts, but want the safety and convenience of checks, especially for transferring money by mail or wire. Because the handling fee is considerably higher, a telegraphed or wired money order normally is used only when the money transfer must be made in a great hurry.

Both the purchaser's name and the payee's name appear on the face of the money order, for sake of easy identification and safety. No earnings or capital growth returns are payable or creditable to the holder of a money order.

Traveler's Checks

Traveler's checks are drafts purchased from banks or other issuers. They are a form of check especially designed for travelers, including vacationers, and are readily accepted in the United States, Canada and many other countries. The checks are preprinted in such denominations as $10, $20, $50 and $100.

At the time of purchasing traveler's checks, a purchaser must sign his or her name in a designated place on the face of each check and in the presence of an employee of the issuer. When a check is cashed later, the purchaser must again sign his or her name in another designated place on the face of the check. This gives whoever is cashing the check easy comparison of the signatures for proper identification and protection against forgery. Thus, traveler's checks are popular money substitutes for those who want that protection, as well as protection from loss or theft while traveling.

Certified and Cashier's Checks

These money substitutes are obligations of the bank that certifies or issues them. Certified and cashier's checks are acceptable as payment by virtually everyone domestically, even those who will not accept a personal check.

A *certified check* is a depositor's check drawn on a bank and on the face of which that bank has written the words "accepted" or "certified" with the date and signature of a bank officer or an authorized clerk. The amount of the check is charged to the depositor's account immediately and immediately becomes an obligation of the bank. The bank cannot legally certify a depositor's check that exceeds the amount the depositor has on deposit with the bank.

A *cashier's check* differs from a certified check in that it is the bank's own check, drawn upon itself. It is signed by the cashier or other authorized bank official. Although used for other purposes—such as to pay the bank's own obligations or to disburse the proceeds of a loan to a borrower if the proceeds are not deposited to the borrower's account—cashier's checks are also sold to individuals wishing to use them to satisfy their debts.

Both certified checks and cashier's checks generally are used when an individual's credit has not been established or when the individual doesn't have any (or a sufficient) checking account, and the payee requires assurance that the funds are available to cover the check before relinquishing title to goods or other properties being purchased.

Credit Cards

Credit cards are simply instruments or devices issued by oil companies, department stores, local banks and other financial institutions, for the use of the cardholders in obtaining cash, goods, services or anything else of value on credit, up to specified limits that vary with individual cardholders.

Some issuers (such as American Express, for example) charge a periodic (usually annual) fee to cardholders. Other issuers, such as Discover, have no annual fee. Most issuers charge a periodic fee (usually monthly) to merchants in amounts equal to a percentage of the charges that they have accepted against the respective credit cards during the period. In addition, interest is charged to the cardholder for amounts not paid after receipt of the monthly statement.

Some issuers offer *travel and entertainment (T&E)* cards that let cardholders charge purchases and pay for them later. These cards also charge an annual fee based on whether the cardholder has a regular, a gold or a platinum card. The higher the card level, the more benefits and services offered. Unlike bank cards, however, T&E cards do not impose a spending limit and the balance is due in full each month.

Some credit card issuers avoid the merchant charges by administering their own credit functions and some do not make any charges (periodically or for usage) to cardholders except for late payments well beyond the stated due dates. These issuers, such as department stores, charge off the expenses that otherwise would be covered by cardholder fees and merchant charges as costs of doing business. But local banks generally do impose the latter charges, even if not the cardholder fees.

In any event, a cardholder receives one periodic billing (usually monthly) per issuer, listing all transactions within the period and the total due, regardless of how many merchants (or others) accepted the cardholder's charges against that issuer's card. The issuer immediately reimburses those accepting the card, charging them a percentage fee based on dollar volume.

Some bank credit cards permit cardholders to obtain cash advances. Or cardholders with checking accounts may be permitted to write checks in excess of their balances, creating *overdrafts*. The bank then treats such overdrafts as cash advances and the amounts appear on the cardholders' periodic statements just as any other credit card transaction.

People sometimes confuse *debit cards* with credit cards. Debit cards are accepted by merchants like credit cards; however, whenever the card is used, the charge is immediately withdrawn from the user's banking checking account. Debit cardholders do not receive a bill, nor do they pay interest. However, they lose the benefit of floating their money during the grace period of a credit card.

Worth noting is that there are sufficient variations in policies and handling (including fees charged, if any, and interest rates) among the several credit and debit card issuers to warrant some shopping by those wishing to use credit cards as money substitutes. Competition in this lucrative field encourages issuers to attract and retain cardholders with "a better deal."

Regular Checking Accounts

Many people meet their cash needs by holding *demand deposits* in a *regular checking account*. These accounts are very liquid, earn no interest and usually have a monthly service charge. In most cases, the service charge can be avoided if the person maintains a minimum balance in the account or keeps a certain amount in a savings or other account at the same institution.

Usually checks are preprinted checking account withdrawal forms, but they actually need not be preprinted or even printed. According to the *Federal Reserve Board*, the seven-member governing body of the central banking system of the United States, a check is a *draft of order upon a bank or banking house purporting to be drawn upon a deposit of funds for the payment of a certain sum of money to a certain person named therein, or to his order, or to bearer, and paid instantly on demand.*

Because a check is a *negotiable instrument* by legal definition, it must meet certain legal requirements. It must: (1) be in writing and signed by the drawer; (2) contain the phrase *Pay to the order of*; (3) be payable on demand; (4) be payable to order or to bearer; and (5) when addressed to a drawee, the drawee must be named or otherwise indicated with reasonable certainty. In the case of a check, the amount shown on its face must be clearly discernible. A check should be dated, but lack of a date does not harm its negotiability.

Checks may be written to the order of other payees, of course, but they also may be written to *cash* and exchanged for cash when presented to anyone who is willing to accept them, or to the bank, which must accept them if there are sufficient funds in the depositor's account. The latter is the common way of making walk-in or drive-in checking account withdrawals at the bank.

■ INTEREST-BEARING ACCOUNTS

We have seen how individuals can satisfy short-term cash needs with vehicles that usually provide little return or growth. Basically, every individual also needs to store safely some funds for *future* needs and, in most cases, these funds are stored in one or more savings/liquidity instruments that produce return. These instruments include various kinds of bank savings accounts, savings and loan accounts, credit union shares, credit balances at brokerage houses, money market fund reserves, U.S. Treasury bills, commercial paper and so on. In general, savings/liquidity instruments have several characteristics in common:

- *They are debt instruments.* These investments represent financial obligations of issuers to the depositors, owners or the assigns of the depositors or owners. There are variations among the instruments relative to their descriptions, provisions, repayment dates and methods and so on; the security behind these debt instruments; their acquisition, holding and disposition; and other aspects.

- *They earn interest.* In general, *interest*—the rate that must be paid by a borrower to a lender for the use of funds—may be paid out or credited as earned (constructive receipt), or it may be represented by the difference between a discounted acquisition cost and the net amount received on disposition (accrued). In this case, *constructive receipt* means that, even though the interest may not be physically received, it is unconditionally available and, therefore, it is usually considered to be current income for tax purposes. *Accrual* means that the interest is earned but neither received nor past due— not unconditionally available currently, as on demand.

- *Interest on these investments is generally taxable.* With respect to *income tax*, net return on these vehicles (interest) generally is subject to both federal and state taxation at the time it is constructively received. Should these vehicles be used to fund retirement plans that meet requirements for tax deferral until retirement age (IRAs, Keogh plans, qualified pension and profit-sharing plans, etc.), however, the investment returns do not become subject to income tax until actually received.

Following are discussions of representative kinds of savings vehicles that are issued by commercial and savings banks, savings and loans and credit unions. Not all financial institutions issue all of these vehicles, nor is this discussion intended to cover every variation that may be offered. We will provide a general description of the vehicle (or type), discuss any special features and note any difference among financial institutions, if appropriate.

Savings Accounts

Traditional savings accounts offer maximum flexibility and liquidity in that they accept deposits and permit withdrawals at virtually any time. They are interest-bearing and are offered by financial institutions to encourage the habit of thrift among their customers as well as to generate funds that the institutions can lend out at higher rates than they pay the account holders.

Savings accounts may be opened and deposits made without charge at virtually any time. Some banks require minimum deposits to open accounts, and credit unions require that depositors become members. Deposits may be made in several ways, the most common of which are walk-in or drive-in, *automatic teller machines (ATMs)* and automatic or direct deposit (usually of periodic items, such as payroll, Social Security benefits and pension income). These various deposit methods are much the same as those associated with checking accounts.

While accounts are active, they generally bear interest, normally compounded daily from dates of deposit until dates of withdrawal and interest is usually credited to the accounts quarterly. Institutions generally provide depositors with statements of accounts (including these interest credits) quarterly on scheduled statement dates. Many institutions may make small charges to accounts for excessive deposit and withdrawal activities or if account balances drop below specified amounts.

Variations in Accounts

There are a variety of savings accounts, but any variation can be associated with one of two types of accounts:

1. those established to satisfy differing needs or to attract certain markets; or

2. those established so that they comply with the laws in certain states.

In the first category: *Christmas (or Hanukkah) Club Accounts* call for the depositors to save regular amounts periodically so that, with any interest accumulation, there will be money for Christmas or Hanukkah presents. *Kiddie Club Accounts* for children, *Budget Club Accounts* as well as *Vacation* and *Travel Club Accounts*—even special clubs to save for annual insurance premiums, taxes or the like—are similar variations that follow the same pattern as Christmas Club Accounts. Most institutions pay interest on these clubs, but some do not.

In the second category: Some state laws do not permit commercial banks to accept savings accounts, but do allow them to accept deposits on which interest is paid and to do so under the same conditions as savings banks. The banks do so under different names such as *Special Interest Accounts* and *Thrift Accounts*. Except for the name, they are regular savings accounts.

ILL. 3.2 ■ *Financial Products Through U.S. Financial Institutions*

Product	Minimum Deposit	Advantages	Disadvantages
NOW Accounts	Varies	Checking privileges Variable interest rate	Minimum balance may be required Service fee may be charged if balance falls below minimum
SuperNOW Accounts	Varies	Checking privileges Variable interest rate	Minimum deposit may be required Service fee may be charged if balance falls below minimum
Passbook Savings Accounts	Varies	Few restrictions Unlimited withdrawals Variable interest rate	Usually pay lower interest rates than money market funds
Money Market Deposit Accounts	Varies	Money market rate of interest	Restricted number of transfers and checks each month—usually six Minimum deposit may be required Service fee may be charged if balance falls below minimum
Certificates of Deposit	Varies	Guaranteed fixed rate of return	Loss of interest for early withdrawal
Treasury Bills	$10,000	Interest exempt from state and local taxes Easily sold	High minimum deposit
EE Savings Bonds	$25 ($50 face value)	Interest exempt from state and local taxes Federal tax deferred until maturity	Lengthy 10-year maturity Penalty for early withdrawal before five years
HH Savings Bonds	$500	Interest paid annual Provides current income	10-year maturity Federal taxes on interest not deferrable

Combination Savings/Checking Accounts

Although these are often called *interest-bearing accounts*, they technically are not. Traditionally, checking accounts have not been permitted to pay interest and savings accounts have not been permitted to allow withdrawals by check. But with creative thinking on the part of the banks, here is what has happened over the past several years.

First, banks physically (but not technically) combined a regular savings account and a regular checking account into the dual savings account/checkbook, with identical account numbers for each and a single statement sheet containing records of both accounts. Although the depositor could not write checks on what was in the savings account portion (only on what was in the checking account), it was relatively simple to transfer funds from one account to the other. An added advantage was that if a stated minimum balance was maintained in the savings account portion, no charge would be made for the checking account entries regardless of the number of transactions. A number of these combined accounts are still in use.

The second step came in 1981 with federal regulations permitting savings institutions to employ *negotiable orders of withdrawal*—the basis for the so-called NOW accounts. Combined checking and savings accounts were again used, but with *all* funds deposited to the savings accounts and *no* funds (zero balance) to the checking accounts. There was one very important addition: authorization by depositors for the banks to withdraw automatically from the savings accounts and deposit in the checking accounts just enough to cover the depositors' checks as those checks became payable.

That is the basis for the interest-bearing checking accounts, sometimes called *NOW accounts* or *SuperNOW accounts*. All deposited funds draw interest in the savings account until automatically transferred to the zero balance checking account to cover checks written by the depositor. Most banks have no flat charge or charge for checks (regardless of number) if a stated minimum balance is maintained, but usually charge after the balance falls below that minimum. With those exceptions, these accounts are virtually the same as combinations of regular checking and savings accounts, as previously discussed.

Certificates of Deposit (CDs)

A *certificate of deposit (CD)* is a receipt, payable to depositors or their assigns, for funds deposited with the issuing banks. In return for a deposit—usually $1,000 or more—made for a specified period, a bank or savings and loan will pay a specified interest rate. The longer the investor leaves the money on deposit, the higher the interest rate. Interest on six-month CDs is typically the same as that paid on money market funds, while the rate on longer-term CDs is usually a percentage point more than the investor could earn on U.S. Treasury securities of the same maturity.

Generally, a CD is the safest, simplest and one of the most popular ways for smaller investors to store extra cash for six months or more. There are usually a wide range of options as to maturity, no fees or commissions are charged and the investment is protected by federal insurance. However, if the investor must withdraw his or her money prior to the end of the certificate term, a withdrawal penalty is assessed. In addition, interest earned on CDs is subject to federal, state and local taxes.

ILL. 3.3 ■ *Selecting a Certificate of Deposit*

- Look for the best yield and the best rate.

- Determine how the institution calculates interest; the shorter the compounding period, the more interest will be paid.

- Compare the fees.

- Invest for the term you can afford; there are penalties for early withdrawal.

Some CDs are payable on demand by the holder, but are really not savings vehicles. They pay no interest and they are used primarily as guarantees of performance, as evidence of good faith or as collateral for loans. However, most CDs are payable to the holder at some specified future date 30 days or more after issuance or (in lieu of a specified due date) on a requested date at least 30 days after notice is given. They do pay interest, at fixed rates, from date of deposit.

Some banks issue larger denomination CDs—from $100,000 up to a million dollars—called *jumbo CDs*. These often pay interest at market rates at their inception and usually mature in one to six months. The federal deposit insurance stops at $100,000, so any amount above that is not insured and is secured only by the bank itself.

Some banks and brokerage firms also offer *zero CDs* in a variety of maturities. This type of CD does not pay interest on a regular basis, but it is sold at a discount from face value. Interest accrues annually until the CD matures and the holder must report the income for tax purposes.

Money Market Deposit Accounts

Offered by most banks as a response to Wall Street money market mutual funds, *money market deposit accounts* provide competitive interest rates as well as liquidity and are insured up to $100,000 by the Federal Deposit Insurance Corporation. They tend to pay slightly lower yields than money market mutual funds and Treasury bills (T-bills). One reason for the lower yields is that banks are required to keep on deposit in the Federal Reserve Bank up to 12 percent of the balance of these accounts, which means that banks cannot loan out and make money on that portion of their deposits. In addition, the interest rates change daily or weekly, along with changes in short-term interest rates.

Holders of money market deposit accounts are permitted to withdraw cash usually as often as needed. However, most accounts limit preauthorized transactions (such as a mortgage payment) or check-writing privileges to three per month. If the holder writes more than three checks or makes more than three transfers, the bank usually assesses fees for each subsequent transaction. Therefore, some institutions have established SuperNOW checking accounts for those who wish to write more than

---

ILL. 3.4 ■ *Selecting a Money Market Deposit Account*

- Look for institutions that consistently pay higher rates.

- Find out how interest is computed.

- Look for hidden fees.

- Compare services and convenience as well as interest.

- Compare minimum balance requirements.

---

three checks a month. The disadvantages of these SuperNOW accounts are higher fees and higher minimum check amounts such as $250 or $500.

Money Market Mutual Funds

Money market mutual funds are pooled investments offered by mutual funds, insurance companies and brokerage firms. Mutual funds are discussed in considerable detail in Chapter 7; however, since these particular funds—money market funds—also are commonly used savings/liquidity vehicles, they should be briefly mentioned here.

Money market funds invest in high-yielding, short-term securities such as Treasury bills, bank certificates or commercial paper. While holding these short-term securities, money market funds pass the net interest earned on to their shareholders (investors) on a per share basis, usually producing a substantially higher percentage of return than regular savings accounts. Moreover, the shares may be liquidated quickly for their current net asset value.

While a fund investor holds shares, the fund pays to, or reinvests in shares credited to the account of, the shareholder (at the shareholder's option) *dividends* that are generally the equivalent of the fund's *net earnings per share* in the past quarter. The

---

ILL. 3.5 ■ *Selecting Money Market Mutual Funds*

- Compare rates among funds. (Beware of funds offering much higher yields than others, which may indicate owner quality securities or extended maturities.)

- Look for quality and diversity of the fund's portfolio by reviewing the prospectus.

- Those in higher tax brackets might consider tax-exempt money funds as an alternative to longer-term, tax-exempt municipal bonds.

---

yield of a money market fund changes on a daily basis because it reflects the current money market rates earned by the underlying securities that make up the fund's portfolio. The yield that the investor receives is *net of the expenses of the fund*—that is, less any charges for advisory or management fees and operating costs during the period.

Money market mutual funds are generally less safe than money market deposit accounts offered at banks and S&Ls, which are federally insured up to $100,000. Overall, however, the risk is considered minimal because the funds are diversified and usually invested in government securities and short-term, high-grade corporate securities.

■ BROKERAGE HOUSE CASH AND CREDIT BALANCE ACCOUNTS

In addition to banks, S&Ls and credit unions, brokerage houses offer various cash and credit balance accounts. A *brokerage house* is an organization involved in the buying and selling of securities, combining the features of a *broker*—someone engaged in the business of transacting securities for another party and earning a commission—and a *dealer*—someone in the business of making a market in a security and offering buy and sell prices to others. We'll discuss traditional brokerage house operations, margin accounts and so on in Chapter 6. Here, only a relatively new type of check or credit card type of side account offered by some brokerage houses will be mentioned briefly.

The essential underlying component of such a vehicle is a *margin account* with the brokerage firm. This is an account wherein securities may be purchased with the aid of credit provided by the purchaser's broker. Establishing the account sometimes requires a minimum combined total (cash or securities) of a certain amount, such as $20,000, in the margin account. Once the minimum requirement is satisfied, the customer may elect to establish his or her choice of several side accounts, the only differences usually being the kinds of securities the side accounts are invested in (regular, tax-exempt or U.S. government money market funds). There may be a modest annual fee for maintaining the account. In case of a firm's liquidation, such an account in a member firm of the *Securities Investor Protection Corporation (SIPC)* is protected up to $500,000 in total cash and securities ($100,000 limit on cash) holdings per customer.

All cash, dividends and free credit balances are thereafter automatically transferred from the margin account to the side account and invested in the money market funds employed by that account. The side account, in effect, then becomes a managed money market fund, with the same kind of privileges, including withdrawals by check—or even by use of authorized debit card.

Should check or debit card obligations, or the customer's desire to invest additionally in the margin account, exceed the funds in the side account, appropriate funds can be loaned or transferred from the margin account. Clearly, this is a very flexible arrangement, comparable to similar services offered by banks and other financial institutions.

Over-the-Counter Market Vehicles

By definition, all securities transactions (stocks, bonds, funds and so on) not done on an organized exchange (such as the New York Stock Exchange) are *over-the-counter (OTC) transactions*. The common term for securities bought and sold that way, as well as the people buying and selling, is the *over-the-counter market*.

All *new* issues of stocks and bonds (including U.S. government and municipal bonds), all new issues of investment company shares (including mutual funds), the securities of many new and relatively small companies, most commercial bank and stock insurance company securities, 95 percent of government bonds, all private placements and many listed securities are bought and sold in the over-the-counter market. Here, we want to mention only *Treasury bills, Treasury notes* and *commercial paper*, all of which are savings/liquidity vehicles and are bought and sold over the counter.

Treasury Bills

Treasury bills, or *T-bills*, are U.S. government securities with 30-day to one-year maturities and are available in amounts of $10,000 to $1 million. *Treasury notes*, or *T-notes*, are the same except with one-year to 10-year maturities and denominations of $1,000 or $1 million. The rates are set by bidding and are generally much higher than those of savings accounts, yet these securities offer the ultimate in safety. They are purchased at a discount. In other words, the price paid for the security is less than its face value.

T-bills and T-notes can be purchased through banks at a modest fee, or from broker-dealers at slightly higher fees. They may be purchased at no fee from Federal Reserve banks or branches, and they may be redeemed at no cost through Federal Reserve banks or branches at maturity.

Commercial Paper

Commercial paper is an IOU from a corporation in exchange for a loan of $25,000 to $1 million or so. The issuing company promises to repay all the money, plus interest, within a specified number of days, usually less than 270. Interest rates are relatively high. Yet these are considered quite safe due to the well-known, reputable corporations that issue them.

Commercial paper may be purchased over the counter from broker/dealers at a fee or directly from issuing corporations. They may be liquidated on the open market at any time for whatever they will bring—usually a fair price—directly or through broker/dealers. On maturity, the commercial paper is collectible from the corporation, just as any other debt or IOU.

Life Insurance Company Products

Although most cash value life insurance policies and deferred annuities are not purchased primarily for liquidity purposes but to satisfy other long-term objectives, these financial resources do have a liquidity feature that should be mentioned here.

That feature, of course, is the *cash* or *loan value*, plus any accumulated dividends and/or prepaid premiums, which may be obtained in cash very readily—and, in case of the loan value, at very reasonable interest rates. In addition, life insurance policies may be used as collateral for obtaining loans.

Of course, policy values should be withdrawn only in times of real need or emergency because of the important, long-range living and death objectives for which the insurance was primarily obtained. In recent years, as will be covered later, a number of life insurance products have been developed in which the policy loan features play a greater role than had traditionally been the case.

■ SUMMARY

Investors should begin their financial program with an emergency fund that consists of cash or cash equivalents such as a savings account, CDs and money market funds. These assets should be highly liquid and as safe as possible. Although there are a number of financial institutions into which depositors may place their funds, commercial banks, savings and loans and credit unions are the most familiar and accessible. In essence, deposits made to the financial institution are then loaned to other people or businesses. In return for the use of its depositors' money, the institution usually pays interest.

In addition to saving between three and six months' worth of living expenses in an emergency reserve, the investor should have health, life and disability insurance and a retirement plan, including Individual Retirement Accounts (IRAs), a Keogh plan and/or a 401(k) plan. In Chapters 4 and 5, we'll discuss ways in which your clients can establish this secure financial base with insurance and annuities before progressing to the next level of the investment pyramid.

■ CHAPTER 3 QUESTIONS FOR REVIEW

1. Which of the following financial intermediaries has no power to make loans to businesses?

   A. Credit unions

   B. Mutual savings banks

   C. Savings and loan associations

   D. Commercial banks

2. Savings/liquidity vehicles share all of the following characteristics EXCEPT

   A. they provide a hedge against inflation

   B. they can be quickly converted to cash in an emergency

   C. they are a convenient way to meet day-to-day expenses

   D. they offer almost complete safety of principal

3. In general, which of the following accounts will likely pay the highest return?

    A. Savings accounts

    B. Regular checking accounts

    C. Money market mutual fund accounts

    D. Money market deposit accounts

4. Federally chartered commercial banks are required to provide depositors with insurance through the

    A. NCUA

    B. SAIF

    C. BIF

    D. FDIC

5. Which of the following is a demand deposit account?

    A. Regular checking account

    B. Certificate of deposit

    C. Money market deposit account

    D. Treasury bill

4

Life Insurance

L ife insurance is a key element in any well-formulated investment plan. Positioned at the base of the investment pyramid, it is a safe, sound and—for most individuals—necessary financial product. Whereas most investments provide a way to store or accumulate investment capital, life insurance goes one step further. It is the means by which an investor can *protect* the assets he or she has accumulated and fill the financial gap that might exist if death occurs before an individual has fully built the investment pyramid his or her family will require in the future. This is the primary function any life insurance product serves. However, if properly selected, managed and used, life insurance itself can serve as an accumulation vehicle to support or fulfill other financial objectives as well.

In this chapter, we will examine life insurance as a financial product and focus on the role it plays in investment planning. Life insurance works best when it is part of an overall plan—when its purchase is based on and its use directed toward specific goals and objectives.

■ ■ ■ ■ ■

■ LIFE INSURANCE AS A FINANCIAL PRODUCT

Life insurance is a financial resource. It is a contract that provides, in exchange for a certain amount of premium, the payment of a stipulated sum in the event of an insured's death. All life insurance products, whether they're temporary or permanent, share this important function—that is, the creation of a stipulated fund. The fact that this fund and its payment are guaranteed is one trait that sets life insurance apart from other types of financial products and enables it to serve a unique purpose in one's financial plan.

Basically, there are two classes of life insurance: temporary (or term) and permanent. Within these two classes are many types of policies that vary in their basic design, including the premium payment method, the duration of coverage, the source of premium payments, the number of lives insured, the underlying account that funds the policy and so on. In fact, some of the newer, nontraditional policies, such as universal life and variable life, go beyond the labels of "term" or "permanent" and are becoming very popular; we will discuss several of these newer policies in this chapter. However, the classifications of term and permanent will provide the foundation to describe how life insurance fits into the investment pyramid. (Annuities, another type of product offered by insurance companies, will be discussed in the next chapter.)

■ TERM LIFE INSURANCE

Term life insurance has been described as the simplest, most basic form of life insurance. It provides protection for a limited period of time and pays its death benefit (i.e., the policy's *face amount* or *value*) only if death occurs during that period. Term insurance is *temporary* insurance in that coverage has a definite expiration date. If death occurs during the policy's term, the policy pays a guaranteed benefit. If, however, death occurs after the expiration of the policy's term, nothing is paid. By the end of the policy term, all premiums have been fully earned (having been fully applied to the cost of protection whether or not death occurs) and the policy has no further value.

Term policies can be written for a period as short as one year or may provide protection to the insured's age 65 or 70. Customarily, term policies are written for specific periods of time, such as 5, 10, 15 or 20 years. Depending on the policy, these policies can be *renewed* at the policyowner's option without evidence of insurability. Premium rates are level for each given period and will increase with each renewal, reflecting the attained age of the insured at the time of renewal. If the insured has *convertible* term insurance, he or she can exchange it for whole life insurance without a medical examination, but at a higher premium.

Because the probability of death increases with age, term insurance premiums increase as the insured ages. At older ages, this increase becomes quite sharp, reflecting the higher death rates at advanced ages. Generally, for people under age 45, term insurance costs about one-fifth as much as whole life, thereby providing maximum protection at minimal cost. However, because premiums rise steadily at each renewal, term insurance is often more expensive than whole life insurance over the long run.

Level Term Insurance

Level term insurance provides level protection for a specified period, after which the policy expires. A $100,000 10-year level term policy provides a straight $100,000 of coverage for a period of 10 years. A $250,000 term-to-age-65 policy provides a straight $250,000 of coverage until the insured reaches age 65. If the insured under the $100,000 policy dies at any time within those 10 years or if the insured under the $250,000 policy dies prior to age 65, their beneficiaries will receive the policies' face amounts as benefits. If the insureds live beyond the 10-year period or past age 65, respectively, the policies expire and no benefits are payable.

Level term is appropriate when the need for protection is temporary and expected to remain constant over the term period. If the need is expected to decline or increase, a different type of term protection is warranted.

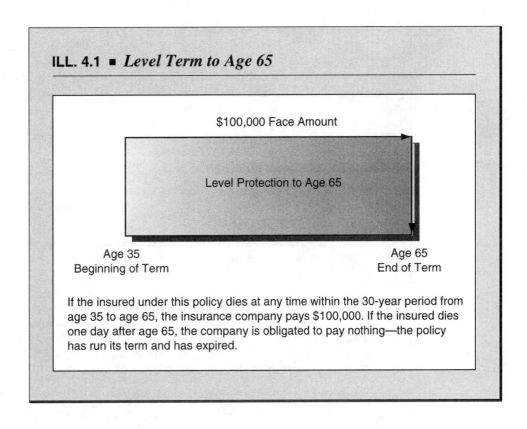

ILL. 4.1 ▪ *Level Term to Age 65*

$100,000 Face Amount

Level Protection to Age 65

Age 35
Beginning of Term

Age 65
End of Term

If the insured under this policy dies at any time within the 30-year period from age 35 to age 65, the insurance company pays $100,000. If the insured dies one day after age 65, the company is obligated to pay nothing—the policy has run its term and has expired.

Decreasing Term Insurance

Decreasing term policies are characterized by benefit amounts that decrease gradually over the term of protection. A 20-year $50,000 decreasing term policy, for instance, will pay a death benefit of $50,000 at the beginning of the policy term; that amount gradually declines over the 20-year term and reaches $0 at the end of the term.

Decreasing term insurance is best used when the need for protection declines year to year. For example, a person with a fixed-period, declining-balance mortgage could purchase decreasing term insurance that would pay off the mortgage balance should he or she die during the mortgage-payment period. The decreasing amount of debt is matched by similarly decreasing amounts of life insurance so that if the insured dies at any point in this period, the amount of insurance in force should equal the balance left on the mortgage.

Increasing Term Insurance

Increasing term insurance is almost always sold as a *rider* rather than as a separate policy. It is used primarily to provide a benefit that increases over time. An example of increasing term is a return of premium policy whereby the amount paid at death is the face amount of the policy plus a sum equal to all (or a portion) of the premium paid. The premium for this type of policy would, of course, be higher than for a policy that does not provide for return of premiums.

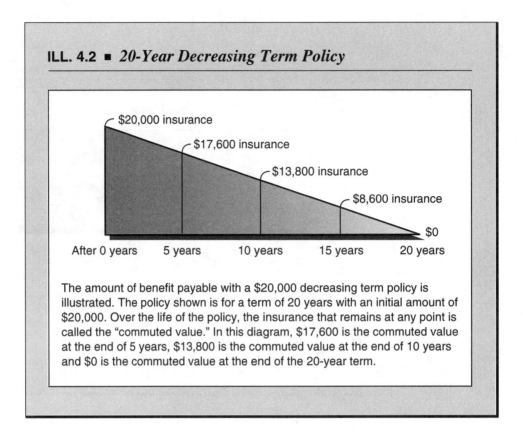

ILL. 4.2 ■ *20-Year Decreasing Term Policy*

$20,000 insurance

$17,600 insurance

$13,800 insurance

$8,600 insurance

$0

After 0 years   5 years   10 years   15 years   20 years

The amount of benefit payable with a $20,000 decreasing term policy is illustrated. The policy shown is for a term of 20 years with an initial amount of $20,000. Over the life of the policy, the insurance that remains at any point is called the "commuted value." In this diagram, $17,600 is the commuted value at the end of 5 years, $13,800 is the commuted value at the end of 10 years and $0 is the commuted value at the end of the 20-year term.

Uses of Term Insurance

Term insurance, providing "pure protection" against death only, fills an essential need when properly used. Many situations exist where term insurance may offer an appropriate solution, especially in certain situations where the need for protection is of short duration. Here are three examples:

1. William receives a substantial loan from the bank that must be repaid at the end of two years. He is afraid that if he dies while the loan is outstanding, his family will be overburdened by the repayment of the loan. William can protect against this danger by buying a two-year term policy (or a one-year renewable term policy, renewing at the end of the first year if the loan is not yet repaid).

2. Mary engages in a speculative business enterprise involving all her available financial resources over a five-year period. Meanwhile, if she dies, her family will lose the capital invested plus personal profits. If Mary purchases a five-year term policy, she both protects against death during the period and is offered the privilege of conversion to permanent insurance.

3. Michael has children in their late teens. Until now, Michael has been unable to set aside a fund for their college education, but for the next four years he will be able to save from increased personal income. However, if Michael were to die at any time during the next four years, the college fund would be insufficient. To protect the children against the risk of loss of a higher

education, Michael can purchase an adequate amount of one-year renewable or five-year term insurance.

Any number of emergencies might arise requiring insurance protection at a critical time, when temporary financial conditions will not permit a person to pay the higher premiums for whole life or some other form of permanent insurance. For example, a person might suffer the loss of a job or some other sudden financial loss from which he or she can recover within a short period of time. In such cases, term insurance fits a very definite need.

In all instances where the life agent finds it wise to place term insurance, he or she should keep in mind that term insurance is simply a *rented* life insurance estate, providing protection for a limited *term of years*. Whenever term insurance is sold, the agent has also created an opportunity for a second sale—the conversion of the term policy to *permanent* insurance that will bring benefits to the policyowner whether the insured dies or lives.

■ PERMANENT LIFE INSURANCE

Permanent life insurance is a class of insurance protection that assures coverage over the insured's lifetime or to the policy's maturity date, if the insured is still alive at that time. As long as the contract remains in force (i.e., as long as the premiums are paid), the insured is covered. Permanent life insurance provides the policyowner with important contractual rights while the insured is alive and the contract is in force. Especially noteworthy among these rights is the availability of a guaranteed *cash value* that increases annually per a schedule and rate included in the policy. This cash value is available at the policy's maturity date—or at any earlier time—upon surrender of the policy or as a loan against the policy. As some experts have described it, the difference between term and permanent insurance is that term provides protection against a contingency (the possibility of death during the policy term), while permanent protects against a certainty (everyone is going to die).

Even though permanent life insurance may be bought primarily for its death protection benefits, its cash value or accumulation feature allows it to also operate as an investment vehicle in several ways:

- *It builds cash value.* Depending on the type of policy, the cash value growth is guaranteed (traditional whole life) or will vary, depending on the underlying investment fund (variable life or variable universal life). These cash values belong to the policyowners and are available to help support their financial objectives.

- *The cash value growth is not taxed while it accumulates in the policy.* Since taxes on the cash value's compounded interest earnings are deferred, these earnings can create a sizable sum over time.

- *Life insurance requires periodic contributions.* Many individuals do not have the discipline to invest or save on a regular basis. Moreover, some investments, such as savings accounts, are too readily accessible to properly serve as long-term accumulation plans. The fact that life insurance requires periodic premium payments and its values are somewhat illiquid makes it a good accumulation vehicle. Because premiums are not considered spendable dollars, they are much more likely to be paid as they should be, generating a cash value fund for the future.

- *Life insurance is a safe investment.* Behind every life insurance policy stand reserving and nonforfeiture laws, state guaranty associations, rating organizations and the strength of the insurance industry itself. Because of these factors, life insurance is one of the safest, most secure investments. Though term insurance can play a role in this investment arena, our focus here will be on permanent plans.

Traditional Whole Life Insurance

Traditional whole life insurance is the most common type of permanent insurance. It is so called because its coverage extends and its premiums are payable for the insured's "whole life"—from the date of issue to the date of death (or to the insured's age 100, whichever comes first*). The benefit payable is the face amount of the policy, which remains constant throughout the policy's life. Premiums are set at the time of policy issue and they, too, remain fixed and *level* for the policy's life. Cash values accumulate in the policy, growing each year at a guaranteed interest rate.

The cash value accumulation of a whole life policy is often described as a "living benefit." To explain, assume that Robert purchases a whole life insurance policy at age 30 with a face amount of $100,000. The premiums for this policy are calculated on the assumption that Robert will pay them for the next 70 years. As shown in Ill. 4.3, the $100,000 face amount in reality consists of what is termed a *pure insurance amount* and the *cash value amount*. For the first few years that the policy is in force, the pure insurance amount remains equal to, or very close to, $100,000, while the cash value is zero or close to zero. As time goes on and the cash value builds within the policy, the pure insurance amount decreases until, at age 100, the cash value of the policy equals $100,000 and the pure insurance amount equals zero.

The ever-increasing cash value is an asset Robert can rely on at any point in the policy's life: it can be borrowed at very reasonable rates; it can be "surrendered" or taken as cash (in which case the policy terminates); it can be applied to purchase alternative forms of coverage; or it can be left intact to grow and support the death benefit. Life insurance cash values can even be used as collateral for a loan. These "living benefits" represent an advantage that cash value life insurance has over term insurance.

Notwithstanding the discussion above, it is important to emphasize that the policy's death benefit (the protection aspect) and its cash value (the accumulation aspect) are not separate elements, separately payable. They are interdependent aspects of the

---

* The significance of age 100 is an actuarial one: actuarially, every insured is presumed to be dead by then. Whole life is designed to mature at that age, meaning that the cash value will have grown to an amount equal to the full face value of the policy and the amount of pure insurance protection will have declined to $0, as it was actuarially designed to do. Any insured still living at age 100 will be issued a check for the full value of the policy, at which point the policy expires. Consequently, the premium rate for whole life is based on the assumption that the insured will be paying premiums to age 100.

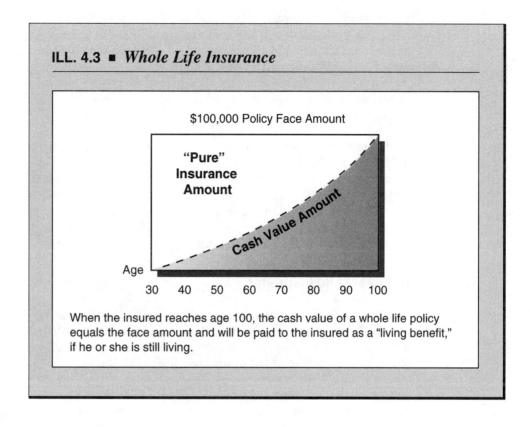

ILL. 4.3 ■ *Whole Life Insurance*

$100,000 Policy Face Amount

"Pure"
Insurance
Amount

Cash Value Amount

Age

30   40   50   60   70   80   90   100

When the insured reaches age 100, the cash value of a whole life policy equals the face amount and will be paid to the insured as a "living benefit," if he or she is still living.

same policy, stemming from a singular financial base. Using the previous example, for Robert's policy to pay the full $100,000 as a death benefit, the cash values must be fully intact. If, for instance, Robert had taken out a loan from his policy and died before it was repaid, the unpaid amount of the loan plus any interest due would be deducted from the $100,000 death proceeds before those proceeds were paid to Robert's beneficiary. A life insurance policy's face amount (death protection) is payable only upon the death of the insured and while the policy is in force. The cash value (accumulation) is available only while the insured is living and upon giving up all or an equivalent portion of the protection initially provided by the policy. However, it is the dual nature of a whole life policy—protection and accumulation—that can make it a valuable financial resource.

Limited Pay Life Insurance

A *limited pay life insurance* policy is actually a whole life policy with its premiums adjusted so they are paid for a specified period. A person who purchases a 20-pay life insurance policy really has a whole life policy for which he or she will pay premiums for 20 years. At the end of this period, the premiums are no longer payable yet the life insurance protection continues for the remainder of the insured's lifetime or until age 100 when the policy would pay its face value. The most extreme form of limited pay policies is a single premium policy. Such a policy involves a large one-time-only premium payment at the beginning of the policy period. From that point, the policy is completely paid. Because the premium-paying period for limited pay policies is shorter than for traditional whole life, the premiums are higher. However, the total paid under either plan should approximate the other.

Limited pay life insurance policies provide faster-growing cash values than straight whole life policies offer. The premiums are adjusted to fit a specified period, such as the insured's anticipated retirement date. Premiums are paid during the insured's most financially productive years, with no premiums due after a specified period. At that time, the insured will have a fully paid-up policy—its values and benefits intact and available—and the premium dollars will be freed up to use for other needs.

For a number of people, the 15-year to 20-year period preceding retirement may be a time when their financial obligations are great—children are in college, mortgages have not yet been paid off, a business may require additional investment—and their incomes may be relatively high. Although these people need permanent, whole life protection, they are also concerned about maintaining their lifestyle after they retire when their incomes may be drastically reduced. These prospects are candidates for limited pay whole life insurance.

Universal Life Insurance

Although technically a permanent life insurance product, a *universal life (UL) insurance policy* has many features that are not associated with traditional life products and, for many prospective insurance buyers, it provides an attractive alternative to a traditional whole life or limited pay life plan.

Unlike whole or limited pay life policies with their fixed face amounts, fixed cash value accumulations and fixed schedule of premium payments (all of which must

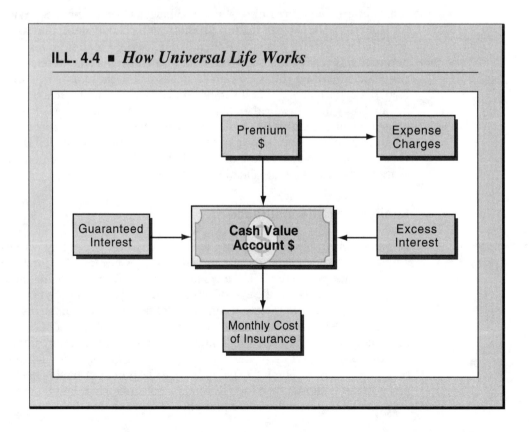

ILL. 4.4 ■ *How Universal Life Works*

be paid or the policy lapses), universal life allows policyowners to determine the amount and frequency of premium payments and to adjust the policy face amount up or down, as needs may dictate. This flexibility characteristic of universal life policies is created by "unbundling" or separating the policy's three basic components: the pure insurance protection element, the accumulation element and the expense (loading) element. Basically, the policy works like this.

The policyowner selects one of two death benefit options:

1. an increasing death benefit (the sum of a level term insurance amount plus the increasing cash values); or

2. a level death benefit (the sum of a decreasing term insurance amount plus the increasing cash value).

Then, based on the amount of insurance (the "amount at risk"), a premium rate is established. From the premium, a predetermined monthly expense charge is taken for expenses (the loading factor). The balance of the premium is directed into the policy's cash value account, where it is credited with interest at a *guaranteed minimum rate* (as specified in the contract) *plus* any *excess interest* the invested values earn (dependent on market conditions). Then, and each month thereafter, a mortality charge is deducted from the cash value account for the cost of the pure insurance protection. (These costs are at term rates.) As long as the cash value account is sufficient to pay the monthly mortality and expense charges, the policy will continue in force, irrespective of any premium payments. This means that a policyowner could pay less than the premium rate established or even skip payments. Of course, premium payments must be large enough and frequent enough to generate sufficient cash values. If the cash value account is not large enough to support the monthly mortality and expense charges, the policy terminates.

At stated intervals (and usually upon providing evidence of good health), the policyowner can increase the face amount of the policy. Similarly, a decreased face amount may be desired. Though there will be a corresponding increase (or decrease) in the monthly pure insurance cost deducted from the cash value account, the premium the insured pays does not necessarily increase (or decrease). Again, as long as the cash value can cover the mortality and expense costs, the policy remains in force. There may be times when the insured wants to pay more into the policy to add to the cash value account. This can be done subject to certain guidelines that control the relationship between the cash values and the policy's face value.

There are other factors that distinguish universal life from whole life. For one thing, UL allows a policyowner to make *partial withdrawals* from the policy's cash value account. (Whole life allows a policyowner to tap cash values only through a policy loan or a complete cash surrender, in which case the policy terminates.) Though there may be tax consequences for partial withdrawals, this option enhances the UL's flexibility. Too, unlike whole life, UL offers the policyowner the choice of two death benefit options as described previously.

From the policyowner's perspective, the flexibility of universal life centers around the amount and timing of premium payments and the amount of insurance. As we have seen, because the cost of the insurance is taken from the policy's cash value, premium payments can (within limits) be increased or decreased or skipped altogether. As long as the cash values are sufficient to support the cost of insurance protection, the policy remains in force. The amount of the insurance and the death benefit can be increased (as long as the insured is healthy) or decreased to adapt to a policyowner's need. Finally, as noted, universal life policies typically allow for partial withdrawals of the cash value (though surrender charges could be applied). This is in contrast to whole life policies that allow a policyowner to tap cash values only through policy loans or complete cash surrender.

Because of its flexibility, universal life has been described as a "cradle to grave" plan. For example, during the years when death protection is most needed, the amount of insurance can be adjusted upward to cover those needs. As the individual nears retirement and perhaps has a greater need for savings and accumulation, the face amount can be decreased. By decreasing premiums, the policyowner can divert the savings to another investment; by increasing the premiums, the insured will enhance his or her cash value growth. The fact that this growth is tax deferred is another benefit.

Variable Life Insurance

Variable life insurance (VL) has some of the features of traditional whole life: level, fixed, permanent premiums and a minimum guaranteed death benefit. However, unlike whole life, which guarantees a certain rate of return on its cash values, variable life is a *securities-based* insurance product with no guaranteed rate of return. The cash values of the policy are maintained in a separate account and invested in a selected portfolio of stocks, bonds or money market funds. A variable life policyowner directs how the cash values are invested, and to this extent, assumes the risk of making the investments. Consequently, cash values are not guaranteed with variable life; they will perform in relation to the underlying investment portfolio. If the portfolio does well, the return will be higher than what the policyowner otherwise would have received with a traditional policy. However, if the portfolio performs poorly, the policyowner could lose a portion of his or her investment funds.

The death benefit payable under a variable policy is also a function of how well the cash values perform. As noted, a minimum benefit is guaranteed; it is the initial face amount of the policy. The actual amount of the death benefit, however, is equal to the minimum death benefit plus the cash value. Thus, if at the insured's death the policy's cash value were $0, only the minimum death benefit would be paid. If the policy's cash value were greater than $0, the death benefit would be that value plus the minimum benefit.

Whether variable life is suitable for any given individual will depend on his or her risk tolerance. Variable life can be an excellent way to accumulate retirement savings while maintaining needed insurance coverage, as long as the individual can accept the risk. Because of the investment risk of these policies, they are considered "securities" as well as insurance and are regulated by state insurance law and the Securities and Exchange Commission (SEC). A person who sells variable life must be licensed to sell insurance and be registered with the National Association of Security Dealers (NASD). In addition, the insurance company must prepare a prospectus, and agents must provide the prospective insured with a copy of this prospectus before or at the sales interview. Strict rules governing the conduct of the sale must be followed.

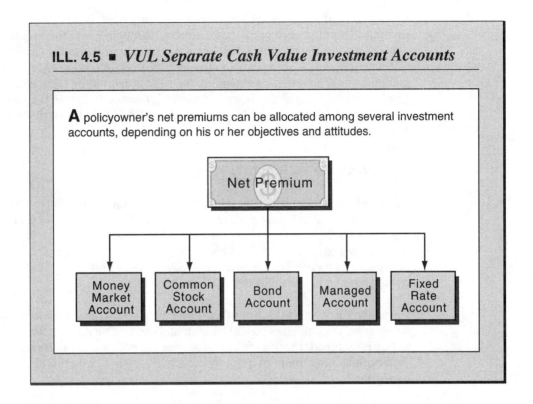

ILL. 4.5 ■ *VUL Separate Cash Value Investment Accounts*

A policyowner's net premiums can be allocated among several investment accounts, depending on his or her objectives and attitudes.

Net Premium

Money Market Account

Common Stock Account

Bond Account

Managed Account

Fixed Rate Account

Variable Universal Life Insurance

One of the most versatile products offered by insurers today, *variable universal life (VUL)* combines features of universal life and variable life into one policy. Specifically, variable universal life policies provide permanent, cash value insurance with flexible premiums, separate cash value investment accounts, death benefit options and no cash value guarantees. Cash values can be moved among the underlying investment accounts, within limits, death benefits can be increased or decreased to meet policyowner needs; and premiums can be increased, decreased or even skipped, as long as the cash value is enough to support the insurance amount. As in the case of variable life, the policyowner—not the insurer—assumes the investment risk for his or her cash values.

The size of the death benefit and the cash value will depend on how well the underlying investment accounts perform. A variable policy gives the investor the chance to boost his or her return more than with other cash-value policies, but there is also more risk. Although a minimum death benefit is guaranteed so that the policy will never fall below its face value, there is no such guaranteed floor on the cash value. Therefore, the policyowner could end up with a smaller cash value than with other policies.

■ RIGHTS AND BENEFITS OF LIFE INSURANCE OWNERSHIP

Very few people purchase life insurance as an investment only and rightfully so. Its primary purpose is not as an investment vehicle, but as protection against loss of income associated with death. No other financial product can guarantee that a specific sum of money will be available precisely when it is needed most. However, owning a life insurance policy means more than being able to designate a beneficiary to receive the proceeds. Life insurance ownership provides many other rights and benefits, which some people may overlook when putting together their financial plans. It is only by understanding the full value of a life insurance policy that it can be properly positioned in an individual's financial plan. In the next section, we'll take a look at some of these rights and benefits, and then discuss the role of life insurance in personal investment.

Life Insurance as Property

Those who purchase life insurance policies are commonly referred to as "policy-*owners*" rather than "policy*holders*" because they do, in fact, own their policies and may do with them as they wish. *Owning a life insurance policy is the equivalent of owning a piece of property.* And one right of owning property is the ability to *assign* or transfer its ownership to someone else. This same ability applies to life insurance ownership and is known as the *right of assignment*.

Basically, there are two types of assignment: absolute and collateral. An *absolute assignment* is complete and irrevocable and the assignee (the person to whom the policy is assigned) receives full control over the policy and full rights to its benefits. An absolute assignment of a life insurance policy is a common charitable gifting technique.

A *collateral assignment* is one in which the policy is assigned to a creditor as security, or collateral, for a debt. If the insured dies, the creditor is entitled to be paid the amount he or she is owed from the policy's death proceeds, with the balance of the proceeds going to the policy beneficiary. Once the debt is repaid, the policy rights assigned to the creditor revert to the policyowner. Being able to use a life insurance contract as collateral can help an individual obtain credit and enhances his or her borrowing power—key ingredients to sound financial planning.

Policy Loan Privileges

As mentioned earlier in the chapter, one of the benefits of owning cash value life insurance is the *policy loan* privilege, under which the insurer, on the security of the contract, will advance to the policyowner an amount up to the guaranteed cash value, at a specified rate of interest. There is no requirement that policy loans have to be repaid, and they cannot be "called" by the insurer. As such, they can be likened more to an "advance" on the policy's proceeds. However, any amount not repaid by the time the insured dies, including interest, will be subtracted from the policy proceeds. By the same token, if a policy is surrendered for cash, the amount paid to the policyowner is reduced by the amount of any outstanding loan plus interest. Despite these restrictions, the policy loan privilege is a valuable option, as it can provide a ready source of cash for emergencies or other needs.

Protection Against Creditors

Another benefit life insurance offers is that the proceeds, if properly arranged, cannot be attached or claimed by creditors of the deceased insured. States have enacted what are called *exemption statutes*, which establish the conditions under which death proceeds go directly to the insured's beneficiaries without being subject to claims of the insured's creditors. A typical example of such conditions is that the beneficiary is a named person other than the insured or his or her estate. There are few other forms of property that one can own at death which are not, to some extent, subject to creditor claims.

Nonforfeiture Rights

Owners of cash value life insurance policies, as we've learned, have access to these values whenever they want them and for whatever reason. The term *nonforfeiture rights* refers to the fact that a policy's cash value cannot be forfeited to the insurer and the policyowner has a number of rights and options as to the use of his or her cash value. The policy can be surrendered and the value taken as cash or used for a policy loan. In addition, there are two other options: reduced paid-up insurance and extended term insurance.

Under the *reduced paid-up* option, the cash value is used to purchase a reduced amount of paid-up insurance, freeing the policyowner from future premium payments. The result is a paid-up policy, the same kind as the original, for a lesser face amount. The reduced policy also builds cash values.

Under the *extended term* option, the cash value is used to purchase a term insurance policy, in an amount equal to the original policy's face value, for as long a period as the cash value will buy. When the term insurance's period of coverage expires, there is no more insurance protection.

Dividend Rights

Life insurance policies can be participating or nonparticipating. *Participating* policies carry slightly higher premium rates, based on conservative assumptions regarding the insurer's investment earnings, mortality (death) experience and expenses. If actual results are better than the assumptions—if actual investment earnings are higher or death claims are lower, for example—the difference is available to be returned to policyowners as a *policy dividend*. These dividends represent *surplus*—an excess of premiums paid over expenses and claims incurred—and must not be confused with dividends paid to holders of corporate stocks. Whether or not policy dividends are payable is determined annually; they are never guaranteed.

Owners of participating policies have a number of choices as to how they may receive policy dividends.

1. They may be taken as cash.

2. They may be applied toward the next premium payment.

3. They can be applied toward the purchase of paid-up additions to the policy (i.e., used as single premiums to purchase as much paid-up insurance as possible, payable under the same conditions as the basic underlying policy).

4. They may be left with the insurer to accumulate as interest.

5. They may be used to purchase one-year term insurance.

Owners of *nonparticipating* policies do not share in the insurer's experience and have no rights to policy dividends. They do, however, have the advantage of slightly lower premium payments on their policies.

Favored Tax Treatment

One of the most significant advantages of life insurance ownership is the favored tax treatment policies receive in a number of respects. First, unlike many other types of savings and investment products, interest earned on accumulating life insurance policy cash values is not currently taxable. Though the guaranteed interest rate is usually low, say 3½ or 4½ percent, it follows that the gross return on taxable savings and investments necessarily must be higher to equal the net return available through an insurance contract. Interest earned in excess of the guaranteed rate is also not currently taxable.

Second, life insurance policy death proceeds paid in a single sum are also exempt from income taxes. To be able to leave a lump-sum, income-tax free benefit to one's heirs or beneficiaries at death can be a significant estate and financial planning consideration. Note, however, that this tax-free status is given only to single or lump-sum payouts; any other payout or settlement option that involves the payment of proceeds plus interest over time will incur tax on the interest portion of the payout. (See Ill. 4.6.)

Third, dividends paid on participating policies are not taxable because dividends are considered a return of premium paid, not investment income. It should be noted, however, that any *interest* that dividends left on deposit with the insurer may earn is taxable.

Finally, with regard to the taxation of surrendered cash values, a policyowner is allowed to receive tax free an amount equal to what he or she paid into the policy in the form of premiums; this is known as the policyowner's *cost basis*. Any amount over the cost basis represents interest earnings, which are fully taxable when received.

Guaranteed Value

Finally, owning a life insurance policy provides the benefit of knowing what its exact value will be at death—something that cannot be known in advance for other kinds of properties or investments. With term or whole life, this value will be the policy's face amount; with variable life, it will be at least the guaranteed minimum. A life insurance owner can count on this value, whether death occurs tomorrow or 40 years down the road.

■ THE ROLE OF LIFE INSURANCE IN PERSONAL INVESTMENT

A person's death produces a need for money—*immediate* money to help pay for the bills associated with that death and for the short-term cash needs of the surviving family members. Then there is also the longer-term need for ongoing *income*—a continuing source of money coming in to cover the surviving family's monthly expenses. Life insurance can cover both immediate cash needs and ongoing income needs, and assure that a family's long-term financial objectives will be met, even if

ILL. 4.6 ■ *Life Insurance Settlement Options*

The proceeds of a life insurance policy can be paid out in a variety of ways. The choice is up to the policyowner, as a right of ownership, or he or she may leave the decision to the beneficiary. Some choose to have the proceeds paid in a single lump sum. However, there are other options that might be more suitable to the needs of the surviving beneficiary or surviving family. These alternate payment options are known as settlement options.

- Interest-Only Option — Under this option, the insurance company holds the proceeds in trust and at interest for a specified period of time and pays the beneficiary the interest earnings at regular intervals. The proceeds themselves are then paid out at the end of the specified period, either in cash or under one of the other settlement options.

- Fixed-Period Option — Under this option, the company pays the beneficiary an equal amount of money—a combination of proceeds and interest earnings—over a specified period of years. The amount of each installment payment is determined by the length of the desired period of income.

- Fixed-Amount Option — With this option, the policy proceeds plus interest earnings are paid out regularly in specified amounts for as long as the proceeds last. The amount of each income payment is fixed; how long the payout period will last is determined by the amount of the payment.

- Life-Income Option — Under a life-income option—of which there are several—the beneficiary receives a guaranteed income *for life*. Essentially, the proceeds are used to purchase a life annuity, the duration of which is based on the beneficiary's lifetime.

the principal wage earner dies. As we've discussed, this is the primary purpose of life insurance and it can be served by both term and cash value plans. A secondary purpose, *accumulation*, can be served by cash value plans. Let's take a look at how life insurance can meet both.

Cash and Income Needs at Death

The death of a family's wage earner creates two distinct financial needs: *cash* and *income*. Cash needs are immediate; income needs are ongoing. Life insurance provides the perfect solution to both and can help assure the financial future of the surviving family.

1. *Final expenses.* Associated with every death are a number of costs: hospital and medical expenses, funeral costs, taxes, debts, estate administration costs,

etc. Life insurance proceeds would cover these costs *immediately* upon proof of death, with little or no administrative work.

2. *Housing*. Life insurance can assure the future of the surviving family members by making it possible for them to stay in their home after the death of the wage earner.

   This can be accomplished by having a death benefit equal to the outstanding balance of the home mortgage or equal to 10 to 12 months' rent on the apartment.

3. *Education*. Life insurance proceeds can be used to fund a child's education, a financial objective that otherwise would be very difficult to achieve if the family's principal wage earner were to die while the child was young.

4. *Emergencies*. While the future cannot be predicted with accuracy, future emergencies can be anticipated. Life insurance proceeds can be used to create a fund that assures the money will be there to cover the cost of the emergency, no matter when, no matter what the situation.

5. *Income*. Surviving family members will have ongoing income needs—the daily, weekly, monthly and annual costs of living will not cease upon the death of the wage earner. Life insurance proceeds can be distributed in exact accordance with the family's income needs, by utilizing the contract's *settlement options*. Basically, settlement options place the policy proceeds in trust with the insurance company, and are paid out, with interest, over time. (See Ill. 4.6.)

Accumulation and Life Insurance

In recent years, an increasing emphasis has been placed on the tax-deferred, internal cash-value buildup of permanent life insurance plans. Newer products, such as universal, variable and variable universal whole life, have attempted to maximize this accumulation aspect of life insurance protection. Having retained generally its tax-deferred status at a time when many tax shelters have lost tax-favored treatment, these forms of life insurance increasingly are being viewed by the public as viable investment vehicles as well as protection for human life values. In this section, we'll discuss how the accumulation element of cash value life insurance can fit into an individual's investment plans.

Wealth Accumulation for Retirement

One of the most common investment priorities for most people is to acquire or have access to enough wealth so that they can comfortably retire and/or pass their wealth on to their dependents. As mentioned in Chapter 2, most financial planners recommend that their clients begin their investment strategy with relatively low-risk, safe investments. The base of the investment pyramid consists of conservative investments—savings and checking accounts, CDs, money market accounts, traditional life insurance products and annuities. Through personal savings and permanent life insurance cash values, individuals have the foundation with which this accumulation begins.

Some might argue that the rate of return on life insurance makes it unsuitable as an accumulation vehicle when compared to other investments that offer potentially higher returns. To some extent this may be true; however, there are a number of counterarguments to this position. First of all, most experts agree that, in the pursuit of retirement funds, for example, individuals should diversify or balance their savings and investment mix. Life insurance provides a balance and minimizes loss because it offers safety of principal, liquidity and, with traditional policies, a guaranteed rate of return. Although many investments can offer a higher rate of return than life insurance, few investments are safer.

Second, life insurance accumulates cash values on a tax-deferred basis, which enhances its growth. Other investments, unless they too are tax deferred, will provide a return that is reduced by an amount equal to the individual investor's tax burden. Through tax-deferred earnings that are compounded year after year, a life insurance policy can generate sizable cash values for retirement purposes. No other form of financial investment product, other than IRAs and tax-qualified or tax-advantaged retirement plans, permits the taxpayer/investor to postpone, sometimes forever, income tax on return on capital invested. Some forms of investment such as tax-exempt mutual funds are free from some income tax; however, they do not have the unique ability to create a sizable, liquid estate, with little or no risk of loss of investment in the manner that life insurance does.

Third, certain types of life insurance policies, such as variable life and variable universal life, *do* offer the potential for higher returns. Through these plans, life insurance products have kept pace with the changing needs and expectations of an increasingly sophisticated consumer who wants long-term investments with appreciation potential.

Income for Retirement

Being able to count on a certain income flow will be another retirement objective for many people. Social Security benefits will not provide the level of income needed to maintain a comfortable standard of living nor will many pension plans (if, indeed, the individual is entitled to a pension). The accumulated cash value from a life insurance policy can help provide additional income. For example, cash values can be withdrawn, surrendered or borrowed and used to pay off a large debt, such as a mortgage. Although the policyowner cannot permanently withdraw the cash-value reserve portion of the policy and still remain insured, he or she can borrow against the cash value at relatively low interest rates.

The policy's cash value may also be used to purchase an annuity. As explained in more detail in Chapter 5, an *annuity* is a contract that pays a regular income for life or for some specified period of time. Policyowners may also elect a *joint and survivor option* that covers two people, usually a husband and wife, until both people have died. Of course, a variety of other annuities (i.e., 10 years certain, 15 years certain and so on) is also available as a source of continuing income.

Business Planning and Life Insurance

Life insurance plays a vital role in the investment and retirement plans of business owners. For most business owners, whether they are sole proprietors, partners or close corporation stockholders, their businesses represent the largest source of their income and the most significant portion of their wealth. Planning for the orderly transition from or succession of their business is a major issue business owners must address.

A business owner can choose when to terminate his or her active involvement in a firm. Many plan to remain active until death. Others may choose to withdraw sooner, to make way for a younger family member or to enjoy the leisure of retirement. Regardless of when an owner withdraws, plans must be made so that the owner's departure does not reduce the value of the business or prevent the family from receiving its full interest at the owner's death. Consequently, financial planning for a business owner should take into account that his or her involvement with the business will eventually cease and his or her ownership interest will have to be sold or transferred. These two certainties may or may not occur at the same time.

Life insurance is an effective planning tool that can address both eventualities. Let's briefly review its applications here:

- Life insurance can be used to fund plans that provide incentives to a key employee the business owner views as a successor to the owner. These plans include deferred compensation, profit-sharing plans or split-dollar life insurance, for example.

- Life insurance can be used to fund retirement plans for the business owner, such as SEPs or Keoghs.

- Life insurance can be used to fund business buy-out agreements, guaranteeing the orderly sale and transfer of the business at the owner's death and providing his or her family with the assurance that they will receive a full and fair price for the business.

- Life insurance can be used to provide estate liquidity, an important consideration for business owners whose assets are tied up in their business.

Estate Planning and Life Insurance

Finally, life insurance is an important estate planning tool and is often the only practical way of guaranteeing that sufficient cash will be available to provide *estate liquidity.* As we've learned, death brings about certain financial obligations that must be met immediately with cash. Final expenses, hospital and medical costs, funeral and burial costs, unpaid debts, bills, taxes, probate costs, attorney fees—all of these obligations must be paid before an estate can be settled and before property and assets can be transferred to the decedent's heirs. Even the most modest estate will likely be faced with thousands of dollars in final expenses. If there is not enough cash in the estate to cover these costs, then assets may have to be sold or liquidated, often at less than market value. Life insurance, however, can provide that needed cash—and it is available at precisely the time it will be most needed. Also, insurance proceeds can be removed from the probate estate (by the policyowner giving up all incidents of ownership), thus reducing probate and administrative costs and lowering any estate tax bill. In planning to meet the liquidity need, no other vehicle is better than life insurance.

■ LIFE INSURANCE COMPANY OPERATIONS

Life insurance is written by a variety of commercial carriers. There are stock insurers, companies owned and authorized by their shareholders, mutual insurers, which are owned and controlled by their policyowners and fraternal associations, which primarily sell to members of their own specific ethnic or religious group. However, to individual policyowners and their families, the type of insurance company is probably far less important than its financial strength, integrity and ability to meet the guarantees its policies promise. In this final section, we'll take a brief look at insurance company investment practices and how individuals can assess an insurer's financial health.

Insurer Investment Practices

To fulfill their many obligations, life insurance companies need large amounts of funds. These funds are necessary to pay death claims and maturing endowments, to provide annuity income payments and to meet the demands of policyowners who want to surrender or borrow their cash values. In addition, life insurers, like all other businesses, have ongoing operational expenses: salaries, overhead, rents, taxes and so on. Basically, insurers receive funds from two main sources: premiums paid by policyowners and earnings on investment.

Most states have laws regulating which investments a life insurance company may make and all require that *reserves* be maintained to back the company's financial guarantees. These laws mention the allowable investments and exclude or limit others. For example, for a bond to qualify as an investment, the issuing corporation must have earned more than the amount of the required interest payment for a specified period of years. Generally, permitted investments are those with security of principal and a yield or return certain in time and amount that is high enough to satisfy the interest guarantees made under the insurance company's contracts. An investment's liquidity, maturity date and marketability are of little importance to life insurance companies because premiums and investment income traditionally have exceeded outgoing payments.

Life insurance companies primarily invest in corporate debt issues, government securities, mortgages and real estate. By making these investments, the insurer is loaning money to a corporation (corporate bonds), the government (U.S. Treasury securities) or to a buyer of real estate (mortgages). In return, the insurer receives secure current income and a guarantee of both interest and principal. Capital gains or losses are excluded from investment income. The conservative nature of insurer investments is necessary to fulfill contractual guarantees the policyholders.

Financial Strength

The true financial health of a life insurance company cannot be determined merely by looking at its annual report, nor does the size of the company always indicate its financial strength. However, the company's growth (or lack of growth) over a number of years can reveal some important information. Some factors to consider in assessing financial strength are the types of business written, the company's business trends over the years, the underwriting and investment strategies, the adequacy of its reserves and the ratio of policyholders' surplus to liabilities. Most importantly, the general quality of the company's management should be considered since it, in large part, determines the direction of the company.

Detailed financial information about an insurer can usually be obtained from either the company itself or the state insurance department. In addition, a company's annual financial statements, ratings and analysis are published by various rating companies, such as *A.M. Best*. This company grades the financial stability of insurance companies from A++ (superior) to F (failed or under state supervision). The lower the rating, the greater the risk that the insurer will not be around when the insured needs to file a claim. *Best's* fee (paid by the insured) is typically $10,000 or more per rating.

Some consumers have expressed concern about *Best's* close ties to the life insurance industry and the insurers' ability to influence whether their financial ratings will be published. This, in conjunction with the large rating fee charged, has prompted many insurers to seek ratings from other rating companies such as *Standard & Poor's (S&P)*, *Moody's Investors Service (Moody's)* or *Duff & Phelps (D&P)*. These organizations have excellent reputations for providing objective ratings of a company's financial situation after a thorough examination of the accounting and investment records and after meeting with senior management.

As shown in Ill. 4.7, *A.M. Best* uses ratings that range from A++ (superior; very strong ability to meet its financial obligations) to F (in liquidation). *Standard & Poor's* rating system ranges from AAA (superior financial security; highest safety) to D (placed in liquidation). *Moody's* offers similar gradings, but with ratings that range from Aaa (exceptional security; unlikely to be affected by change) to C (lowest security; extremely poor prospect of offering financial security). Finally, *Duff & Phelps'* ratings range from AAA (highest claims paying ability; negligible risk) to CCC (substantial risk regarding claims paying ability; likely to be placed under state insurance department supervision).

ILL. 4.7 ■ *Insurance Company Rating Systems*

	A.M. Best	Standard & Poor's	Moody's	Duff & Phelps
Superior to Good	A++, A+	AAA	Aaa	AAA
	A, A–	AA	Aa	AA+, AA, AA–
	B++, B+	A	A	
	B, B–	BBB	Baa	BBB+, BBB, BBB–
Fair to Below Minimum Standards	C++, C+	BB	Ba	BB+, BB, BB–
	C, C–	B	B	
Under State Supervision, in Liquidation or Failed	D	CCC	Caa	
	E	CC, C	Ca	
	F	D	C	CCC

You should be aware of the rating differences among these rating companies and what each rating means. Whenever possible, consult multiple sources to get other views of an insurer's financial condition. Not all insurers are properly financed or expertly managed by qualified personnel. If an insurer offers the needed coverage but the agent doubts the insurer's ability to remain solvent, another insurer should be selected. The agent should avoid insurers that are underfinanced, underreserved and undermanaged.

■ SUMMARY

People buy life insurance because other accumulation plans too often do not work. They realize that every person either dies or grows old and, in either event, earning power is destroyed and a new source of income dollars must be ready to take its place. They buy life insurance because a continuous lifelong income is absolutely essential for decent, comfortable living; because they want the right to live, not only today while earning power continues but in some distant day after earning power has ended or been destroyed.

Cash value life insurance can also be used to create an accumulation for future consumption. Though cash values are meant to be used to maintain the insurance, they are available in emergencies and when the insurance no longer is needed. Objectives that can be met partly or completely by the purchase of life insurance include providing for survivors or heirs, eliminating debts acquired during life, disposing of a business and paying final taxes and expenses relating to death.

In Chapter 5, we'll look at another financial product that can help meet your prospects' financial needs—an annuity. Covered are the basic forms of annuities and how these annuities serve different income needs. We'll also look at ways to evaluate annuities in terms of their potential as investments.

■ CHAPTER 4 QUESTIONS FOR REVIEW

1. Which of the following is NOT a true statement regarding term life insurance?

    A. It is the simplest form of life insurance.

    B. The premium is based on the beneficiary's age.

    C. The policy is issued for a specified number of years.

    D. It usually has a option to renew.

2. Traditional whole life insurance is based on an actuarial life span of

    A. 75 years

    B. 100 years

    C. 150 years

    D. 200 years

3. Life insurance may be used as a retirement vehicle for all of the following reasons EXCEPT

A. the cash value growth is taxed at a low rate while it accumulates in the policy

B. life insurance requires periodic contributions

C. it builds cash values that belong to the policyowners

D. life insurance is a safe investment

4. The life insurance product that combines a protection element with an investment element is called

A. whole life insurance

B. universal life insurance

C. variable life insurance

D. term life insurance

5. Cash value life insurance provides all of the following rights and benefits EXCEPT

A. protection against creditors

B. policy loan privileges

C. tax-free status, regardless of payout option selected

D. guaranteed value at death

5
Annuities

I n this chapter, we look at annuities—a subject with which you are probably already well versed. In its simplest terms, an *annuity* converts an accumulated sum of money into a series of payments over a number of years or a lifetime. The duration of the payments can be structured to extend over a definite period of time or over the lifetime of one or more recipients. Because they can provide a regular, periodic income stream and they enjoy certain tax advantages that other financial products do not, annuities have become popular investments. They are particularly suited for retirement planning and retirement savings.

In this chapter, we'll briefly review some of the key concepts related to annuities. We'll also take a look at the workings of specific types of annuities and at annuity policy evaluation. The central objective is to evaluate this type of resource using similar criteria applied to other investments.

■ ■ ■ ■ ■

■ WHAT IS AN ANNUITY?

An *annuity* is an income stream—a regular, periodic payment for life or another defined period. It is a mathematical concept that begins with a lump sum of money that is deposited, earns interest over time and is paid out over time. Each payment consists partly of *principal*, which the annuity owner contributed in the form of premiums, and partly of *interest* earned on the yet-to-be-distributed principal. Although annuities are issued by life insurance companies, they are not considered life insurance because they offer no insurance protection. In essence, annuities are the opposite of life insurance. While the principal function of life insurance is to *create* an estate (an "estate" being a sum of money) by the periodic payment of money into a contract, an annuity's principal function is to *liquidate* an estate by the periodic payment of money out of a contract. While life insurance protects people who die too soon, annuities protect people who live too long.

Life Annuities vs. Term Certain Annuities

An annuity can structure its payout for a fixed number of years or for the duration of one or more lives. If the payments are contingent upon a life or lives, the annuity is known as a *life annuity*. If the payments are fixed for a certain number of years, without regard to a life contingency, the annuity is a *term certain* or *period certain* annuity. For example, Ralph, age 65, owns an annuity that will pay him $100 a month for as long as he lives; his is a life annuity. Diane, also age 65, owns a term certain annuity that will pay her (or her beneficiary) $500 a month for 10 years, after which there are no more payments. Life annuities can also provide a term certain feature. For example, a life annuity with 10-years certain provides for lifetime payments, but also guarantees a minimum payment period of 10 years, even if the annuitant were to die prior to the end of the 10-year period.

How and why can life insurance companies accept a certain amount of capital and guarantee that it will pay a specific lifetime income? Life insurance companies as chartered in the individual states are authorized to provide financial products that deal in *life contingencies*. Actuarial science has become an advanced form of mathematics that is recognized for objectivity in dealing with large statistical samplings of the population. These accurate, scientific methods can be used to predict length of life. Death is certain; it is *when* death will occur that is unknown.

To estimate how long a male or female of a given age is expected to live, insurance companies use *annuity tables*, based on the law of averages and the record of life spans compiled over generations. The *mortality table* is the basis for calculating the *risk factor*, which in turn determines the gross premium rate. These tables are based on large numbers of people and cannot, of course, predict how long any one particular individual will live.

As shown in Ill. 5.1, some people will die sooner than expected, and some will live longer than the table predicts. However, the company's annuity transactions will

ILL. 5.1 ■ *2000 Individual Annuity Table**

Attained Age	Life Expectancy		Deaths per 1,000 @ Attained Age	
	Men	Women	Men	Women
45	37.94	41.44	1.75	0.94
55	28.89	31.99	4.53	2.46
65	20.45	23.02	9.94	6.25
75	13.16	14.86	28.30	17.56
85	7.75	8.37	73.28	57.91
95	4.35	4.50	162.18	156.85

*Projected to 2000. The mortality rates for this table are conservative as related to the actual and projected experience upon which they are based.

Source: 1998 *Life Insurance Fact Book*, American Council of Life Insurance.

average out over a period of years. In this way, insurers can guarantee the lifelong payments annuities are designed to provide. This means that annuities can be used primarily as *retirement income* vehicles—protection against the risk of outliving one's income. For example, although a man age 45 might "expect to live" almost 36 more years, he might be one of the unfortunate number who die before reaching age 46. On the other hand, he might live well into his 90s. Other members of his age group may also live longer—or shorter—lives than indicated by mortality tables.

■ ANNUITY BASICS

An annuity is a cash contract with a life insurance company. In addition to the insurer, there are usually three parties involved: the contractholder, the annuitant and the beneficiary. The *contractholder* is the owner of the contract and responsible for premium payments; the *annuitant* is the one by whose life the contract (and payments) are measured and who typically is the recipient of the income payments; the *beneficiary* (if one is named) is the individual who stands in line to receive payments only if the annuitant dies before the contract has paid its full benefit or if the contractholder dies before any payments commence. In many cases, the contractholder and the annuitant are one and the same, just as the policyowner and the insured are often the same person under a life insurance contract. It's important to make the distinction, however, since the rights, responsibilities and benefits are different for contractholders and annuitants. The contractholder controls all decisions relating to the annuity and could, for example, choose to surrender the contract before any payments are made to the annuitant.

An annuity is purchased in one of two ways: with a single premium payment (some prefer the term *deposit*) at the beginning of the contract or through a series of periodic premium payments over the years. These funds represent the annuity's *principal*. The principal is either credited with a certain established rate of interest or grows in response to its underlying investment base, depending on how the owner chooses to invest the premium deposits. Neither the interest credited nor the accumulating principal is currently taxable to the contractholder, a significant benefit of annuity ownership. The combination of (1) principal, (2) compounded interest or investment earnings and (3) tax deferral is the way an annuity grows and the ultimate amount available for payout is, in part, a reflection of these factors.

With any annuity, there are two distinct time periods: the accumulation period and the payout, or annuity, period. The *accumulation period* is that time during which funds are being paid into the annuity, in the form of premiums by the contractholder, and interest is earned on those premiums. An annuity's accumulation period can be as short as one month or as long as several years, depending on when the contract is scheduled to begin making payouts. The *payout* or *annuity period* refers to the point at which the annuity ceases to be an accumulation vehicle and begins to generate benefit payments on a regular basis. Typically, benefit payments are made monthly, though quarterly, semi-annual or annual payments can be arranged.

The above describes the basics of the annuity product. However, there are a number of options and designs available to the annuity purchaser that will enable him or her to structure the product to best suit his or her own needs. These four designs include:

1. the funding method—single premium or periodic premiums over time;

2. the date the annuity payments begin—immediately or deferred until a future date;

3. the payout options—a specified term of years or for life or a combination of both; and

4. the underlying investment configuration—a fixed (guaranteed) rate of return or a variable (nonguaranteed) rate of return.

Funding Method

As mentioned previously, an annuity begins with a sum of money invested by the contractholder, which is its principal. Annuity principal is created or funded in one of two ways: all at once with a single payment or over time with a series of periodic payments. Annuities funded with a *single, lump-sum premium payment* at the beginning of the contract might be appealing to individuals who have a moderate to large sum available for investing and who wish to do so on a tax-deferred basis. Most insurers require some minimum amount, such as $5,000, to purchase a single premium annuity.

Annuities can also be funded through a series of *periodic payments* that, over time, will create the annuity principal fund. At one time, it was common for insurers to require that periodic annuity payments be fixed and level, much like traditional insurance premiums, and some contracts may still require fixed premium contributions. Today, it is more common to allow annuity owners flexibility as to when and how much they pay into their contracts. An initial deposit of $500 or $1,000 may be required, but from then on, the annuity owner could make premium payments of as little as $25 or $50, whenever he or she chooses. The insurer will likely send out regular premium notices but these serve primarily as reminders to set money aside on a regular basis.

Date Annuity Payments Begin

Every annuity has a scheduled maturity or *annuitization date*, which is the point the accumulated annuity fund is to convert to the payout mode and the benefit payments to the annuitant are to begin. This date is selected on the application. Basically speaking, there are two options: immediate or deferred.

An *immediate annuity* is designed to make its first benefit payment at one payment interval from the date of purchase. Thus, since most annuities make monthly payments, an immediate annuity would typically generate its first payment one month from the purchase date. As you might guess, an immediate annuity has a relatively short accumulation period and can only be funded with a single payment. An annuity cannot simultaneously accept payments by the contractholder and pay out income to the annuitant.

An immediate annuity is a common choice for those nearing retirement, whose financial focus has shifted from products designed to protect or accumulate wealth to those designed to generate income and who have the lump-sum amount necessary for its purchase. For example, an individual nearing retirement could surrender his or her cash value life insurance policy and use that amount as a lump-sum payment to purchase an annuity. A distribution from a company pension plan, a matured CD or the proceeds from the sale of a home could also be used to purchase an immediate annuity. An immediate annuity is really nothing more than a *distribution vehicle*— a way to convert a sum of money into a stream of income.

A *deferred annuity* is designed to provide income payments beginning at some specified *future* date. It can be funded with either a single payment or with periodic payments over time. In this way, a deferred annuity can serve as a tax-deferred accumulation vehicle, since the premium or premiums deposited will have a chance to accumulate, earn interest and grow, without being subject to tax. Most insurers impose some restrictions on how far into the future benefit payments may be deferred. Usually, deferred annuities must be *annuitized* (that is, converted from the accumulation period to the payout period) before the annuitant reaches a maximum age, such as 85.

Annuity Payout Options

Once an annuity matures and its accumulated fund is to convert to an income stream, a payout schedule is established. There are a variety of ways in which this schedule can be structured. It can be for a specified period of years, for the duration of one or more lives or a combination of both.

Period or Term Certain Option

As mentioned at the beginning of this chapter, the *period* or *term certain payout* is not based on life contingency; instead, it guarantees payments for a certain period of time, such as 10, 15 or 20 years, whether or not the annuitant is living. At the end of the specified period, payments cease. In the event the annuitant dies before the end of the specified period, the beneficiary becomes the recipient of the income until the end of the term.

Straight Life-Only Option

The *straight life-only option* represents the purest form of life annuitization. It provides a series of guaranteed payments for as long as the annuitant lives; when death occurs, payments cease. If at the annuitant's death there is any principal remaining that has not been paid out, it is forfeited. On the other hand, the annuitant cannot outlive the payments. Of all the payout options based on a life contingency, the straight life-only option produces the largest payout per $1 of principal.

Life-Only with Guaranteed Minimum Option

This payout option provides income for the annuitant's life and guarantees a certain minimum payout. This "minimum" can take the form of a specified number of years or the "refund" of the annuity principal if the annuitant dies before the premiums paid into the contract are fully liquidated. For example, a "life with 10-year certain" payout would provide payments for the annuitant's life and guaranteed for 10 years. If the annuitant lives beyond 10 years, payments continue until his or her death. If, however, the annuitant were to die six years after annuity payments begin,

---

ILL. 5.2 ■ *Annuity Payout Options*

There are a number of ways in which an annuity's payout can be structured. However, for any given annuity fund, the more "guarantees" the payout option provides, the smaller each payment will be. Below are the approximate monthly payments that a $100,000 annuity fund would generate, for eight different payout options.*

If the Payout Option Were . . .	The Monthly Payment Would Be . . .
Life-only	$789
Life-only with 10-year term certain	$737
Joint and one-half survivor	$708
Joint and full survivor	$664
Joint and one-half survivor with 10-year term certain	$698
Joint and full survivor with 10-year term certain	$663
Five-year term certain	$1,802
10-year term certain	$1,077

*The assumption is that the annuitant is a 60-year-old male; his spouse/survivor is also 60. The annuitant's life expectancy is 17.5 years; joint-life expectancy is 25.7 years.

---

payments would continue to the beneficiary for four years. A "life with refund" payout would guarantee payments to the annuitant for life, and, if the annuitant dies before the annuity's principal is completely paid out, would provide the beneficiary with either a lump-sum cash amount or continuing payments equal to the principal remaining.

Joint-Life Options

There are several joint-life options which provide for annuity payments to two people, typically a husband and wife. A *joint and full survivor* payout provides for the same monthly payment as long as either of the two people are living. It is only at the death of the second individual that payments cease. A variation of this is the *joint and one-half survivor option*, which provides regular income payments to two people while they are both living and, upon the death of the first, continues payments of half the original amount to the survivor until his or her death.

Underlying Investment Configuration

Finally, annuities can be selected based on their underlying investment base: fixed or variable. Actually, this is probably one of the first decisions an annuity investor will make, and the choice depends to a large extent on his or her investment objectives and risk tolerance.

Fixed Annuities

A *fixed annuity* provides a guaranteed fixed benefit amount to the annuitant, expressed in terms of dollars per payment period (i.e., "$500 a month"). During the accumulation period, the insurer invests the annuity premiums and principal in fixed securities and earns a certain, known return. An established rate of interest, which will never be less than a stated minimum, is credited to the annuity on a regular basis. At annuitization, the total amount of the annuity fund when applied to the selected payout option determines the guaranteed level of benefits. Once established, this payout level remains fixed and unchanging.

Fixed annuities are the more traditional products. Because they provide a specified, guaranteed benefit payable for the life of the annuitant (or other selected period), fixed annuities can offer security and financial peace of mind. On the other hand, since the benefit amount is fixed, annuitants may see the purchasing power of their payments decline over the years due to inflation. For this reason, an equity indexed annuity—with its potential for higher returns—may be more appealing.

An equity-indexed annuity (EIA) is a fixed annuity that offers all the advantages of traditional fixed annuities plus the potential to achieve greater growth and inflation protection. EIAs offer safety of principal, a guaranteed minimum return and some gains from the stock market. What distinguishes an EIA from traditional fixed annuities is the method used to credit interest. For a traditional fixed annuity, the insurance company sets the interest rate each year. For EIAs, the interest rate is determined by applying an interest crediting formula that is linked to the performance of a stock market index. Thus, an EIA can be defined as a fixed annuity that earns interest at a rate based on the performance of a stock market index. Most EIA formulas are linked to the Standard and Poor's Composite Stock Price Index (the S&P 500).

An EIA's performance is not identical to an investment in the S&P 500, however, because the S&P 500 index only reflects increases and decreases in the price of the stocks in the index. Because the S&P 500 is a price index, it does not reflect dividends paid on those stocks or the compound reinvestment of dividends in those stocks. EIAs that tie their return to the S&P 500 will not reflect the effects of dividends. This is important since dividends can have a dramatic effect on total return over a number of years. They always represent a positive number; therefore, the effect of their compounding is also always positive. As a result, the return on an EIA whose performance is tied to the S&P 500 could be much less than the return obtained by making a direct investment in the stocks that make up the index. However, an investment in the stock market involves risk. There is no risk with an EIA.

EIAs are designed for people who want to keep a portion of their savings safe for several years and who don't need access to that money while it's invested in the EIA. Before EIAs were available, people invested such savings in financial products like certificates of deposit, savings accounts and traditional fixed annuities. Although these products guarantee principal, they offered a relatively low rate of return. An EIA provides the same protection, plus, because of the link to the stock market index, it has the potential for greater growth and inflation protection.

Variable Annuities

A *variable annuity* shifts much of the investment risk from the insurer to the contractholder because there is no certainty—and no guarantee—as to its return. Unlike a fixed annuity that invests all its premiums in the insurer's general account, a variable annuity directs all or a portion of each premium payment into a *separate account*, which houses the variable investment options. Whereas the general account holds all the assets of the insurer (which, in turn, are invested and used to support guaranteed interest rates and guaranteed payouts), the separate account is maintained for the purpose of making investments for the contractholder.

With a variable annuity, it is the contractholder who determines how his or her premium will be invested. For example, it may be invested in a stock fund, a bond fund or a money market fund. Most variable annuities permit switching among the different types of funds at the owner's option, though limits are usually set on how often these changes may be made without incurring additional fees. The return on a variable annuity will depend on how well these underlying investments in the separate account perform. If they do well, the contractholder will likely realize growth and returns that exceed what a fixed annuity would offer.

To accommodate the variable annuity concept, a different way of accounting for both premiums and payouts is necessary. During the accumulation period, premiums paid by the contractholder are converted into *accumulation units* and credited to the contractholder's account. The value of each accumulation unit varies, based on the value of the underlying investments. For example, assume that the accumulation unit is initially valued at $10 and the owner of a variable annuity makes a $200 premium deposit. This means she has purchased 20 accumulation units. Six months later, however, she makes another premium deposit of $200, but the underlying stocks in her variable annuity have declined and the value of an accumulation unit is $8. This means that the $200 premium payment will now purchase 25 accumulation units.

At annuitization, the accumulation units in the annuity owner's individual account are converted into *annuity units*. At the point of the initial payout, the annuity unit calculation is made and, from then on, the *number* of annuity units remains the same for that annuitant. The *value* of those units will change, depending on the actual performance of the separate account. For example, let's say that our annuity owner was credited with 100 annuity units at annuitization. The dollar values of an annuity unit for each of the first three months of her payout were $9.50, $9.25 and $10.10, reflecting the fluctuation in the underlying account. The monthly payments the annuitant received were $95, $92.50 and $101, respectively.

The disadvantage of a variable annuity is that its lack of guarantees leaves the owner open to the ups and downs of market risk. On the other hand, the theory behind variable annuities, which has generally held true over the years, is that by tying their return to the market, they are able to outdistance or at least keep pace with the cost of living, thereby maintaining the annuitant's purchasing power. With slight modifications, the payout options described above are all available to the variable annuity owner.

Because of its underlying investment structure, a variable annuity is considered a "security" and can only be sold by agents who have a securities license as well as a life insurance license. All variable annuities must be registered with the Securities and Exchange Commission (SEC) and any sales proposal or presentation must include a prospectus.

■ OTHER ANNUITY FACTORS

The discussion to this point has explained the basics of annuities. Keep in mind that their ultimate purpose—their unique function—is to generate an income stream. When that income will be needed (immediately or deferred), how the annuity will be funded (single premium or periodic), the type of investment return desired (fixed or variable), the type of payout desired (fixed or variable) and how that payout should be structured (term certain or for life; single or joint) are all decisions that will point the investor to the type of annuity that will best suit his or her purpose. However, there are additional factors—some positive, some negative—the annuity investor should consider.

Surrender Charges

Almost all deferred annuities carry a *surrender charge*. This is a charge applicable during the early years of the contract's accumulation phase in the event the contractholder surrenders or cashes in his or her annuity before the insurer has had the opportunity to recover the cost of obtaining the business and issuing the contract. Typically, the surrender charge is a percentage of either the accumulated value of the annuity or the total premiums the owner has deposited. For example, assume Annuity XYZ assesses the following schedule of surrender charges based on premium deposit:

Year 1	7%
Year 2	6%
Year 3	5%
Year 4	4%
Year 5	3%
Year 6	2%
Year 7	1%
Year 8 and after	0%

Now assume Sam purchased Annuity XYZ with a $50,000 single deposit. If he were to surrender the contract in its third year, his surrender charge would be 5 percent of his premium deposit, or $2,500. If he surrendered the contract in its seventh year, the charge would be $500. After eight years, no surrender charges would be applied.

Withdrawal Privileges

Many annuities today offer limited *withdrawal privileges* during the accumulation period, prior to annuitization. Insurers made this option available, in part, to overcome the perception that, due to surrender charges, annuities are illiquid investment vehicles. A typical withdrawal provision allows the contractholder, after the first year, to withdraw up to 10 percent of his or her annuity fund each year without incurring any surrender charges. It should be noted, however, that though the insurer does not assess any charges on such withdrawals, the Internal Revenue

Service (IRS) might take a different position. This is discussed later in the section on taxation.

Death Benefit

Most annuity contracts contain a provision for the payment of a *death benefit* if either the contractholder or the annuitant dies before the contract's maturity or annuity date. This is not a "benefit" in the sense of a life insurance benefit; it is simply the total premiums contributed (less any withdrawals) or the contract's accumulated value, if greater. If the annuitant dies after income payments have begun, those payments will either cease or continue, depending on the payout option in effect.

Contract Loans

A number of newer annuity contracts contain a *loan provision*. This provision allows a contractholder to borrow up to a certain amount of the contract's accumulated value, say 75 percent, at an established rate of interest. A loan provision adds a measure of liquidity to an annuity; however, there may be tax implications as we will discuss.

Fees

An insurance company has expenses related to the acquisition, maintenance and disposition of any block of business. Annuities are no exception. General overhead as well as direct marketing expenses must be recovered. The personalized services offered by an insurance agent are paid for by commission. Other expenses are directly attributed to policy issue: assembly of the policy, mailing costs and establishment of records. Then there are billings, records storage and policy services (change of beneficiary, ownership assignments, loans, periodic notifications and information return and responses to consumer inquiries). There are also the recordings of premium deposits received and interest credited.

Most fixed annuities are sold as back-end loaded contracts, meaning that no fees are assessed at the time of the product's purchase. The insurer makes its money—and covers the cost of issuing such contracts—on the "spread" between the interest it earns on invested premiums and the amount that it credits to an annuity. To assure that expenses are covered if a contract is surrendered in its early years, the insurer will assess a surrender charge, as explained above.

Variable annuities, like fixed annuities, are usually issued without a front-end load; however, they do carry certain unique administrative and servicing costs that are ultimately charged to the contractholder. These costs would include, for example, the costs of transferring invested premiums from one account to another and for issuing quarterly or annual statements to the contractholder. There are also the costs associated with managing and investing the separate account funds. These latter costs are not passed on to the contractholder directly; instead, they are deducted from the fund itself before the value of an accumulation unit is calculated. Similar to fixed annuities, variable annuities also assess surrender charges, applicable during the contract's first few years.

Taxation

With regard to the taxation of annuities, it's helpful to discuss the subject in terms of the contract's accumulation period and its payout period, since different rules apply.

Accumulation Period

During the accumulation period, no matter how long or short it may be, interest credited or earned on an annuity is not currently taxable to the contractholder. (This is similar to the tax treatment of the cash value in permanent life polices.) Though this may have little impact on immediate annuities, it is a significant benefit for owners of deferred annuities. Because of tax deferral, funds accumulate more rapidly than they would with a comparable taxable investment. For example, let's say John, age 50, deposits $50,000 in a certificate of deposit at his local bank. Jane, also age 50, purchases a $50,000 single-premium deferred annuity. Both earn a 6.5 percent rate of return; however, because John is in the 31 percent tax bracket, the earnings on the CD are taxed every year at this rate. This means that John realizes a net yield of only 4.49 percent. Consequently, he has a smaller fund available for continued growth and compounding than does Jane with her annuity. For the sake of simplicity, assume that both the CD and the annuity earn a constant 6.5 percent compounded annually over a 15-year period. The result, when John and Jane are ready to retire at age 65, is a fund of $99,295 in the CD and $128,592 in the annuity. The difference is attributed to tax deferral.

As long as the funds remain in the annuity, they preserve their tax-deferred status. However, if the contractholder accesses those funds prior to the contract's maturity—if he or she takes a withdrawal or loan or complete surrender—it may be a taxable event. To the extent that a withdrawal, loan or surrender consists of any interest earnings (as opposed to principal), it will be considered taxable income.* Furthermore, if funds are taken before the contractholder is age 59½, a 10 percent "premature withdrawal penalty" will be assessed as well. The only exceptions to this penalty are withdrawals or surrenders due to death or disability or if the contractholder annuitizes the contract over a life expectancy.

Payout Period

Once an annuity matures and its fund is annuitized into a series of periodic payments, a different tax rule applies. Each payment consists partly of principal and partly of interest earnings. The objective is to provide the contractholder with a tax-free return of his or her principal while taxing the interest earnings. Consequently, annuity income is taxed in accordance with an exclusion ratio, which excludes a portion of each payment from tax and taxes the balance.

---

* Prior to maturity, any annuity distribution—withdrawal, surrender or loan—will be considered first as a fully taxable distribution of interest earnings until all interest has been withdrawn and only then will any amounts over this be considered a nontaxable return of principal. This treatment applies to any annuity issued after August 14, 1982.

ILL. 5.3 ■ *IRS Table V—Ordinary Life Annuities One Life—Expected Return Multiples*

For annuities with starting date on or after July 1, 1986.

Age	Multiple	Age	Multiple	Age	Multiple
5	76.6	42	40.6	79	10.0
6	75.6	43	39.6	80	9.5
7	74.7	44	38.7	81	8.9
8	73.7	45	37.7	82	8.4
9	72.7	46	36.8	83	7.9
10	71.7	47	35.9	84	7.4
11	70.7	48	34.9	85	6.9
12	69.7	49	34.0	86	6.5
13	68.8	50	33.1	87	6.1
14	67.8	51	32.2	88	5.7
15	66.8	52	31.3	89	5.3
16	65.8	53	30.4	90	5.0
17	64.8	54	29.5	91	4.7
18	63.9	55	28.6	92	4.4
19	62.9	56	27.7	93	4.1
20	61.9	57	26.8	94	3.9
21	60.9	58	25.9	95	3.7
22	59.9	59	25.0	96	3.4
23	59.0	60	24.2	97	3.2
24	58.0	61	23.3	98	3.0
25	57.0	62	22.5	99	2.8
26	56.0	63	21.6	100	2.7
27	55.1	64	20.8	101	2.5
28	54.1	65	20.0	102	2.3
29	53.1	66	19.2	103	2.1
30	52.2	67	18.4	104	1.9
31	51.2	68	17.6	105	1.8
32	50.2	69	16.8	106	1.6
33	49.3	70	16.0	107	1.4
34	48.3	71	15.3	108	1.3
35	47.3	72	14.6	109	1.1
36	46.4	73	13.9	110	1.0
37	45.4	74	13.2	111	.9
38	44.4	75	12.5	112	.8
39	43.5	76	11.9	113	.7
40	42.5	77	11.2	114	.6
41	41.5	78	10.6	115	.5

For federal income tax purposes, the taxpayer excludes from gross income each year a fixed, unchanging fraction of the guaranteed annual sum received under the contract. To quickly determine a year's exempt annuity income, the total investment is divided by the annuitant's life expectancy or, if the payments are only for a fixed period, by such period. The life expectancies used to determine expected returns are taken from annuity tables prescribed by the IRS (see Ill. 5.3).

This IRS table is the one used to estimate an annuitant's life expectancy for purposes of determining the taxable and nontaxable amounts of fixed lifetime annuity income. To determine the taxable and nontaxable amounts of his annual income, an *exclusion ratio* is determined, using the following equation:

$$\frac{\text{Investment in the Contract}}{\text{Expected Return}} = \text{Exclusion Ratio}$$

The "investment in the contract" is the total premium amount the contractholder paid into the annuity; the "expected return" is the total amount the annuitant will receive over his or her lifetime.

For example, Ed has contributed $20,000 in premium to an annuity, which will provide him with $200 a month for life, beginning at age 65. Based on certain IRS-prescribed life expectancy and annuity tables, which apply a "multiplier" to annuity income (see Ill. 5.3), Ed is expected to receive a total of $48,000 in annuity payments over his lifetime. ($200/mo. × 12 mos. × 20.0). Dividing Ed's investment ($20,000) by the total amount he is expected to receive ($48,000) produces the exclusion ratio. In this case it is 41.6 percent. This means that 41.6 percent of each $200 annuity payment Ed receives is attributed to principal and is excluded from tax; the balance represents interest earnings and is taxable. This approach applies until the total of all exclusions Ed takes equals his $20,000 investment. After that, if Ed is still alive and receiving payments, each will be fully taxed.*

Variable annuities that provide payments that vary from month to month and year to year require slightly different calculations and follow slightly different rules, but the basic principle of taxing interest earnings and excluding the annuitant's investment still applies.

■ THE ROLE OF ANNUITIES IN INVESTMENT PLANNING

The advantage of a structured, guaranteed life income stream is obvious and is one of the primary reasons the annuity is so popular. Many individuals, especially those in retirement, may be reluctant to use the principal of their savings, fearing it may become depleted. However, if they choose to conserve the principal, they run the risk of never deriving any benefit from it at all—and ultimately are obliged to pass

---

* It should be noted that contracts that annuitized prior to 1987 are allowed to carry an exclusion ratio indefinitely, no matter how long the annuitant lives or how much he or she receives in benefit payments. It's possible these annuitants may receive tax free more than what they paid into the annuity. This permanent exclusion ratio does not apply to annuities with a post-1986 maturity date.

it on to others at their deaths. An annuity is designed to liquidate principal—but in a structured, systematic way that guarantees it will last a lifetime.

Annuities appeal to uninsurable individuals since an annuity forces a person to set aside certain amounts on a regular basis. If these individuals should die before the contract is annuitized, their beneficiaries would receive at least the sum total of the annuity premiums plus interest. There are also individuals who, in case of their deaths, have made adequate provision for their financial obligations to others and now need only consider their own old-age income requirements:

1. the middle-aged to elderly widow or widower who has inherited a substantial sum of money, has no dependents and is concerned about losing principal funds;

2. the career person who earns a good income, but has realized that age, business pressures or desire may force his or her early retirement;

3. persons whose earnings are unusually high for a relatively short period, such as actors, entertainers or professional athletes;

4. children who are obligated to provide for the needs of a dependent parent as long as the parent lives; and

5. an owner of a small company with just a few employees who wants to provide a guaranteed income at retirement for his employees, but does not want to pay a high cost for administering a formal retirement program.

Guaranteed Income

An annuity is the only vehicle that can offer the investor a guaranteed lifetime income, either immediately or at some future date. Therefore, many individuals purchase annuities to ensure that income will be received for a definite period of time or for life. An annuity helps to solve some of the central problems to funding an adequate retirement income, including:

• maintaining real purchasing power against rising prices;

• creating an income that lasts for life (risk of longevity); and

• using accumulated wealth efficiently to provide such income (with no shortage, but also no excess residual at death).

Tax-Deferred Savings

Besides being able to guarantee a lifetime income, annuities make excellent investment planning products for many other reasons. During the accumulation period the principal builds through investments and returns on investments, while benefits and taxes are deferred. Tax deferral gives the annuity an edge over other products such as CDs or taxable bonds. For example, a CD that earns 6.5 percent will actually yield 4.68 percent to an individual in the 28 percent tax bracket. If that same individual purchases an annuity crediting 6.5 percent, he or she would actually realize a 6.5 percent return because of tax deferral. The combination of tax-deferred growth and interest earnings on the fund compounded over the accumulation period can generate significant retirement funds.

Flexible Investment Options

Although the insurance company manages the available funds, as we have seen, variable annuities allow the annuitant to select from a variety of investment vehicles during the *accumulation phase*. For example, contributions may be allocated to one or more bond funds, stock funds or money market funds. Often, the contributions may be transferred among funds without charge or tax consequences. This flexibility allows the annuitant to choose the most appropriate investment at any given time, thereby maximizing investment growth. For example, if an annuitant contributed $5,000 to a money market fund, which grew to $8,000, the entire $8,000 could be transferred to a another fund within the annuity, such as a bond fund, without the $3,000 gain being subject to current income tax. However, assume the same $5,000 invested in a common stock mutual fund had appreciated to $8,000 and then had been sold and reinvested in a CD. The gain would be subject to tax in the year of transfer.

Liquidity

As explained earlier, the deferred annuity offers a number of liquidity options for those who need access to their funds prior to retirement. Because most annuities carry some kind of surrender charge, many people believe that once they purchase an annuity, their funds are out of reach until they retire or the product is annuitized. In fact, surrender charges for most annuities are of limited duration, applying only during the first five to eight years of the contract. Second, for those years in which surrender charges are applicable, most annuities provide for an annual free withdrawal, which allows the annuity owner to withdraw up to a certain percentage of his or her annuity account with no surrender charge applied.

Deferred annuity owners can also take out loans from their contracts. Typically an annuity loan provision allows the owner to borrow up to a specified percentage of the annuity's fund value at comparatively low rates. Contract owners who consider this option should know that annuity loans are taxable and, if taken prior to age 59½, they would be subject to a 10 percent penalty.

■ RISKS ASSOCIATED WITH ANNUITIES

Annuities are as safe as the insurance company selling the product. Insurance companies are strictly regulated and must maintain reserves. However, there is a small risk that the insurer may go bankrupt. Although there are generally arrangements made to minimize losses, it is a risk that should be noted. In most cases, annuities of established companies are very low risk, although no federal insurance is available at this time.

When an individual saves with an annuity, he or she defers taxes on the interest but they are not eliminated. Investors in higher tax brackets may find they will be better in municipal bonds (discussed in Chapter 7), where the interest is completely exempt from taxes.

When immediate annuities are purchased, annuitants are betting that they will live long enough to recover more in income than they invested. If they want to guarantee that money will pass on to a spouse, dependent or other survivor, they will have to accept lower income payments. And, because income payments on annuities are fixed, they generally will not keep pace with inflation. Finally, the investor is dependent on the management ability of the insurance company issuing the annuity. If the investor selects a stock fund, the selection of funds is restricted to those offered and managed by the issuer. The value of the stock fund may even decline due to poor management.

■ ANNUITY POLICY EVALUATION

The evaluation of annuity policies must be done with awareness of fundamental differences between this and direct "investments" discussed in later chapters. The *yield* or return on premium deposits is a primary consideration in evaluating deferred annuities. Perhaps even more important to some individuals is the security of their *principal*. Most annuities guarantee the contractholder's principal interest.

The evaluation of annuities should also include how they are marketed and what expenses the annuitant pays. Lastly, in evaluating annuities, the method of distribution affects the total return evaluation. Before individually evaluating the specific types of policies, a general evaluation of these subjects may be helpful.

Return on Annuity

Immediate annuities have no accumulation period but do have some internal rate of return. This type of evaluation was covered briefly with the settlement options and policy distribution periods.

The *net premium, after expense loads*, if applicable, may begin earning interest immediately. If the policy effective date precedes the issue date, interest generally is credited only from the latter date. Future premiums are credited (net of any load) as received. Annuities typically do not credit interest like a passbook savings account. The interest might be based on an average balance in the cash value account, with posting at the end of the period (typically one year).

Guaranteed or Floor Interest Rates

To attract new premium dollars, most insurance companies provide attractive guarantees. These may apply to net cash value attributable to all new premiums they received during the given policy year, or may apply only to premiums received during a specified period. The rate might continue to be credited to those cash values for a full 12 months (from the date premiums are received) or only until the end of that policy year.

Some policies provide a graduated scale of interest rates. During the first policy year the stated rate may approach current Treasury bill yields.

Actual Account Performance

In the case of separate accounts for variable annuities, floor guarantees are not available. The rate changes daily since the account's yield rate varies with the dividend and interest rates of underlying securities divided by the total market value of the assets. A decline in stock or bond average prices increases the rate as would an increase in declared dividends by the corporations in which stock is held.

Separate-account funded annuities (unlike those invested in the insurance company's general reserves) directly credit corporate cash and stock dividends, bond interest and returns on "cash balances" held in money market instruments. In addition, a separate account credits the annuity with its share of short-term and long-term capital gains (or losses). This means the annuitant, rather than the insurer, bears the risk of investment losses in exchange for possible gains. Since these yields are credited directly to annuity cash values, the insurance company pays no income tax on the investment earnings.

Excess Interest and Policy Dividends

When an insurance company bears the investment risk, it only can assume interest rates on a fairly conservative basis. If it contractually guaranteed to credit 10 percent interest and rates fall to 5 percent, it would be forced to invest future premiums at a loss. On the other hand, if interest rates rise to 15 percent, without policy flexibility, most annuitants might stop paying premiums or replace the contract with a new one issued by another insurance company.

For annuities to remain attractive, most new contracts allow the company to credit excess interest or dividends. *Excess interest* (as defined by the Internal Revenue Code) is the difference between the *actual declared* rate of interest (established periodically by the insurance company) and the contractually guaranteed interest rate.

To be income tax deductible by the insurance company, to the extent of limits provided, certain qualifications must be met. One such condition is that for policies falling within its provisions, interest either must be guaranteed by rates or by procedures for definitely determining these outside the discretion of the insurer.

A *dividend* is an amount, based on a block of business, that is a return of premium. This is caused by savings on operating expenses, favorable mortality experience and excess interest earned on reserves above what is required to provide the contractual benefits. With fixed monthly annuity benefits, dividends were paid to reflect mainly the excess interest earned, keeping the monthly income fixed. If dividends were applied to purchase additional benefits, the net effect was similar to that of a contract crediting interest. Although annuity policy reserves receive favorable tax treatment, payment of dividends does not offset income to the same extent as crediting interest.

The key point to understand is the general methods used by various insurance companies to credit cash values with increases permitted because of high net rates of return experienced on the investments made by the insurer. The individual annuity contractholder generally is unaware of the taxation of insurance company reserves. The rate of interest actually credited is tax deferred until taken in distribution.

Dividends, whether received in cash by the contractholder or credited back to increase the deferred monthly annuity, also are not taxed currently as income. This means an annuity can be used to compound interest advantageously. Annuities issued to fund certain tax-qualified retirement plans may be credited higher rates of interest or dividends reflecting the absence of tax on reserves held under these policies.

Most policies credit interest *from the date actually received*, or for administrative ease may assume they are received on a policy billing date. However, the actual method of tracking deposits and crediting interest varies widely by company.

Security of Principal

Security of principal (net cash values) is generally the primary consideration when the insurance company invests reserves. The same mixture of investments backs life insurance policies. The types of investments and the adequacy of these reserves are regulated by state insurance departments. To attest to the security of these reserves, the Internal Revenue Code specifically exempts from actuarial valuation and certain minimum funding standards those retirement plans funded entirely with life insurance company reserves. For example, by law, an annuity satisfies diversification requirements because the reserves include a wide range of investments, both long term and short term, equity types as well as debt instruments and real property. Professional investment analysts manage these for the company and have proven to be very capable. As discussed in Chapter 4, *A.M. Best*, among other rating companies, rates the general security and performance of insurance companies for prospective policyowners' use.

How Annuities Are Sold

Though annuity policies with lifetime guaranteed income provisions only can be issued by life insurance companies under state charter, the method of distributing products varies widely. The most available source of annuities is the life insurance agent. Because policy provisions vary from one insurance company to another, an agent who represents one company can digest thoroughly the details of the products and that company's procedures for crediting interest, underwriting, processing conversions, loans and changes in beneficiary. The agent must be licensed in the state where the policy is sold and the policy has been approved.

Many stockbrokers are also licensed to sell annuities. Several insurance companies have developed specialized products to suit this market. Also, the client may initiate the sale or contact. Personal contact by the broker usually is not required. Annuities traditionally have not been marketed aggressively by brokerage houses.

Banks sometimes make annuities available to customers. The bank may act only as a conduit between the purchaser and the insurance company, or it may try to have a portion of the annuity policy reserves flow into its bank. In addition, financial planners either are licensed personally to sell annuities or can refer clients to a reliable source. Though insurance companies have traditionally sold products only through licensed agents and brokers, some take a more direct route, soliciting and accepting applications from the purchaser (annuity contractholder).

Premium Consideration

As presented earlier, annuities can be purchased with a single premium or by periodic premium payments in a variety of modes. Annual and monthly billings are used most commonly. Even on flexible premium annuities, these billings remind the contractholder to put money aside on a regular basis. Insurance companies have been very innovative in making premium payment convenient. Quarterly and semi-annual billing modes are available. In addition, payroll savings units may have special billings. An authorization may allow the insurance company to pay premiums directly from the policyowner's checking account.

Single premium contracts usually have a fairly high minimum amount, but they do offer an advantage. These contracts credit interest at higher rates than other types (except group annuities of considerably higher premium) because the insurance company receives a large sum that can be invested immediately. This determines to a large extent the interest rate that may be credited for many years.

Multiple or flexible premium contracts also have minimum levels. Insurers have, for the most part, kept these quite low. It may be possible to pay as little as $25-$50 per payment. Irregular premium payments typically are accepted only on flexible (or variable) annuities. Thus, where it may take thousands of dollars to purchase bonds or CDs directly, the annuity purchaser can get high rates conveniently. The purchase of an annuity funded by general reserves indirectly provides instantaneous dollar cost averaging depending on how reserves affect actual credited interest. Also, because periodic payments may be credited different "new money" rates by sophisticated computer technology, regular premium payments (instead of single premium payment) provide additional averaging.

Another advantage to annuities is the elimination of personal reinvestment. If an individual buys a bond that pays coupon interest, the investor must reinvest these small amounts if compounding of interest is to be realized. This can be inconvenient and expensive. Amounts to be reinvested (outside of a qualified retirement plan) normally are reduced by income taxes. Inside the annuity, the interest is credited to cash values without the need to reinvest distributions, and it is unreduced by income tax.

Expenses

Just as an insurance company has expenses related to acquisition, maintenance and disposition of its life insurance business so too does it incur expenses in its annuity business: office overhead, advertising, promotional literature and personnel expense related to getting the prospect to buy. The personalized services offered by an insurance agent are paid for by commission. Other acquisition expenses are attributable directly to policy issue. These include the physical assembly of the policy, mailing costs and establishment of records. Commissions have been reduced by competitive pressures to very modest amounts. Computers have enabled all costs related to records and processing to be kept low.

In addition to acquisition expenses, it costs the insurance company money to maintain annuities. This includes billing, records storage and policy services (change of beneficiary, ownership assignments, loans, periodic notifications and information returns; responses to consumer inquiries). The agent/broker typically visits the policyowner periodically to review the policy or policies purchased.

An insurance company also incurs expenses at the time proceeds are distributed. Though a lump-sum distribution requires only one check, the records must be converted (to inactive policy status), income tax forms and other information generated, and the agent typically delivers the proceeds. Death claims may involve multiple beneficiaries, problems in locating persons and completion of estate information forms. Payment of a monthly life income requires conversion, usually to a supplemental contract (to take advantage of higher current annuity income options than are available using policy guaranteed settlement options).

The purchaser of an individual annuity does not see these actual expenses, except where commission disclosure is required for most retirement plans. Instead, the insurance company recovers these in four possible ways: loads, penalties, investment activities or service charges.

Loads

Acquisition expenses may be recovered partially by a *front-end load* charge. An amount (usually a percentage) is removed from premiums and the net amount is credited to cash value. It is only the net amount that is credited with interest. To correspond with the actual acquisition expenses, many contracts have a front-end load only in the first policy year or when premiums during a renewal year exceed those of any previously largest year's premium. A *policy fee* is a small fixed-dollar, front-end load. To increase the net cash values receiving interest, some contracts *level the load*, either over the first few years of the contract or over the life of the contract. Some charge no loads.

Penalties

Another method for recovery of expenses, primarily related to distribution, is the *back-end load* or *early termination charge* or *withdrawal penalty*. This also is typically a percentage. It is the amount removed from cash values before payment is made to the owner. This may decline contractually to zero (or a modest rate) over a stated number of policy years. Certain contracts waive this charge if distribution is taken through exercise of certain settlement options. Some charge no loads on surrenders or distributions.

Investment Activities

Insurance companies, like banks, do not let funds remain idle. The premiums ultimately are loaned out in the form of mortgages, loaned to policyowners or used to invest in securities or real estate. Another method for recovering expenses is from these investment activities. A company invests its reserves at a higher rate of return than that which is credited to policies. A few percentage points in spread, on millions of dollars, creates a significant contribution to offsetting overhead expenses (and perhaps a modest profit).

Service Charges

Lastly, some annuities may impose service charges. These may be a percentage of average cash value or a fixed-dollar amount or a combination. For example, a company might charge $25 annually for general maintenance costs. Charges for specific policy services generally are not made, perhaps because these might be rejected by state insurance departments. Thus, an annuity contractholder normally can change the designated beneficiary, call and ask questions and demand other services for no charge.

From the annuity contractholder's viewpoint, the total actual expenses related to a block of business is (or should be) of some interest. However, except for commission disclosure on qualified retirement plans and expense information on some large group annuities, this information generally is not made available to purchasers of contracts. *Best's Reports* does give the consumer a guideline to overall levels of expense for most insurance companies. Probably even more important is how successfully an insurance company manages its investments. It stands to reason that the better its own return on investments, the more interest or dividends, net of investment expenses and after taxes, can be passed on to the annuity contractholder.

The relative weight of the various expense charges depends on the specific nature of the contract. It is sometimes better, for example, to pay a front-end load than be credited a lower rate of interest. For very small premiums, a fixed-dollar charge may become a relatively greater consideration. In general, a back-end load (withdrawal charge) is preferred over a large (or larger) front-end load because more dollars enter the contract cash values to earn interest. This is true if the annuity stays in force until termination charges decline. Withdrawal charges also allow the insurance company to invest policy reserves in longer maturity bonds at generally higher yields.

■ SUMMARY

Annuities provide a unique vehicle for the accumulation and distribution of wealth over a period of years covering one, two or even multiple life spans. This tool can be used to convert one form of wealth into another, for example, a capital item subject to income tax on capital gains into an income for life with most of the payments not taxed as income.

In simplest terms, whereas life insurance provides protection against premature death, annuities insure against outliving one's resources. No other vehicle perfectly allocates a sum of money over a group of lives so that each individual receives an income that is guaranteed to continue, and use up the principal, precisely for so long as he or she (or the beneficiary) lives, according to contract terms.

After investors have established a solid investment base of savings, life insurance and annuities, they can safely advance to the next level of the investment pyramid. In Chapters 6 and 7, we'll discuss the next level of the pyramid—income-producing investments such as corporate stock, municipal bonds and Treasury securities, which offer investors low to moderate risk in exchange for moderate to potentially high return.

■ CHAPTER 5 QUESTIONS FOR REVIEW

1. Which of the following phrases best describes an annuity?

   A. Tax-sheltered vehicle from which cash can be removed tax free as needed

   B. Life insurance policy that accumulates tax deferred

   C. Stock certificate issued by an insurance company

   D. Contract issued by an insurance company to allow for tax-deferred growth for retirement

2. During the accumulation period of a variable annuity, the value of the account increases or decreases, based on which of the following?

   A. Variable premium deposits

   B. Number of annuitants involved

   C. Investment results of the insurance company

   D. Company expenses

3. Generally speaking, purchasers of annuity contracts tend to

   A. live longer than those who purchase only life insurance

   B. fear that they will outlive their income

   C. purchase fairly conservative investments

   D. allocate their resources between life insurance and annuities

4. All of the following are annuity characteristics that investors look for EXCEPT

   A. short-term investment

   B. safety

   C. tax deferral

   D. guaranteed income

5. To calculate the exclusion ratio, you must know the expected return and the

   A. investment in the contract

   B. date of purchase

   C. tax bracket of the owner

   D. All of the above

......6

Investing in Stock

M oney market accounts, certificates of deposit and other guaranteed or insured investments assure that money set aside for the future will be safe. Individuals will have immediate liquid resources to draw upon in the event of a financial emergency or to create an estate for their survivors if premature death occurs. However, although these investments are relatively risk-free, almost everyone hopes to make a bit more than the return available from insured and guaranteed investments. And unless an individual is extremely risk averse, there is no reason why he or she shouldn't venture into the arena of higher risk and higher return. The key to investment success is to set specific objectives, learn the facts about various investments, use common sense when selecting from among investment options and be patient.

In this chapter, we examine stock investments: the reasons people purchase stock and some factors to consider when deciding to buy, hold or sell a particular stock. We discuss ownership rights in publicly held corporate stock—including common stock, preferred stock and foreign stock. Finally, we look at how stock is traded on the exchanges, over-the-counter and in other markets, as well as stock rights and warrants.

■ ■ ■ ■ ■

■ WHAT IS STOCK?

At some point, almost every investor considers purchasing stock to achieve greater gains—more than the limited fixed-interest income that bank accounts and bonds provide. *Stock* is a security that gives the purchaser part ownership or an *equity interest* in a business. For the issuing company, stock represents a means of acquiring cash without going into debt. For the investor, or stockholder, a *stock certificate*—the document identifying the registered owner, the security and the number of shares owned—represents a share of the risks or rewards of that company. The more shares of stock the investor holds, the greater his or her interest—and often, participation—in the affairs of the company.

Investors primarily profit from stock ownership in two ways: through growth or income. Growth from stock investing occurs when the market value of the security increases. When stock is sold at a profit, the investor realizes a capital gain and is taxed accordingly (more on that later). The investor may also realize income from stock over the course of the investment, before it is sold. This income is from distribution of earnings in the form of *dividends*. Income-oriented stocks generally pay a high dividend in relation to the amount invested. Dividends come in three forms: *cash dividends* (a proportion of quarterly earnings in cash); *stock dividends* (additional shares of stock in the corporation); or *property dividends* (usually securities of a corporation other than the company paying the dividend).

Whereas investors may select income-oriented stock for its dividend potential, growth in the value of the stock, not dividend income, is the primary reason most investors buy common stock. In fact, people looking for growth often select stock in rapidly growing companies that pay little or no dividends per share.

■ DECIDING TO PURCHASE STOCK

After three to six months' worth of living expenses are safely stored in liquid investments and after the financial risk of premature death has been covered by the purchase of life insurance, investors may begin to look for investments that offer a higher rate of return.

Investors contemplating a stock market strategy first should assess their temperament. If they are averse to risk or can't afford to lose their investment capital, they are poorly suited to stocks. However, many investors purchase shares of stock because they:

- offer the possibility of keeping ahead of inflation;

- offer the possibility of price appreciation;

- can be an excellent source of income; and

- tend to outperform bonds over the long run.

Once their soul searching is complete, investors adopt different stock strategies, depending on their theories of how the market works and their own temperaments.

When individuals invest or trade in stock (or have decided to do so), two important personal considerations generally underlie their decisions to buy, hold or sell a given stock: (1) their personal objectives and (2) their personal appraisals of the stock. In most cases they will (or should) use professional advice in making their decisions.

Individual Objectives

When an investor buys shares in a company, he or she can make money in one of two ways: through dividends or through price appreciation when the stock is sold. Generally, *dividends*, a distribution of earnings, are declared when the company is profitable. The company's board of directors decides on the dollar amount that will be distributed. This amount is then divided by the number of shares outstanding.

The second way to make money is price appreciation. The value of the stock may *appreciate* for a number of reasons, including company profitability, the introduction of a new product or the rumor of a company takeover. Conversely, the value of a stock may decline for a number of reasons, including poor overall earnings, ineffective management or negative publicity.

Although there may be other objectives (such as liquidity, tax shelter and so on), the three major objectives that motivate an individual to purchase, own or sell a security are: *income, growth* and *safety.* The income objective places emphasis on substantial and regular dividend payments; the growth objective emphasizes appreciation in value; and the safety objective emphasizes minimum risk of loss of principal.

The ideal stock would satisfy all three objectives, but such a stock seldom, if ever, exists. Generally, the higher the dividend payout, the less cash remains to plow back into the company for growth and vice versa. Moreover, the higher the dividend payout as *income* or the more rapid the expansion of plant and equipment for *growth* (that is, the less conservative the corporation), the greater is the *risk* to principal in most cases. The general axiom is the higher the income or the more rapid the growth, the greater the risk, and vice versa.

Because few stocks offer high dividends, outstanding appreciation potential and safety of principal, investors must decide whether it is more appropriate for their investment strategy to purchase a stock that offers high cash dividends or one that will appreciate in price over time.

Industry Analysis

As stated at the beginning of this chapter, stock is usually purchased because it generates income or appreciates in price. To determine which stock is likely to fare best as the economy proceeds along its upward or downward course, investors look for industries that offer better-than-average, long-term investment opportunities. Some industries are more affected by business cycles than others. Investors find it useful to distinguish between the four types of industries and investments: defensive, cyclical, growth and special situation.

Defensive Industries

Defensive industries are those industries that are least affected by normal business cycles. Most defensive industries involve the production of nondurable consumer goods such as food, insurance, pharmaceuticals, tobacco and energy. Public consumption of such goods remains steady throughout the business cycle, regardless of inflationary or deflationary economic factors. Stock in companies in these industries offers investors some protection against the inevitable downturns in the economy.

During recessionary economic periods and bearish markets, stocks in defensive industries generally decline less than stocks in other industries. During inflationary periods and bull markets, however, defensive stocks show less growth and return.

Investment in defensive industries tends to involve less risk and, consequently, less opportunity for a high return on investment.

Cyclical Industries

Cyclical industries are in many ways the opposites of defensive industries: they are highly affected by business cycles and price changes. Most cyclical industries produce durables such as capital goods, raw materials (e.g., steel, cement, aluminum and paper) and heavy equipment. During periods of tight credit or high inflation, manufacturers postpone investing in new capital goods. Likewise, consumers postpone purchasing durable goods like automobiles, recreational vehicles, appliances and houses. From an investment perspective, such industries producing such goods are considered cyclical.

Stocks in cyclical industries move directly with the business cycle and are known as *cyclical stock*. Generally they pay excellent dividends and their prices advance sharply as business conditions improve. But their dividends and prices fall off sharply when business slackens. Chemical, textile and machinery stocks are examples that usually fall in this category. Their primary appeal, of course, is the rapid rise in their dividends and prices when the business cycle is on the rise.

Growth Industries

Every industry and product passes through four phases during its existence: introduction, growth, maturity and decline. An industry is considered in its growth phase if the industry is growing faster than the economy as a whole because of technological changes, new products or changing consumer tastes. Computers, soft drinks and bioengineering have all been growth industries in the recent past. Because most companies in this phase retain nearly all of their earnings for expansion, stocks in these industries usually pay little or no dividends.

The stock of a corporation whose earnings have increased consistently over a number of years, and which shows every indication of continuing to expand, is termed a *growth stock*. Most growth stocks provide relatively low dividend yields because earnings are being plowed back into the companies. However, when interest rates are high, even growth stocks may have to issue dividends if they wish to attract capital. Growth stocks, nonetheless, are primarily attractive for price appreciation potential, especially from a long-range standpoint—usually not for income or a quick profit.

Special Situation Stock

Special situation stocks are stocks of a company with unusual profit potential due to nonrecurring circumstances. Examples include an expected business recovery under new management, the discovery of a valuable natural resource on corporate property or the introduction of a new product.

Investor Types

Depending primarily on their attitude relative to the income, growth and safety objectives, but also on how they arrive at their decision to buy, hold or sell a stock, individuals divide themselves into three broad (sometimes overlapping) types: gamblers, speculators and investors.

1. *The Gambler.* Gamblers dream of fantastic growth in a hurry. They give virtually no thought to income or safety. In fact, they give virtually no thought to their actions. Like flipping a coin or buying a raffle ticket, they play their hunches or take their chances, without investigating the probabilities (and often without considering the extent or consequences) of success or failure.

2. *The Speculator.* Speculators, like gamblers, hope for rapid growth (or rapid decline, in the case of short selling), with virtually no concern for income, and generally with only modest, if any, concern for safety. But unlike gamblers, they figure the odds of success or failure very carefully and govern their actions accordingly. They usually are *in and outers*, buying and selling frequently, normally holding stocks for only brief periods of time and trying to make quick profits on each transaction.

3. *The Investor.* Investors are primarily interested in substantial and stable dividend incomes or in substantial rates of growth, or a combinations of moderate amounts of both over relatively long periods of time. In any event, investors virtually always place maximum emphasis on a high degree of safety. Like speculators, investors carefully investigate each stock in which they are interested, weighing the probability of its satisfying their objectives and governing their actions according to their conclusions. Unlike speculators, they generally are interested in the long haul, the income or growth probabilities over a number of years. When they buy a stock, they usually intend to hold it until their objectives are satisfied. They tend to sell stock earlier only if it fails to live up to expectations, or can be replaced with something better.

General Sources of Information

Investors gain their impressions of the general health and trends of the economy and businesses by following financial articles and published national statistics. Of particular interest are items indicating amount and direction of changes in national income amounts, such as: *gross* or *net domestic product (GDP* or *NDP)*; personal income; new construction; equipment spending; inventory changes; current and estimated government expenditures and taxes; price indexes; production indexes; unemployment rates; department store, chain store, and mail order sales; and new orders and inventories of manufacturers.

A favorite indicator, considered by many to be the first clue to economic trends and business cycles, is the index of *durable* goods sales, or sales of such raw materials as pig iron, which is a principal ingredient of many durable goods. Because metals, lumber, hardware and other durable goods may be stocked up, or their purchase or replacement may be delayed indefinitely, their sales tend to fluctuate quickly, widely and directly with consumer demand, and thus serve as a barometer of the current business cycle.

ILL. 6.1 ■ *Market Indexes*

Dow Jones	New York Stock Exchange	Standard & Poor's
• 30 Industrials	• Composite	• 500 Index
• 20 Transportation	• Industrials	• Industrials
• 15 Utilities	• Utilities	• Transportation
• Equity Market Index	• Transportation	• Utilities
	• Finance	• Financials
		• 400 MidCap

Investors generally expect the overall stock market to follow much the same trends they see for the national economy and business, and rightfully so, for the market reflects the nation's economic and business health. In addition, investors usually pay particular attention to market news stories, analyses and averages that appear in the financial sections of their newspapers or financial publications. Investors also rely on a number of *indexes* that act as barometers of the overall market. As indicated in Ill. 6.1, the major indexes include the *Dow Jones Industrial Averages (DJIA)*, the *Standard & Poor's 500* and the *New York Stock Exchange (NYSE)* indexes.

Expected Return on Stock

After assessing the health of the economy and businesses in general, investors will look closer at the specific stocks they are interested in. As a general rule, investors should look at several measurements to determine a corporation's financial strength and its stock's potential return. When determining whether to purchase a particular stock, investors should consider the following:

- *The stock issuer should be researched carefully.* Before investing any money in stock, investors should know exactly what type of business the company is in, how profitable it is, how much debt it has, which companies are competing with it and which new products or services it intends to introduce. In addition, the investor should be familiar with the company's management team and its philosophy.

- *Outstanding shares should be 10 million or more.* A large supply of common stock shares ensures an active and liquid market in which the company's stock can easily be bought and sold.

- *The trend over the past five years of earnings per share should be upward.* The company's net income (income after taxes and preferred stock dividends) divided by the average number of common stock shares outstanding is called its earnings per share. The earnings per share of stock should continue to increase over time.

- *Increased earnings should be accompanied by increased dividends.* Although some corporations reinvest most of their earnings for future growth, many pay at least modest dividends to stockholders on a quarterly basis. Investors should also consider a stock's *yield*—its current dividend divided by the current market price of a share. Generally, the yield should be higher for a stock purchased for income than one chosen for potential price appreciation.

- *The price-earnings ratio (P/E ratio) should indicate safety.* The *P/E ratio* is calculated by dividing the previous year's earnings per share (or the current year's estimated earnings) by the current price of the stock. The ratio reflects investor opinion about the particular stock and the market in general. For example, a P/E ratio under 20 is usually considered safe, although a low P/E of 5 or 6 usually means that investors have little confidence in the stock. A P/E ratio above 30 usually indicates a potential for the stock's future growth and investors' interest in the future of the company.

- *Potential earnings and profits from stock splits should be evident.* A corporation's board of directors may approve a stock split when it feels the price of its stock is too high. A *stock split* is a change in the number of shares of common stock of a corporation, without changing the actual dollar value of total shares. In a *stock split*, the number of shares owned by existing stockholders are "split" to create a larger number of shares. For example, four thousand shares valued at $100 per share can be split two for one (producing eight thousand shares valued at $50 per share). The lower market price often enhances the stock's trading appeal.

In some cases, the board approves a *reverse split*, which reduces the number of shares outstanding. (Four thousand shares valued at $2 can undergo a reverse split of 1 for 10, resulting in 400 shares valued at $20 each.) Although reverse splits are not common, it may be done to boost the price of a stock that the company feels is undervalued.

Risks of Investing in Stocks

Investors must also recognize the risk that the stock's future dividend and price performance may fall short of predictions, resulting in anything from less gain than expected to total loss of principal. Unfavorable variation in the stock's future performance could result from unfavorable changes in the economy and/or overall business conditions, new technical developments or innovations or stronger competition from other companies. Finally, investors should understand that there is no guarantee that they will earn a profit in stocks.

■ CHARACTERISTICS OF CORPORATE STOCK

How is it that stock—which is a unit of fractional ownership in a corporation—can be acquired and held by individual investors? Basically, when a company wants to raise capital to expand, it can borrow the money from the bank, from another corporation or from individuals, or it can issue or sell stock to the public. For the issuing company, stock represents a means of acquiring cash without going into debt. The maximum number of shares that a corporation may issue is limited technically by its charter, but usually is limited practically by the number of shares that investors are willing to buy and that the corporation decides to issue. As a holder of corporate stock, the investor has a part ownership, or equity, in that corporation. That is why stocks are called *equity securities*.

Types of Corporations

Basically, two types of corporations issue stock—*publicly held corporations* and *privately held corporations*. The major difference between the two is in the degree of managerial control exercised. Private companies do not register their stock on any national exchanges. Their board members usually control the majority of the stock and are the sole determinants of management policy. When they sell stock, it is only in limited amounts and then usually only to employees and persons of their choosing, such as those who are or will be active in the management and operation of the business.

In contrast, publicly held corporations usually issue larger amounts of shares of stock, which are bought and sold at will by members of the general public—people who may be, but usually are not, actively engaged in the management and operation of the business. The aggregate shares of capital stock issued by the corporation and owned by its stockholders represent the total ownership of the corporation. To the extent of the relationship a stockholder's shares bear to all shares, the stockholder is an owner of the corporation. For example, if a stockholder holds 100 shares in a corporation that has 10,000 shares outstanding, that stockbroker is a 1 percent owner of the corporation.

The Nature of Publicly Held Stocks

By definition, a *share* of stock is *one of the equal parts into which the capital stock of a corporation is divided and represents the owner's proportionate interest in the corporation*. As such, a share of stock entitles its holder to certain ownership rights, including the right to share in distributions of the corporation's earnings when such dividend distributions are declared by the board of directors, the right to share in the distribution of net assets upon dissolution of the corporation and usually the right to vote for members of the board of directors.

Once issued, a share of stock generally may be sold or transferred freely from one person to another, with the ownership interests and rights it represents passing to the new shareholder. A major exception arises when the corporation purchases some of its own previously issued shares and retires them or holds them for resale or merger purposes. During such period as the corporation owns the shares, they are known as *treasury stock* and represent no ownership interest or rights except the right to resell the shares, in which case the shares regain their original status in the hands of new owners.

Generally, a share of stock may be sold, given, bequeathed by will or otherwise transferred by its owner without restrictions, and upon completion of the transfer, all ownership interests and rights represented by the share pass intact to its new owner. The corporation normally continues business as usual, uninterrupted and unaffected by such changes.

The Stock Certificate

Because a share of a corporation is invisible and intangible, some tangible evidence of its existence and ownership is necessary for both legal and practical purposes. To document the fact that a stock has been purchased, companies used to issue a *stock certificate* to each shareholder. This piece of paper showed the number of shares owned by that person. For the investor, or *stockholder*, the certificate represented a share of the risks or rewards of that corporation. As stated earlier, the more *shares* of stock the investor held, the greater his or her interest in the affairs of the company. The stock certificate, *an engraved document representing legal evidence of ownership of a stipulated number of shares of stock in a corporation*, provided this tangible evidence of investment.

In form, the typical stock certificate was a single sheet of quality paper, carefully engraved with an ornamental and unique design to minimize the possibility of counterfeiting as well as for sake of appearance. The face of the certificate contained the certificate number, the name of the issuing corporation, a brief recital of the name of the owner and the number and kind of shares, the issue date, signatures of the proper corporate officers, the corporate seal, appropriate notations and signatures of the transfer agent and registrar.

Stock certificates are rare these days and may be eliminated in the next few years. Ownership of stock today is represented by electronic means. In fact, 90 percent of all individual investors allow their brokerage firms to hold their stock *in street name*; that is, registered in the name of the brokerage firm and evidenced by a confirmation and an entry on the stockholder's monthly statement. For most purposes, this statement clearly and adequately identifies what ownership interest is represented and who owns it. If a detailed statement of rights is desired, it ordinarily is necessary to refer to the corporation's charter and bylaws, copies of which generally are available on request.

Kinds of Stock

Stocks issued by corporations may be divided into *common* stocks and *preferred* stocks. Within these two broad classifications, there are variations. There are also *rights* and *warrants*, which are not types of stock, but which represent certain privileges or options with respect to stocks. Discussion of these two major classes, variations and related privileges and options follows.

■ COMMON STOCK

Common stock, as its name implies, is the most prevalent and frequently traded of the two types of stock. It represents residual ownership in the issuing corporation, that is, claim to what remains of corporate earnings and assets after all prior claims and other obligations of the corporation have been satisfied. Thus, the holder of common stock has a true, basic ownership interest in the corporation.

Because it represents residual ownership, common stock is issued by all corporations. It is the only class of stock issued universally. In number of shares issued and traded, common stock is overwhelmingly predominant and generally is the class of stock intended when the word *stock* is used without qualification as to class.

Holders of common stock, as residual owners, are the primary risk bearers in the corporation. They have the opportunity to enjoy the net benefits of the corporation's profits, growth and overall success—but at the risk of loss, to the extent of their committed investment, if the corporation fails or is not sufficiently profitable.

Common Stock Ownership Rights or Privileges

In keeping with their risk-bearing function and basic ownership interest, common stockholders generally possess certain fundamental ownership rights. These rights include the following:

1. *Right to transfer ownership.* The stockholders have a legal right to transfer their stock certificates, usually as they wish. However, statutes may permit the directors to restrict the freedom of transfer to safeguard the interests of the corporation and of the stockholders.

2. *Right to limited liability.* Common stockholders are not personally liable, legally or financially, for the corporation's activities or obligations. Thus, although the stockholders bear the risk of loss, the extent of their losses normally is limited to the amounts they have paid or committed themselves to pay for their stock.

3. *Preemptive right to purchase newly issued stock.* When a corporation raises capital through the sale of common stock (or securities convertible into common stock), it may be required by law or its corporate charter to offer the securities to its common stockholders before it offers them directly to the public. Stockholders then have what is known as a *preemptive right* to purchase enough newly issued shares to protect their proportionate ownership in the corporation. To illustrate, a person who already owns 1 percent of the stock of Microscam Corporation (MCS) will have a preemptive right to purchase 1 percent of any new stock issue. Preemptive rights help ensure that stockholders' rights (such as voting rights) are not diluted at the issuance of new stock.

4. *Right to vote.* Common stockholders generally have the right to participate in the affairs of their company by voting for directors and on other corporate matters, such as the issuance of senior securities (all debt and equity securities having priority claim over common stock), stock splits and substantial changes in the corporation's business. These voting rights, the matters requiring a stockholder vote and the mechanics of voting are established by the corporation law of the state in which the corporation is chartered or by the corporation's charter and bylaws.

5. *Right to inspect corporate books.* Common stockholders have a right to inspect the books of the corporation and a right to a list of the names and addresses of the other stockholders. In actual practice, the right to see the books generally is satisfied by an audited annual statement furnished by management.

6. *Residual claim to assets.* When a corporation ceases to exist, the stockholders, as owners, have a right to the assets of the corporation. The right is

residual in that a common stockholder may make a claim only after all debts and other security holders have been satisfied.

7. *Right to take legal action against management or the board of directors.* Stockholders may take the company's management (including members of the broad of directors) to court if they believe management has committed wrongful acts that could harm the corporation. Stockholders may also take legal action against the board of directors to restrain it from acting in a manner inconsistent with the corporate charter.

Advantages of Common Stock Ownership

Investors buy common stock because an investment in common stock can increase in value. Stock tends to keep pace with inflation and, although it is riskier than bonds or preferred stock, common stock has many advantages.

- *Safety.* As long as the issuing company retains its financial strength, growth and profitability, the investor's money is safe. Typically, the company will pay dividends and the value of the shares will increase over time.

- *Liquidity.* Common stocks are often easily traded on major stock exchanges and over-the-counter at clearly stated prices.

- *Capital appreciation.* Many investors buy stock because they expect the price of the stock to grow over time. As the corporation prospers, the market value (or the current price of the stock) increases.

- *Growing dividends.* Investors expect the income distributed to stockholders of the corporation to increase as the corporation's overall earnings increase. Corporations tend to boost their payout to keep stockholders satisfied with their stock investment.

Risks of Common Stock Ownership

As with other investments, there are some risks associated with owning common stock. These risks are lessened when the stock of a quality corporation is purchased. Some of the more common risks include:

- *Permanent loss of capital.* In the long run, investments in common stock have outperformed investments in other capital markets. However, it is possible to lose all of the profits and some of the capital when an investment is made in overpriced stock. When the price begins to fall, many investors are reluctant to sell and hang on to their stock in hope of a price increase that may not materialize.

- *Stock market risk.* There is a risk that a stock's price will increase or decrease because of changes in the overall stock market. Over time, the prices of most stocks tend to move in the same direction, up or down. In essence, the strengths, weaknesses and uncertainty of the overall economy are some of the causes of volatile stock prices.

- *Interest rate risk.* Interest rate risk is associated with a loss or gain on a fixed-rate security because interest rates in general rise or fall after the security is purchased. Many stocks, such as those of utilities, banks or finance companies, are *interest rate sensitive*, which means that they are directly affected by changes in interest rates. For example, an investor pays $1,000 for a bond with an 8 percent interest rate; a year later, the investor decides to sell the bond, but finds interest rates on comparable bonds have risen to 9 percent. No one will now pay the investor $1,000 for an 8 percent bond if a similar bond paying 9 percent can be purchased. However, interest rate risk can also work in the investor's favor. If interest rates decline, bond prices generally rise.

■ PREFERRED STOCK

The second major classification of stock (which corporations frequently do, but are not required to, issue) is preferred stock. It is so named because its holders are given prior rights to dividends (and sometimes other prior rights) over holders of common stock. Preferred shareholders, for example, receive their dividend payment after all bondholders are paid and before dividends are paid on common stock.

Preferred stock confers many of the same rights as common stock on purchasers, such as limited liability and transfer rights, but usually does not allow them to vote. The trade-off is in the level of safety and income: preferred stock pays a fixed dividend that usually does not vary from quarter to quarter. This makes a preferred stock investment more interest rate sensitive than common stock, but it is regarded as a good income security.

Preferred stock rights also differ in the event of corporate dissolution. The holder has *prior claim over assets*, which means that, in the event of corporate bankruptcy or dissolution, he or she can claim a share of remaining assets before common stockholders. Another term for this right is *senior security*.

■ PREFERRED STOCK VS. COMMON STOCK

Except for some minor variations, the mechanics, form and terms relative to preferred stock are virtually identical to those previously discussed in connection with common stock. Let's look at five ways in which preferred stock may vary from common stock.

1. *Preferred dividends.* Preferred stock provides for a specified dividend per share that must be paid before any dividends may be paid on the common stock of the corporation. This dividend may be stipulated as a specific amount per year (such as $4 per share) or as a *percentage of par* or stated value (such as 5 percent of $100), usually payable quarterly.

2. *Preferred claim to assets.* Preferred stock has a prior claim to corporate assets in the event of liquidation, that is, its claim must be satisfied in full before the residue of the liquidation value may be distributed to common stockholders. In the absence of such specific provisions, however, preferred and common stock share equally in the priority of their claims to assets.

ILL. 6.2 ■ *Reading Stock Market Listings*

Stocks are listed alphabetically by their full name and then abbreviated; ticker symbols are not used. Prices are equivalent to dollars and fractions of dollars (e.g., 35⅞ = $35.87).

Prices and volume figures in the NYSE composite listings comprise price and volume from the New York Stock Exchange, five regional exchanges including the Chicago Stock Exchange, and over-the-counter trading in NYSE-listed stocks. NYSE stocks that didn't trade on a given day are not listed.

All dividends are calculated on an annual basis by multiplying the latest reported payment times the frequency of payment.

	365-day High	Low	Stock	Div	Yld	PE Ratio	Sales [hds]	High	Low	Close	Chng
↑	35⅞	18³⁄₃₂	**Mattel s**	0.20	0.5	20	3824	u36⅞	35⅞	36⅜	+1⅜

Arrow	Latest close is a new 365-day high (↑) or low (↓).
365-day High/Low	Highest and lowest intraday price during preceding 365 days.
Stock	Abbreviation of company name. A letter appearing after a name indicates a footnote.
Div	Indicates annual dividend per share, based on latest periodic dividend.
Yld	Indicates annual dividend as a percentage of latest price, computed daily.
PE Ratio	Price/earnings ratio, derived by dividing current price per share by earnings per share from continuing operations over previous 12 months.
Sales (hds)	Number of shares traded as of 5:15 p.m. New York time that day, in hundreds of shares. An underlined listing indicates that volume on this day was greater than 1 percent of the company's shares outstanding.
High	Highest price of the session; u indicates 365-day high was surpassed during the day.
Low	Lowest price of the session; indicates 365-day low was surpassed during the day.
Close	Price as of 5:15 p.m. New York time.
Chng	The difference between closing price this day and closing the previous trading day. If stock appears in **boldface**, price has changed by more than 3 percent from previous close.

3. *Limited voting rights.* Except in a state where all stock must be given voting power, the right to vote generally is withheld from preferred stockholders—or at least restricted. The underlying logic is that because of their preferred and relatively secure position, they need not have a voice in management, except when special questions arise that particularly affect their position, such as the right to vote on any question relative to creation of additional long-term corporate debt or issuance of new preferred stock with claims equal

to or superseding their own—or any charter or bylaw amendment that materially would alter their current preferred position.

4. *No preemptive rights.* Because preferred stock usually is nonparticipating, its holders generally are not given preemptive rights in new common stock issues or issues convertible to common stock. However, when preferred stock is participating, it offers the holder a share of the earnings after all senior securities have been paid, and it has full voting power. It sometimes is given preemptive rights to subscribe to new common stock issues (or securities convertible to common stock).

5. *Callable by the corporation.* Representing an ownership interest, preferred stock has no maturity date. However, it is sometimes callable by the corporation—that is, the corporation retains the right to redeem (repurchase and retire) the preferred stock if and when it wishes.

Corporations may choose to redeem stock because: (1) it improves the position of the common stockholders by eliminating the prior claims to earnings and assets; and (2) it can reduce the corporation's liabilities for payment of higher than market dividend rates, which reduces the corporation's overall *cost of capital*—the cost of alternative sources of financing to the firm.

Types of Preferred Stock

Preferred stock may be issued in different classes and types. The *class designation* applies to the stock's stated rate of return—one issue will pay a higher dividend than another. Therefore, it differs from common stock whose shares all amass an identical dividend determined by the corporation's board of directors.

There are four types of preferred stock:

- cumulative

- noncumulative

- participating

- convertible

Cumulative Preferred Stock

As we have seen, an advantage of many preferred stocks is that all current and past dividends will be paid to preferred stockholders before common stockholders will be paid their declared dividends. Because preferred stock represents an ownership interest rather than a debt, no preferred dividends must be paid when corporate earnings do not justify them. However, when not paid in full on scheduled dates, they normally *accumulate* and all such accumulated unpaid preferred dividends must be paid in full before dividends may be paid on common stock. Usually, preferred stock is noncumulative only if so specifically provided.

Noncumulative Preferred Stock

This stock is closer to common stock—its holders receive a dividend only if the board chooses to declare one. Holders have no right to future or unpaid past dividends, but have other preferred rights. The amount of their dividends usually remains constant, leaving the claim to varying residual earnings to common stockholders.

Participating Preferred Stock

This form of preferred stock promises its holders dividends of a specified amount, plus extra dividends in some cases. Extra earnings are often shared between participating preferred and common stockholders.

Convertible Preferred Stock

Convertibles may be bonds or preferred stock that can be exchanged for a number of common shares of the same corporation. This option enables the holder to receive fixed income until the market offers an opportunity for growth. Convertibles are considered a conservative investment and will yield a lower rate of return than non-convertible bonds or preferred stock.

Disadvantages of Preferred Stock

Although preferred stock usually has an excellent safety record with relatively high yields, it has some disadvantages. There are four common disadvantages.

1. Because the dividend is fixed, preferred stock does not offer stockholders the opportunity to share in the good fortunes of the company.

2. Preferred stock does not have a maturity date, as does an issue of bonds, so there is no assurance that the investor will get back his or her initial investment at some point.

3. In the event of corporate bankruptcy, preferred stockholders are paid after bondholders if the company is liquidated.

4. A rise in interest rates will have a negative impact on the price of preferred stock. As overall interest rates rise, the price of stock usually falls. The price will also drop if it appears the company will be unable to meet its dividend payments.

■ FOREIGN STOCK

In addition to stocks offered by U.S. corporations, there are stocks of *foreign corporations*, that is, of companies domiciled in countries other than the United States. These stocks may be bought, held and sold by U.S. citizens. As discussed later in this chapter, some of these stocks are traded only on the over-the-counter markets and/or exchanges of the countries in which those companies are registered. But many foreign stocks are also traded on the over-the-counter market or stock exchanges of the United States.

Major foreign markets are in Toronto, Montreal, London, South Africa, Frankfurt, Brussels, Milan, Tokyo, Paris, Zurich, Amsterdam, Hong Kong and Sydney; these markets trade in their own respective currencies, except African mines that trade in U.S. dollars.

American Depositary Receipts

A U.S. investor interested in buying stock of foreign corporations need not always receive the foreign certificates. Instead, the investor can, in many cases, buy *American depositary receipts (ADRs)*, also know as *American depositary shares (ADSs)*.

An *American depositary receipt* is a negotiable security and represents a receipt for a given number of shares of stock (typically one to ten) in a non-U.S. corporation. American depositary receipts facilitate the trading of foreign securities in U.S. markets. The ADR itself is an instrument that can, like a share of stock, be bought and sold in the U.S. securities markets on an exchange or over-the-counter.

Foreign corporations often use ADRs as a means of generating U.S. investments in their securities and companies. A major benefit of issuing ADRs is that the foreign corporations do not have to go through the entire Securities and Exchange Commission (SEC) registration process typical for new U.S. issues. Issuers of ADRs do, however, have to meet all of the qualification requirements of Schedule D of the NASD bylaws. To be included in the NASDAQ system, the ADR issuer must, at a minimum, make available to its stockholders an *annual balance sheet* and an *operations statement*. It must also work to maintain a fair and orderly market for its securities and protect its stockholders by coordinating its regulatory activities with the NASD.

Custodian Bank

American depositary receipts are issued by foreign branches of large commercial U.S. banks. The actual shares of foreign stock that the ADR represents are held by a custodian (typically a foreign bank in the home country of the issuer). The stock must remain on deposit as long as the ADR is outstanding, because the ADR is the depository bank's guarantee that it holds the stock.

American depositary receipts are registered on the books of the U.S. bank responsible for them. The individual investors in the ADRs are not considered the registered owners. In addition to holding the underlying securities, the depository bank must provide other services to ADR holders. Of great importance to holders of foreign-based securities, the bank must provide information to the ADR holders about any developments in the foreign corporation or the country of registry that could affect the ADR.

Counter Cyclical

The major reason for getting involved in foreign stocks, as contrasted with U.S. stocks, is that many investors believe that foreign stocks act *counter cyclical* to U.S.

stocks (i.e., they tend to rise when U.S. stocks are declining and vice versa). Thus, those investors believe foreign stocks provide good hedges in a balanced investment portfolio.

Some investors consider foreign countries more favorable climates for business and investment. Some of their reasons are obvious, others less so. For example, labor costs are much lower in many parts of the world. Some say that the work ethic and pride in quality has deteriorated in the United States. The continuous deficits and inflation in the United States led some investors to investments and securities of companies in countries with strong currencies. Some resources, such as metals, exist in small quantities or not at all in our country.

Although foreign securities offer substantial rewards, they also have significant risks. In addition to the risks inherent in most stock investing, international stocks are especially susceptible to political risk. Everything from how effectively a foreign government promotes private enterprise to wage levels and employee benefits has an affect on an international stock's value. For example, in Great Britain, when the Conservative party is the majority party, it, unlike the Labour party, tends to encourage foreign investment, which results in a sharply rising stock market.

Of course, the specific equity selected makes returns differ drastically from averages. Many fortunes have been made, regardless of country, in identifying small companies whose earnings growth was exceptional. Due to the difficulty of finding such opportunities in a foreign market, many investors purchase shares in a mutual fund that specializes in this special kind of investment. Mutual funds are covered in Chapter 8.

■ SECURITIES MARKETS

A *securities market* is the location in which, or system through which, trades of securities occur. The term *Wall Street* is sometimes used to represent the collective marketplace in which employees and customers of the financial industry interact to buy and sell stocks, bonds and other instruments.

For the purposes of our discussion, there are two stages in which corporate stocks (and bonds, which are discussed in Chapter 7) are marketed: (1) when they are first being issued and (2) when they are being sold as previously issued securities. How stocks are marketed in each stage may vary, generally depending upon the combination of prevailing factors, including any legal requirements that may pertain. The market in which securities are bought and sold is also known as the *secondary market* (as opposed to the *primary market* for new issues).

All of the securities transactions in which people, corporations, governments and institutions engage take place in one of four markets:

1. an exchange;

2. the over-the-counter (OTC) market;

3. the third market; or

4. the fourth market (INSTINET).

Following a brief introduction of these four markets, we'll discuss the exchange and OTC markets in more detail.

Exchange Market

The *exchange market* is a centralized marketplace where securities (primarily previously issued securities) listed on that exchange are bought and sold. The term *listed security* refers to any security listed (quoted) for trading on an exchange. An exchange provides its members with certain services, such as standard hours of operation, a trading floor, access to specialists (or *market makers*), minimum standards for listed securities, rules and regulations, an orderly market, electronic quotations and even computerized trading systems. The best known and largest U.S. exchange is the *New York Stock Exchange (NYSE)*. Other stock exchanges include the *American Stock Exchange (AMEX)* and the regional Boston, Cincinnati, Chicago, Pacific and Philadelphia exchanges.

Over-the-Counter Market

The *over-the-counter (OTC) market* (also known as the *unlisted market*) is a decentralized marketplace in which brokers and dealers conduct business by telephone and through computerized quotation systems rather than at a centralized place of business. More than 15,000 different securities are traded OTC (including all municipal and U.S. government securities), compared to the 4,500 or so securities registered for listed trading on the various exchanges. The OTC is a negotiated market in which buyers and sellers work out prices acceptable to both.

Third Market (OTC-Listed)

The *third market* is a trading market for institutional investors in which *exchange-listed* securities are bought and sold (usually in large blocks) in the OTC market. These transactions are arranged and negotiated through the services of a broker-dealer registered as an OTC market maker in listed securities.

All securities listed on the NYSE and AMEX plus most exclusively traded securities listed on the regional exchanges are eligible for OTC trading, provided that trading information (volume and execution price) is reported for public display on the *Consolidated Tape* within 90 seconds after the execution of any transaction. The Consolidated Tape system is designed to deliver real-time reports of securities transactions to subscribers as transactions occur on the various exchanges.

Fourth Market (INSTINET)

The *fourth market* is a market for institutional investors in which large blocks of stock (both listed and unlisted) change hands in privately negotiated transactions between banks, mutual funds, pension managers and other types of institutions, unassisted by a broker-dealer. Those trading in the fourth market are connected and serviced by a computer network developed and operated by INSTINET, a Reuters PLC company. Operating since 1969 as an SEC-registered broker-dealer, INSTINET allows buyers and sellers to negotiate trades directly and anonymously with one another. *Black box* or *screen trading*, as it is sometimes called, is becoming an increasingly important market for all types of listed and unlisted securities.

■ THE EXCHANGES

The exchange has a location—a specific address where it is housed and at which it operates its *trading floor*, where trading (buying and selling) is conducted as a two-sided auction with competition between both buyers and sellers (buyers competing with each other for the lowest prices and sellers for the highest). Buyers and sellers may be working for themselves (as *principals*) or on behalf of others (as *agents*).

Common stock of approximately 4,500 publicly held corporations can be bought or sold on the exchanges. About 2,000 of these corporations have their shares listed on the NYSE or AMEX. In addition, a number of regional exchanges such as the Chicago Stock Exchange and the Pacific Stock Exchange trade listed stock. In addition to domestic stock exchanges, there are a number of foreign stock exchanges.

Membership and Privileges

Organizationally, most exchanges are registered as not-for-profit corporations operating under their own constitutions, bylaws and rules. Exchange membership, which is limited in number and highly exclusive, is composed of individuals who have been accepted for membership by the exchange, who have paid for their memberships called *seats* on the exchange and who continuously maintain the high standards of business conduct and integrity set by the exchange.

Brokers

A securities *broker* is an individual or firm, who, for a commission, acts as an agent or intermediary between sellers and buyers of securities. The broker is a member of the exchange who executes the buy or sell order on the floor of the exchange. In no stage of the overall transaction does he or she own the securities. The broker merely sells and buys them for clients and handles the details of these services.

Dealers

A securities *dealer* is an individual or a firm that deals in securities as a principal. That is, he or she purchases securities from and sells them to clients at net prices. In the interim between purchase and sale, brief as it may be, he or she owns the securities. The dealer charges no commission, but derives his or her compensation from the profits realized on any excess of net sale prices over net purchase prices.

Members of the national exchanges may effect a transaction as either a broker or a dealer. These *broker-dealer* members enjoy the privilege of buying and selling listed securities on the trading floor of the exchange, and they may make such purchases and sales either for their own accounts or for the accounts of their clients.

Scope of Trading

In addition to trading on the exchange as broker-dealers for their own clients, members may similarly trade for nonmember broker-dealers and thus indirectly for their clients. Moreover, many exchange members have branch offices through which they extend services to clients, other broker-dealers in a number of principal cities.

Thus, although only members may actually trade on the floor of the exchange, virtually any investor may buy and sell listed securities on the exchange, either directly through a member or indirectly through a nonmember dealer or broker who, in turn, employs the services of a member.

Listing Requirements

Usually only the securities of well-established corporations are listed on exchanges. In most cases, only they can meet and maintain the stringent listing requirements of the exchanges. For example, the *initial* requirements for any corporation that wants its stock listed on the NYSE include:

- The market value of its publicly held shares must be at least $18 million.

- At least 1.1 million shares must be publicly held.

- Two thousand stockholders must each hold 100 shares or more (2,000 *round-lot owners*).

- Corporate earnings before federal income tax must be at least $2.5 million for the latest fiscal year and at least $2 million for each of the two preceding years.

Listing requirements have been modified from time to time in the past, and may be modified in the future.

Primary Functions of the Exchange

From the standpoint of the *issuing corporation*, the primary function of the exchange is the creation of wider markets for, and interest in, any new securities that the corporation may issue in the future by providing ready marketability of the corporation's previously issued, outstanding securities. The exchange is principally a market for already issued securities.

From the standpoint of the investor, the primary function of the exchange is the provision of prompt marketability and liquidity for listed securities. The holder of a listed security can usually sell it promptly on an exchange. It is important to note that the exchange makes no guarantee of the value of a listed security or of the price it will bring. It only assures that the security may be sold promptly at whatever the market price may be at the time.

■ THE OVER-THE-COUNTER MARKET

The *over-the-counter (OTC)* market is a *negotiated* market where buyers seek out sellers with the lowest prices and sellers seek out buyers offering the highest prices. A negotiated market is competitive; one brokerage firm is competing against a number of other brokerage firms, each trading for its own inventory. When a customer wants to put in an order to buy or sell securities, his or her brokerage firm will call one of more *market makers* (or principals) in that security and negotiate a price.

Unlike the exchanges, the OTC is a decentralized market. Trading takes place over the phone, over computer networks and in trading rooms across the country; it is essentially trading without a *floor*. It consists of millions of buyers and sellers and thousands of securities houses and branch offices, all linked together by a vast communications network.

The quality of a company and the integrity of its management never should be judged by which method of trading is employed for its shares. For example, many banks and insurance companies of the highest quality trade over-the-counter. To easily locate buyers and sellers, OTC dealers use the *National Association of Securities Dealers Automated Quotation Service*, a computerized system that provides up-to-date bid and ask prices on over 5,400 actively traded OTC stocks representing over 4,600 corporations. Securities that can be traded in the OTC market include, but are not limited to the following:

- American depositary receipts (ADRs);

- bank stocks and insurance company stocks;

- most corporate bonds;

- municipal bonds;

- U.S. government securities; and

- common and preferred stock.

The OTC market is principally a seasoning ground for the securities of new or relatively small corporations, but it also has its share of old-line, blue chip issues. It is the sole market for the initial issue of new stocks, bonds (including U.S. government and municipal bonds) and investment company shares and is often the venue for liquidating large blocks of listed or unlisted securities.

OTC Stock Listings

So many stocks are traded over-the-counter that it would probably require an entire newspaper to list all of them. Some low-priced and infrequently traded over-the-counter stocks are not on the NASDAQ system and, therefore, are not published in newspapers. These so-called *penny stocks* may sell for a fraction of a cent per share; however, some people use the term to describe stocks that sell for under $5 a share. Broker-dealers receive the bids and asks for these stocks on lists called *Pink Sheets* (because they are printed on pink paper). These are interdealer quotations and are subject to change.

Only the most actively traded issues are listed in financial sections of newspapers like *The Wall Street Journal*. For example, OTC stocks with widespread interest may be listed in the newspaper under *Additional OTC Quotes*, which usually displays only the bid and ask of the day.

Those OTC securities that have a national interest are listed on the NASDAQ system in one of two tables: (1) *The NASDAQ National Market Issues* table gives detailed information on the most actively traded OTC stocks; and (2) *The NASDAQ*

ILL. 6.3 ■ *Reading the NASDAQ Tables*

The *National Market Issues* tables show the high and low price of the issue for the year, annual dividend per share, current yield, price/earnings (P/E) ratio, sales volume and net change. For example, assume that the table shows the following:

	52 Weeks Hi	Lo	Stock	Sym	Div	Yld %	PE	Vol 100s	Hi	Lo	Close	Net Chg
s	27	16½	FstFedMich	FFOM	.52	2.2	11	1780	24	23½	23¾	+ ¼
s	27¼	17⅝	FstFedFin	FFSW	.48	1.9	6	1	25¾	25¾	25¾	+ 1¼

FstFedMich had a *high* price of 27 ($27) and a *low* price of 16½ ($16.50) during the past year. Its annual *dividend* is $.52; its current yield is 2.2%; its *P/E ratio* is 11. *Sales volume* the previous day was 178,000 shares. During that day's trading, the stock sold as low as 23½ per share and as high as 24 per share, where it closed. The *net change* was ¼ point higher than the previous quoted closing price.

Bid & Asked Quotations table provides the stock name and dividend, sales volume, the last trade and the net change for the day.

OTC Regulation

The over-the-counter market is closely regulated by both federal and state laws and is constantly supervised by the *National Association of Securities Dealers (NASD)*, a voluntary self-regulatory organization that sets high standards for its members and handles any necessary disciplinary action. NASD members may transact business with other firms at rates below those charged to nonmembers. Any securities firm that is not a member of the NASD is supervised directly by the SEC, which has the same power over the NASD as it does over the exchanges.

■ HOW THE MARKET OPERATES

After an investor selects a stockbroker, he or she opens an account to buy or sell stocks. Investors may establish a cash account or a margin account. A *cash account*, similar to a retail charge account, allows an investor to buy securities through a broker and pay for them within five working days of the purchase. A *margin account* allows the investor to borrow a portion of the purchase price of the securities.

Placing an Order

Investors can begin trading after opening an account. They may *enter an order* with their broker to buy or sell 100 shares (called a *round lot*) or for less than 100 shares (called an *odd lot*). Three types of orders investors may place with their broker-dealers include market orders, limit orders or stop orders.

Market Order

A *market order* instructs the broker-dealer to buy or sell securities immediately at the best price available. When the investor enters a transaction, the broker-dealer quotes him or her the price at which the security is being traded. The investor then decides whether to buy or sell the security and gives the broker-dealer the order. Within a few minutes, the order is executed on the floor of the exchange or OTC. Because of the speed with which market orders are executed, the investor can be somewhat assured that the price at which the order is filled will be close to the current market price at the time the order was placed.

Limit Order

A *limit order*, unlike a market order, instructs a broker-dealer to buy or sell a security for a customer at a *specified* price, and usually within a limited period of time—as within a week or month—or the order may be *good til canceled*.

The broker-dealer may execute the buy or sell order only if, within the time limit, it can be executed at the specified price, or at a price *more* favorable to the customer, that is, higher than the specified price if selling or lower than the specified price if buying.

Stop Order

A *stop order* instructs a broker-dealer to buy (or sell) a security as soon as its price reaches the price specified in the order. As soon as this specified price is reached, the stop order becomes a market order and the broker-dealer buys (or sells) the security. A stop order frequently is used to protect a paper profit or to prevent a larger loss.

Opening a Position

When investors enter a transaction to buy or sell a security, they are *opening a position*. The most common type of transaction is the *long position*, in which investors buy securities that they feel will increase in value and which can be sold at a later date at a profit. When a decline in securities prices is anticipated, investors may take a *short position*, in which they sell stocks with the intention of repurchasing those stocks at a lower price in the future. When investors sell securities they originally bought, or buy securities they originally sold, they are *closing the position*.

Long Sales

As stated earlier, many securities purchases are made with borrowed funds rather than on a cash basis. When traders are optimistic about business and the stock market, they are called *bulls*, and they generally buy long—they buy securities in anticipation of rising prices. If investors feel strongly bullish about particular stocks, they may *buy those stocks on margin*. This means they may buy them by making down payments and borrowing the balance of the purchase price from their broker-dealers through their margin accounts.

To make such loans to customers, the broker-dealers (in theory) borrow the money at the going rate of interest and charge this interest (plus ½ percent to 1 percent for handling) to the customers' margin accounts. Moreover, the broker-dealers hold the stocks purchased on margin while there are loans against them, with the right to *hypothecate* them—that is, to pledge those stocks as security for loans.

When customers buy on margin, they usually plan to sell the securities later at anticipated higher prices, and from the excess of the selling price over the buying price, pay off the loans with interest to their broker-dealers, recoup their down payments and realize some profits. Thus, by involving their own money only in *portions* of the purchase prices, they hope to realize the profits on the *total amount* of the securities purchased, including those purchased with borrowed money.

Of course, investors can be wrong—the prices of the securities could go down. In such cases, the customers would sustain losses—but more importantly, the customers will be required to repay all of the loans with interest.

Short Sales

Somewhat less typical is the *short sale*. An investor who sells short has the same profit motive as an investor who buys long, but does everything in reverse. The short-selling investor initially borrows stock from a broker-dealer, then sells the stock at the current market price. The investor anticipates that the price of the stock will go down enough to allow replacement of the borrowed stock at a cheaper price at a later date.

The broker-dealer, if able to find shares of that security to borrow, loans the shares to the client and lets the client take the chance that the stock will indeed become cheaper in the future. The client takes a *short position* by selling shares of stock he or she does not own.

Short sales are considered risky. The seller must buy stock to repay the loan and is thus at the mercy of the market. If the stock price rises instead of falls, the investor may have to pay a great deal of money to buy the shares necessary to repay the loan.

■ STOCK RIGHTS AND WARRANTS

Stock rights and warrants are special types of securities issued by a corporation in certificate form that entitle the holder to purchase common stock (or sometimes other securities issued by the corporation) at a stipulated price, within the amount and time limits specified by the terms of the certificate. Purchasing a right or a warrant is not the same thing as purchasing stock: investors have no ownership interest in the underlying company.

Rights

A *right* is a security representing a stockholder's preemptive right to purchase new securities in proportion to the number of shares already owned. The term *preemptive right* refers to the right of an existing stockholder to purchase shares of a new issue of stock in proportion to the number of shares the investor already owns. A concern is that if new shares are issued by a corporation, the present stockholders' ownership of the company will be diluted if they are not able to purchase a proportionate share of the new issue; their voting percentage, earnings per share and net worth per share will be reduced. Furthermore, the additional supply of stock available to the market may cause the market price of the stock to decrease.

Rights, also known as *stock rights*, are stock purchase options issued to existing stockholders only. The right is an option to purchase a company's new issue of stock at a predetermined price (normally for less than the stock's current market price). The right is issued for a short period of time, normally for 30 days, with the option expiring after that time. Stock rights entitle the stockholder to purchase common stock below the current market price at issue date. This means that the rights are valued separately and trade in the secondary market during the subscription period.

Rights Offering

A *rights offering* is a short-term (typically 30 to 45 days) privilege a stockholder receives from a corporation, and a subscription right is the actual certificate representing that privilege. One right is issued for each share of common stock the investor owns. Therefore, an investor with 100 shares of common stock receives a certificate representing 100 rights.

The terms of the offering are stipulated in the subscription rights, which are mailed to stockholders on the payable date. The rights describe the new shares to which the stockholder is entitled to subscribe, the price, the date the new stock will be issued, the name of the rights agent that will send the subscription and the final date for exercising those rights.

Corporations issue rights as a convenient way to raise additional capital. When issuing new shares of common stock, a corporation may choose to sell its shares to existing stockholders before going to public investors. This may be because the company believes its stockholders would be the best prospects to buy additional shares of the company, or it may be because the corporation's stockholders have preemptive rights. To illustrate how a stockholder might benefit from a company's decision to issue rights, let's look at an example.

Assume that Midwest Public Light's stock is trading at $30 per share, that stockholders get one right for every five shares and that each right entitles the holder to buy one new share at $22 each. To calculate the value of one right *before* it expires and becomes worthless, the following formula is used:

$$\text{Value of a right} = \frac{MP - EP}{NR}$$

where
  MP = a stock's market price
  EP = exercise price of new stock
  NR = number of rights needed to buy one share

In the Midwest Public Light example, the calculation is:

$$\text{Value of a right} = \frac{\$30 - \$22}{5} = \$1.60$$

Therefore, the value of each right is $1.60 and each share is worth that much more to current stockholders. A stockholder who receives rights may exercise the rights to buy stock by sending the rights certificates and a check for the required amount to the rights agent; sell the rights and profit from their market values (rights certificates are negotiable securities); or let the rights expire and lose their value.

Warrants

A *warrant* is a certificate giving the holder the right to purchase securities at a stipulated price from the issuer. Unlike a right, a warrant is usually a long-term instrument, affording the investor the option of buying shares at a later date at the subscription price, subject to the warrant's expiration date.

Warrants may be detachable from the underlying security, or they may be nondetachable. If detachable, they may trade separately in the market purely as speculation on the price of the underlying stock (because the warrants do not receive dividends or represent any other right of a corporate owner). While the exercise price is set above the market price of the stock when the warrant is first issued, the investor hopes the stock's price will increase, at which point the investor can (1) exercise the warrant and buy the stock below the price he or she would have to pay in the market or (2) sell the warrant in the market at a price based on the benefit the purchaser can get by exercising the warrant and buying the stock below market price.

Warrants are usually offered to the public as a sweetener in connection with other securities (usually debentures) to make these securities more attractive to investors. Investors enjoy the security of owning a bond, note or preferred stock, but might also benefit from the opportunity to participate in the appreciation of the common stock. However, warrants have no voting rights, pay no dividends and have no claim on the assets of the corporation. The value of a warrant is based on anticipated future gain—that is, on the expectancy of a rise in the future market price of the underlying stock to a point substantially above the stated price during the life of the warrant.

A warrant is exercised for a much longer period than a right, sometimes for years into the future or perpetually. Also, the price at which an investor can buy stock by exercising a warrant is normally *higher* than the market price of that stock at the time the warrant is issued; whereas the price at which an investor can buy stock by exercising rights is normally *below* the price at which the new stock is being placed on the market.

A number of investors buy and sell warrants with no intention of exercising them, but for the sole purpose of realizing a profit on the changing market prices of the warrants. Leverage works both ways: warrant prices go up or down faster than the underlying stock. Since these prices usually are extremely volatile, such trading generally is considered speculative in nature.

ILL. 6.4 ■ *How Dollar Cost Averaging Works*

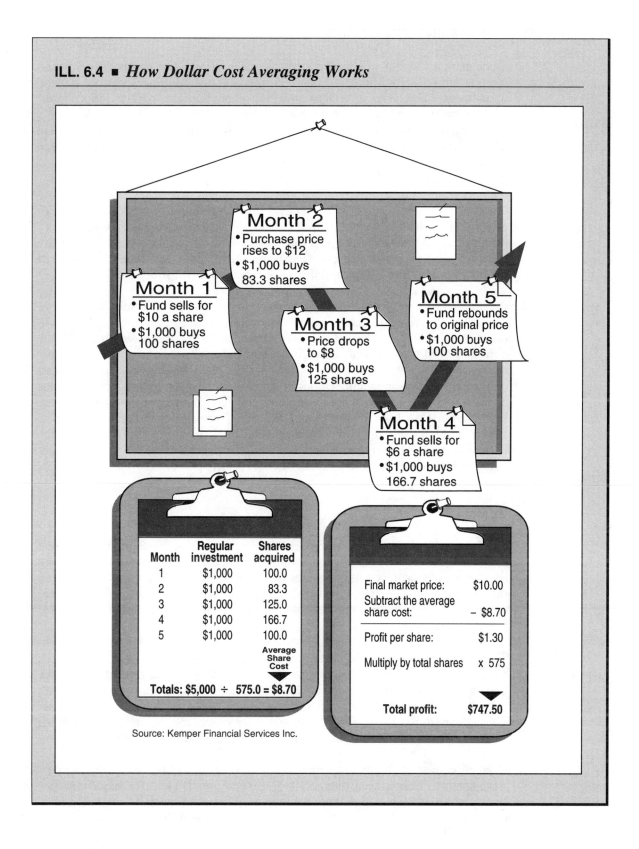

Source: Kemper Financial Services Inc.

■ INVESTMENT STRATEGIES

Stock market investment strategy is often condensed to a few words: *diversify* and *buy low and sell high*. Strategies for selecting stocks and building a portfolio depend upon investor objectives as well as on beliefs about how the market works. If the investor's objective is growth, his or her strategy in selecting stocks can be very fundamental, identifying promising small companies with proprietary products and aggressive marketing officers. These firms generally invest their profits in research and development and consequently don't pay dividends.

Another strategy is to employ *dollar cost averaging*, a plan of investing that involves the periodic purchase of stock, mutual fund shares or other securities. An established dollar amount is invested rather than a number of shares or units. For example, an investor buys a regular block of stocks each month (say $1,000 worth), no matter what the price. The average cost per share will be less than the average of the prices paid. The concept of dollar cost averaging is illustrated in Ill. 6.4.

A third investment strategy that some investors use is to select stocks they believe are inflated in price and likely to drop. As explained earlier, investors use a technique called *selling short* to actually profit from the drop in a stock's price. To make a short sale, an investor with a margin account selects a stock he or she thinks is overpriced. The investor borrows the shares from his or her broker-dealer, with an obligation to return an identical block of stock at a future date. The borrowed shares are then sold. If the price of the stock rises, and stays high, after the investor sells, he or she must buy back the shares at a loss. But if the price drops, as he or she gambled it would, the investor can purchase them for less than he or she received for the borrowed stock. The difference between what the first block of stock sold for and what the investor paid for the second block is profit.

■ SUMMARY

There is inherent risk in any investment that grows and increases in value. No one can accurately predict what the market price of a security will be at any future point in time or even, with certainty, whether it will be up or down in relation to the current price. As we've stated, in general, the greater and faster the *growth*, the higher the risk, and each investor must decide how much risk is acceptable in relation to potential return.

Thus, trading in securities represents both an *opportunity for gain* and a *risk of loss*, depending solely on the market at the time of purchase and the time of sale. If the market sets a low price at time of purchase and a high price at time of sale, the result is profit. If a high price is set at purchase and a low price at sale, the result is loss. This simple truth is fundamental to an understanding of trading and trading results, and it is a vital fact of life to anyone investing in securities of almost any type.

In addition to stock, many corporations and state, local and federal governments issue bonds to finance their operations. In general, bonds are safer than common stock and usually pay a higher annual income. They are especially appealing to retired investors or pension funds that must plan for the retirement of its participants. Unlike stock whose return varies based on market conditions, bonds provide a fixed return if they are held to maturity. We'll look more closely at bonds in Chapter 7.

■ **CHAPTER 6 QUESTIONS FOR REVIEW**

1. All of the following are rights of common stock shareholders EXCEPT the right to

   A. vote for the election of directors
   B. transfer shares freely, unless there is an agreement to the contrary
   C. receive dividends regardless of corporate earnings
   D. inspect the books

2. An order that is sent immediately to the floor to buy or sell securities without restrictions is known as a

   A. market order
   B. limit order
   C. stop order
   D. good-til-canceled order

3. All of the following are typical characteristics of preferred stock EXCEPT

   A. subordinate claims to assets
   B. dividend preference
   C. limited voting rights
   D. callable by corporation

4. For investors, the primary purpose of a stock exchange is to

   A. prevent speculative security offerings
   B. protect investors from misrepresentation and fraudulent activities by issuing corporations
   C. provide a ready market for buying and selling listed securities
   D. administer and enforce various federal laws relating to securities

5. With respect to foreign stocks, what is perhaps the greatest additional risk for the investor?

   A. Market risk
   B. Liquidity risk
   C. Purchasing power risk
   D. Political risk

7
Investing in Bonds

I n Chapter 6, we discussed common and preferred stock, two investments purchased because of their dividend income and appreciation of value. In this chapter, we'll consider another investment alternative—bonds. We'll look at bond characteristics in general and at corporate, U.S. government and municipal bonds in more detail.

One underlying fact to keep in mind throughout this chapter: Every investment discussed here technically represents the investor's loan of money to the borrower, whether the borrower is a bank or other business, the federal government, a municipality or an individual. In contrast to *equity-type* investments, like stocks, that give the investor part ownership in a company, bonds are *debt-type* investments that make an investor a lender to a company or the government (borrowers). Whoever owns a bond holds the issuing corporation's IOU. Bondholders are lenders who expect not only repayment of the loan (principal), but also returns for the risks of lending and rewards for postponing consumption.

Consequently, these debt-type investments pay *interest* and make *specific promises with respect to repayment(s)*, in contrast to equity-type investments that typically pay *dividends* or shares of *profits*, if any, and offer *no promises regarding return of principal*, except for residual net assets in event of liquidation.

■ ■ ■ ■ ■

■ WHAT IS A BOND?

A *bond* is a long-term debt obligation of a corporation or government that is secured by specified assets or a promise to pay. Bonds are popular securities that, in one or another of their varieties, enjoy widespread ownership among people in virtually all income brackets. Consequently they may be found in portfolios and estates of all sizes. Although there are basic differences, bonds are frequently mentioned in the same breath with stocks, are discussed in much the same terminology and, generally, are marketed, traded and selected in the same manner.

From the standpoint of the issuing organization, the primary purpose of a bond (like stocks) is to obtain capital. When companies or the government need to raise cash, they may issue bonds. Under this strategy, capital is obtained by *borrowing* it from the purchaser of the bond, and, unlike stocks, no change in ownership of the issuing organization is involved.

From the standpoint of the investor, the primary purpose of purchasing a bond is to earn long-term income. As with most loans, the borrower pays *interest* to the lender. Traditionally, bonds have been considered conservative investments that offer a steady source of income, but little prospect of an increase in value. However, many investors now choose bonds because these investment alternatives are more attractive than depositing money in a savings account or investing in stock.

Bond Issuers

Corporations issue bonds to raise capital to pay for operating expenses, expansion and modernization. In addition, corporations may issue bonds to borrow large sums of money that are needed to finance a takeover of another corporation.

The federal government issues U.S. government bonds that pay for a wide range of government activities. Federal government agencies, such as the Federal National Mortgage Association and the Government National Mortgage Association, issue bonds that are indirect obligations of the U.S. government. In addition, states, cities, counties and towns issue bonds to pay for a wide variety of publicly beneficial projects—schools, highways, stadiums, sewage systems, bridges and so forth.

Finally, many foreign companies and governments issue bonds specifically to U.S. investors. International bonds offer interest income as well as the potential for gains from appreciation in the value of the currency. Although many international bonds offer lower yields than U.S. bonds, large numbers of investors have diversified their bond portfolios with international bonds.

Bondholders' Rights

As we have said, bondholders do not possess ownership interests in the corporations or other issuers by virtue of owning their bonds, so they generally do not enjoy the ownership rights of stockholders. But they do have a right to receive interest and repayment of principal, according to the terms of the bond, and to that extent, they (as creditors) have claims prior to that of stockholders (as owners) on the income and assets of the organizations that issued the bonds.

In the event of an organization's bankruptcy or liquidation, bondholders' claims must be satisfied before there are any residual assets for distribution to owners. In fact, the bondholders generally may force liquidation of assets if they do not receive their interest and principal payments as scheduled, according to the terms of the bonds they own.

Most bonds (with the exception of U.S. Savings Bonds and Savings Notes) are *negotiable*. This means outstanding bonds generally may be sold or otherwise transferred by one bondholder to another, with all of the issuing organization's obligations represented by the bond passing intact to the new bondholder.

Effects of Inflation

Bonds, like other debt investments, generally promise rates of interest and fixed redemption values when the principal is repayable. Consequently, *inflation* tends to reduce the earnings and principal values of bonds in terms of purchasing power.

In addition, bond prices, just like stock prices, tend to fluctuate. Their market value changes daily in reaction to the availability of money. As interest rates rise or decline, bond prices change. This happens because the bond coupon, or interest rate, is *fixed*; the only way the bond market can accommodate changes in interest rates is by changing the bond's current market price. Basically, *bond prices move in exactly the opposite direction from interest rates*. When interest rates increase, bond prices fall. When interest rates decline, bond prices go up. Let's look at an example.

Assume the overall interest rate is 6¾ percent and most investments are paying a 6¾ percent return. An investor purchases a bond issued at 6¾ percent. Four years later the interest rate rises to 8 percent; however, the rate of the existing bond remains fixed at 6¾ percent. Because the bond is paying less interest than is generally available for a new bond issue, investors will be willing to pay less to own this existing bond. Therefore, the value of the bond falls. Conversely, if the overall interest rate falls to 5 percent, investors will be willing to pay more to purchase an existing bond that pays 6¾ percent since its return is higher than a new bond's rate would be.

Because interest rates may affect the price of issued bonds, many investors feel that a mix of stock and bond holdings makes for a well-balanced, diversified portfolio. The appropriate mix of stocks to bonds depends on the investor's age and needs. Stocks provide an opportunity for growth; bonds provide stable income.

■ COMMON CHARACTERISTICS OF BONDS

Corporations, governments and municipalities may issue a variety of bonds at any given point in time, but virtually all bonds contain certain basic characteristics, the chief of which are listed and described next.

The Promise to Pay

A bond is the IOU that the issuing organization gives in exchange for a loan. As such, it contains a *promise to pay*—both the principal of the loan and interest at a stated rate until the principal is repaid, according to the terms specified in the bond. This is the fundamental difference between a bond and a share of stock—satisfaction of the debt represented by the bond, according to its promise to pay and terms, takes precedence over a share of stock's claim to earnings and assets.

The bond itself is also a *certificate of indebtedness* that provides tangible evidence of the issuing organization's obligation to the bondholder or the promissory note that states: (1) the amount of the loan; (2) the rate of interest; (3) how and when the interest is payable; and (4) how and when the loan principal is to be repaid. The certificate also shows the dollar amount (or *face value*) of the bond and the maturity date.

The Denomination

The *face value* or denomination of a bond is also known as the *par value* and is usually $1,000. This means bonds are usually sold at a price near $1,000 when they are first issued. After that their prices may vary, moving up and down depending upon the prevailing market conditions. As discussed in more detail later, a bond sells near its par value when it is first issued and for as long as the market interest rate remains the same as the bond's *coupon*—the annual interest payable on the bond. For example, a bond sells at par if both the bond's coupon and the market interest rate equal 5 percent. Bonds may also be sold or traded *at a premium* (that is, *above par* or over $1,000), or *at a discount* (that is, *below par* or less than $1,000).

Bond Interest

As stated, most bonds specify an interest rate or *coupon* that remains the same throughout the term of the bond, with the interest payable at regular intervals (usually semiannually) on specified dates. Most interest payments are automatically sent via check to the holder.

Other bonds, such as zero-coupon bonds and U.S. Savings Bonds, pay no interest until the bond is redeemed. These bonds are sold at a discount from their face value. The value of these bonds increases each year and at maturity the bondholder receives the full face value. The difference between what the investor originally paid for the bond and what he or she receives at redemption is the equivalent of interest.

Bonds with lower coupons and/or longer maturities are more affected by changes in overall interest rates than bonds with higher coupons and/or shorter maturities. When market interest rates fall, bond prices rise; when market rates rise, bond prices fall. The greater the change in interest rates, the greater the change in bond prices.

Bonds are sometimes issued without specific interest pledges, particularly in event of the reorganization or readjustment of the financial structure of a corporation. Such bonds generally provide that interest is payable "in such amounts as the Board of Directors shall determine" for each interest period. Or, in the case of *income bonds*, the bonds specify that interest is paid out of surplus income, if any, and the bond also includes limiting definitions of what constitutes "surplus income."

Maturity Date

In essence, a bond investor lends money to the bond issuer. In return, the issuer promises to pay interest periodically and to repay the principal at *maturity* (typically 10 or more years from the date of issue). Many bonds designate a definite date when, regardless of other considerations, the principal is to be *redeemed* or repaid. At the maturity date, the bondholder returns the bond to the issuing corporation and receives in cash the bond's face value.

Serial bonds, issued on the same date by the same issuer, contain the same provisions, except that they have different maturity dates extending over a series of years so that the issuer does not have to repay all of the bonds at the same time.

ILL. 7.1 ■ *Example of Bonds with Serial Maturities*

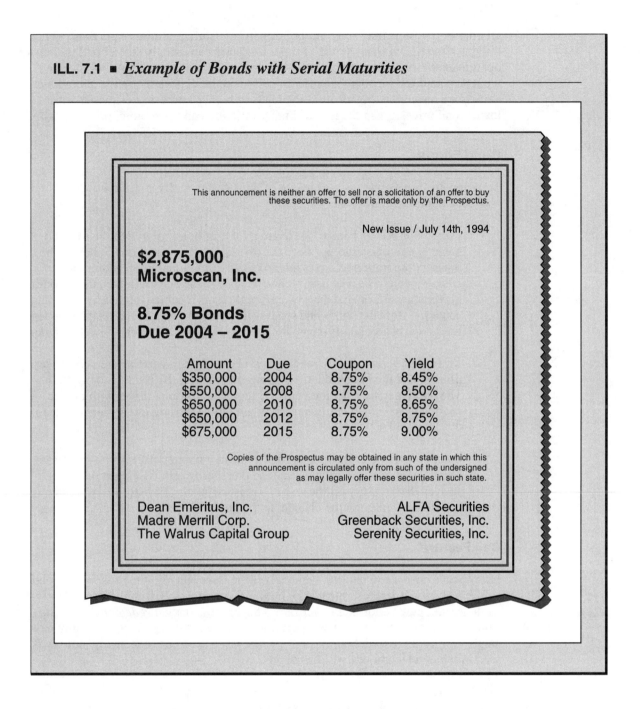

This announcement is neither an offer to sell nor a solicitation of an offer to buy these securities. The offer is made only by the Prospectus.

New Issue / July 14th, 1994

**$2,875,000
Microscan, Inc.**

**8.75% Bonds
Due 2004 – 2015**

Amount	Due	Coupon	Yield
$350,000	2004	8.75%	8.45%
$550,000	2008	8.75%	8.50%
$650,000	2010	8.75%	8.65%
$650,000	2012	8.75%	8.75%
$675,000	2015	8.75%	9.00%

Copies of the Prospectus may be obtained in any state in which this announcement is circulated only from such of the undersigned as may legally offer these securities in such state.

Dean Emeritus, Inc.
Madre Merrill Corp.
The Walrus Capital Group

ALFA Securities
Greenback Securities, Inc.
Serenity Securities, Inc.

Still other bonds set up a period of years in which repayment may be made—and then specify a definite date at which, if repayment has not already been made, it is to be made. A few bonds provide for extensions beyond their specified maturity dates, sometimes by mutual agreement between issuer and bondholder, sometimes solely at the option of the bondholder.

Bonds frequently run for 10 or 20 years and even much longer. When the period to maturity extends more than 40 or 50 years into the future, the specified maturity date assumes relatively little importance.

Of course, investors may sell their bonds before maturity, although the issuer is not obligated to redeem them ahead of time. Investors can usually sell a bond in the open market through a stockbroker—but it is possible that they will not receive what they paid for the bond because the price is quite dependent on the overall market. As we have seen, higher inflation leads to higher interest rates, which means lower bond prices. Even the hint of higher inflation can cause bond prices to fall.

Bond Forms

Traditionally, bonds were issued in one of three forms with regard to how the bond was held and how interest was paid.

1. *Coupon or bearer bonds.* These are a form of bond for which the owner's name is not registered nor does the owner's name appear on the bond. The issuing corporation will pay interest to any individual upon submission of a *coupon*, which is a promissory note payable to the bearer. In fact, these bonds get their name from the days when bondholders received interest by "clipping coupons" from the bonds and sending them to the issuer for payment. Coupon bonds and bearer bonds are no longer being issued, although a few still trade.

2. *Registered bonds.* These bonds are issued with the owner's name on the certificate, and the bondholder is also registered with the issuing corporation. The bond may be redeemed only by the owner or transferred with proper endorsement. The bond issuer automatically mails any interest payments to the bondholder.

3. *Book-entry bonds.* These securities are sold without delivery of a certificate. Evidence of ownership is maintained on records kept by a central agency, such as the Treasury on the sale of Treasury bonds. Transfer of ownership is recorded by entering the change on the books.

Call Feature

Many bonds have a *call feature*, which gives the issuer the right to redeem the bond before maturity. If interest rates drop, bond issuers can pay off the original debt while issuing new bonds at a lower rate. This process (called *redemption*) can be compared to refinancing a house to get lower interest rates and lower monthly payments. If only some of the bonds of a specific issue are to be redeemed, a lottery is used to select which bonds will be called.

The conditions for calling in a bond are given in the *trust indenture*, a written agreement between a corporation and its creditors that details the terms of the debt issue. These terms include such things as the rate of interest, the maturity date, the means of payment and the collateral.

The call privilege usually provides for payment of a *premium* if exercised, normally expressed as a percentage of the maturity value. For example the agreement might read, "The issue may be called at 105 percent from 1994 to 1999, 104 percent during 2000, 103 percent during 2001, 102 percent during 2002, 101 percent during 2003, and up to the date of payment in 2004." In this example, a bondholder with a bond worth $1,000 at maturity would receive $1,050 if the issuer redeems the bond between 1994-99. Typically, the call feature is not exercised if the current interest rate is the same or higher than the bond coupon rate.

A *sinking fund* is an account to which payments are made over a period of time to accumulate a predetermined amount of capital by a known date in the future. Corporations use sinking funds as capital reserve accounts to redeem bonds at maturity, in some cases protecting investors against the risk of default and as an alternative to other means of redemption or retirement, such as payment from current earnings.

The Security Behind the Loan

Every bond contains a statement describing the security or collateral on which the loan rests. If the issue is secured and backed by a legal claim on some specific property of the issuer, it is called a *secured bond*. An issue backed only by the promise of the issuer to pay interest and principal on a timely basis is called a *debenture* or unsecured bond.

Secured bonds include issues that are secured by real estate, such as *mortgage bonds* where the properties covered by the mortgage are listed and the relation of the present mortgage to other mortgages is set out. Other secured bonds include *collateral trust bonds*, which are backed by securities owned by the issuer but held in trust by a third party; *equipment trust bonds*, which are backed by specific property, such as certain warehouses, plants, rolling stock, forests, mines or equipment; and *first and refunding bonds*, a combination of first mortgage and junior lien bonds, which are secured in part by second or third mortgages on other properties. These types of bonds will be discussed in detail later in this chapter.

Unsecured bonds include *debentures*—long-term bonds that are unsecured and backed only by the good faith and reputation of the issuing corporation—and *subordinated debentures*—unsecured bonds that have a claim secondary to other debentures.

Certainly it is important that the investor understand exactly the security upon which the future of his or her bonds rests. A bond accurately described as a first mortgage bond might be quite appealing to an investor, whereas a bond clearly described as a second, third or fourth mortgage bond, or one resting upon the earnings and financial status of some other corporation, might be relatively unattractive. We'll look at both secured and unsecured bonds in more detail later in this chapter.

The Conversion Privilege

Some bonds specify that they may be converted to stock at a given time or within a stated period of time, at the option of the bondholder. The *conversion privilege* will provide for a ratio by which the exchange of bonds for stock is to occur. As a rule, when bonds are given conversion privileges, it is to make them more marketable.

For example, assume Corporation A issues $1,000 bonds with the right for five years to convert each bond into 20 shares of its stock with a market price of $40 a share at the time the bond is issued. At the time of issue, each bond is worth 20 shares or $800 worth of stock. In theory at least, if the price of the stock goes up to $55 a share, each $1,000 bond becomes worth $1,100.

ILL. 7.2 ■ *Bond Definitions and Features*

A bond may have some special provisions or features and be subclassified further accordingly. Some common definitions are given below.

- *Baby bond*—Any bond issued in a denomination of less than $1,000 par (face or maturity) value
- *Bearer bond*—A bond that does not have the owner's name registered on the books of the issuing company and that is payable to the holder
- *Callable bond*—A bond containing a call provision, under which the issuer has the right to retire the bond before its stated maturity date
- *Convertible bond*—A bond that can be exchanged for the issuer's common stock according to a stated ratio, at the bondholder's option
- *Junk bond*—Bond rated BB or lower by *Standard & Poor's* or another investment rating service (the lower the rating, the more speculative the investment)
- *Registered bond*—A bond whose owner is registered by the issuing corporation, and may be redeemed only by that owner or transferred with proper endorsement, unlike a *bearer* or *coupon* bond
- *Sinking fund*—A fund to which payments are made over a period of time, to accumulate a predetermined amount of money to pay off the bond on or before its maturity date
- *Tax-exempt bond*—A bond issued by municipalities, with interest exempt from current income taxes
- *Zero-coupon bond*—A bond that is sold at a deep discount from par value and therefore appreciates substantially but makes no payments of interest (the bondholder, therefore, does not receive any payments until maturity, although the annual accrued appreciation is taxable, unless the bond is a municipal zero, which is tax-exempt)

In many cases, conversion privileges are important and have a real bearing on the value of bonds. But the whole matter frequently is so intricate and involves so many factors that the investor is often confused and should rely upon professional advice.

■ MARKETING AND TRADING BONDS

Bonds (except U.S. Savings Bonds) are marketed and traded much the same as stocks. A *new issue* of bonds is typically sold and distributed by or through an investment banker (who normally assists in preparation of the issue). Or it is sold directly by the issuing organization, often to an institutional investor, when a corporation offers bonds for the first time to the public. Institutional investors, such as banks, pension funds, mutual funds and insurance companies, then trade these securities in large blocks.

Most *previously issued bonds*, including almost all U.S. government bonds, are marketed over-the-counter by broker-dealers. However, some bonds (primarily corporate and public utility bonds) are listed on exchanges and traded much as listed stock. While they own the bonds, the investors are creditors of the issuing organizations.

Bonds may be traded in the *primary market*, a market in which an investor purchases financial securities, via an investment bank or other representative, from the issuer of those securities. Issuing companies and broker-dealers must comply with Securities and Exchange Commission (SEC) regulations regarding disclosure and registration.

The *secondary market* for corporate bonds is a market for existing financial securities that are currently traded between investors. It operates at two levels: national exchanges and over-the-counter. Bonds that trade on the national exchanges are listed there at the request of the corporation. Companies may choose not to list their bonds, in which case they trade *over-the-counter (OTC)*. Both markets are closely monitored by the financial media, and current yields and market prices are listed in the securities columns.

Bond Ratings

One of the important factors in determining the interest rate a bond must pay to attract investors is the *credit quality* of the bond. The two most important companies evaluating bonds, *Standard & Poor's* and *Moody's Investors Service*, generally reach the same conclusions about each bond. Illustration 7.3 provides the rating classifications used by these two companies and a general description of the ratings.

As shown in Ill. 7.3, bonds rated AAA by *Standard & Poor's* or Aaa by *Moody's* are the highest-grade obligations, meaning they possess the highest degree of principal and interest protection. Bonds rated below BB or B are speculative in nature and are called *junk bonds*. These lower-quality bonds must pay higher yields to attract investors.

■ BOND MATURITY VALUES AND YIELDS

As explained earlier, the face or par value and the maturity date of a bond generally are stated on its face, and typically that face or par value is payable in full on that stated maturity date. This is true regardless of the type of bond or the way it was purchased (new issue or on the market, at par, at a discount or at a premium).

Bond Yields

A *bond yield* is the percentage of return an investor earns from a bond, not considering capital gains or losses. The yield is not the same thing as the interest rate; it may be higher or lower than the bond's interest rate. As shown in Ill. 7.4, a bond's yield may shift over time because of changes in overall interest rates. When a bond paying 8 percent interest is purchased at par ($1,000), it returns an annual interest payment of $80, or an 8 percent yield. If the same bond is purchased at a discount ($800), the annual interest payment remains the same but the yield rises to 10 percent ($80 ÷ $800). On the other hand, if the bond is purchased at a premium ($1,200), the interest payment results in a yield of only 6⅔ percent ($80 ÷ $1,200).

ILL. 7.3 ■ *Bond Ratings*

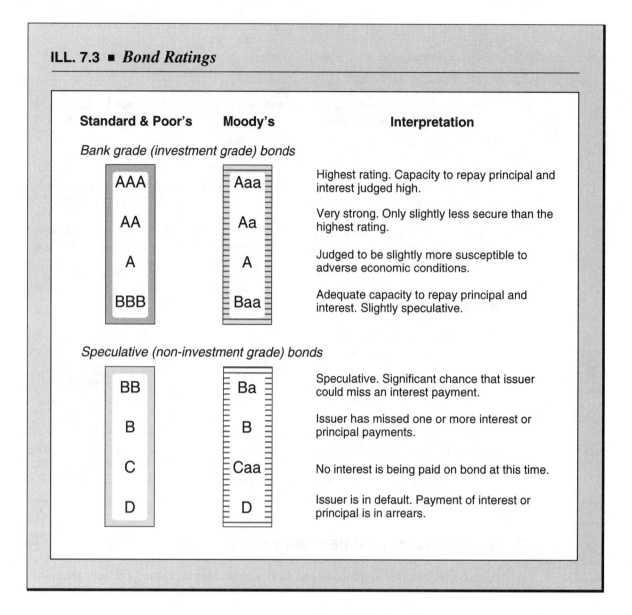

Standard & Poor's	Moody's	Interpretation
Bank grade (investment grade) bonds		
AAA	Aaa	Highest rating. Capacity to repay principal and interest judged high.
AA	Aa	Very strong. Only slightly less secure than the highest rating.
A	A	Judged to be slightly more susceptible to adverse economic conditions.
BBB	Baa	Adequate capacity to repay principal and interest. Slightly speculative.
Speculative (non-investment grade) bonds		
BB	Ba	Speculative. Significant chance that issuer could miss an interest payment.
B	B	Issuer has missed one or more interest or principal payments.
C	Caa	No interest is being paid on bond at this time.
D	D	Issuer is in default. Payment of interest or principal is in arrears.

There are frequent complications as to: (1) the payment of scheduled interest prior to the full repayment of par at maturity; and (2) the possibility of an issuer's calling a bond at a premium before its maturity date. Because of these possible (and in some cases, certain) complications, bond investors may compute any one or more of four types of bond yield.

Coupon or Nominal Yield

The *coupon* or *nominal yield* is the interest rate stated on the face of the bond. Thus, a bond with a par value of $1,000 paying a 4 percent fixed rate will yield $40 annually regardless of what happens to the price of the bond.

ILL. 7.4 ■ *How Bond Yield Fluctuates*

Assume an investor purchases a bond at par ($1,000) that pays 8 percent interest. Note how changing purchase prices will affect the yield.

Bond Purchase Price		Interest Payment	Yield
At par	$1,000	$80	8 percent
At a discount	$800	$80	10 percent
At premium	$1,200	$80	6⅔ percent

Current Yield

The *current yield* compares the bond's annual return with its current market value. This helps bondholders compare bond returns with other investment options. Current yield is calculated by dividing the annual interest income (in dollars) by the bond's current market price. Thus, if a corporate bond with a 4 percent coupon rate is currently selling at a discount price of $950 (95 percent of par), the current yield would be 4.2 percent ($40 ÷ $950). Note that the current yield on a discounted bond is always above the nominal yield; it is below the nominal yield of a bond sold at a premium.

Yield to Maturity

The *yield to maturity* is the expected rate of return that will be earned on a bond if it is held until maturity. Like current yield, it weighs the cost of the bond against return, but over the life of the bond. When buying or selling bonds on the secondary market, it helps investors to calculate or to find the yield to maturity in the *Bond Basis Book*. The formula provides an adjusted annual yield used in judging the viability of bond purchases. For example, a bond bought at $900 with a 10 percent interest rate and a 10-year maturity would have a yield to maturity of more than 11 percent.

Yield to Call

The *yield to call* is the rate of return on an investment that accounts for the cash difference between a bond's acquisition cost and its proceeds, as well as interest income calculated to the earliest date that the bonds may be called in by the issuing corporation. Any premium payable on redemption (in excess of face or par value) must be included in the yield.

■ UNDERSTANDING BOND TABLES

Corporate bond listings appear in a number of financial newspapers; however, the most complete listings usually appear in *The Wall Street Journal*. Typically, the listing will look like this:

Bonds	Cur Yld	Vol	Close	Net Chg
Dole 8⅝ 96	8.9	70	96⅞	+¼

Let's look at what this listing means. The first column shows the name of the company or organization issuing the bond—in this case *Dole*. The name may be fully spelled out (Dole, Exxon) or abbreviated (MerLy for Merrill Lynch, for example) and may be different from those used in stock tables.

The first column also notes the *interest rate*, or *coupon rate*, and the year of maturity for this issue. In this case, the 8⅝ percent Dole bond is due in 1996. Some companies have a number of bonds outstanding from a number of bond issues. These issues, with different interest rates and maturity dates, are listed separately.

The next column (Cur Yld) gives the *yield*. The yield for this Dole bond is 8.9 percent, which means that the annual interest payments will be 8.9 percent of what the investor will pay for the bond today. (The interest rate is obtained by dividing the coupon rate by the latest price.)

The third column (Vol) indicates the *volume of trading* during the previous day in thousands of dollars rather than in number of shares sold. The figure is read by adding three zeroes. In this case, $70,000 worth of Dole bonds were traded the previous day.

The last two columns provide the *closing price* and the *net change*, which represents the difference between the closing price of the previous trading day and the price of the day before that. Bond prices are quoted as a percentage of face value. In the example above, the closing price of 96⅞ means that the actual price of the bond is 96⅞ × $1,000 face value, or $968.75 for each bond. The figure always refers to a fraction of par value. For example, Dole was *up ¼ point*, which means the closing price given here is ¼ percent of par value greater than the closing price given the previous day. Since par is $1,000, the closing price shown here is $2.50 (¼ percent of $1,000) more than the last closing price. This closing price is given as 96⅞ or $968.75; therefore, the closing price from the previous day must have been $966.25 to allow for an increase of $2.50 per bond.

In discussions of bonds, the term basis point is sometimes used. A *basis point* is ¹⁄₁₀₀th of 1 percent and is a convenient way to discuss changes in yields. For example, an increase in yield from 9.5 percent to 10 percent is a 50 basis point increase.

Typical bonds consist primarily of: (1) *corporate bonds*, issued by both public utility and privately owned corporations; (2) *U.S. government securities*, issued by the federal government; and (3) *municipal bonds*, issued by local governments or units of local governments. In the next sections, we'll look at each of these bonds in more detail.

■ CORPORATE BONDS

Corporate bonds are debt securities issued by corporations when they need money—to expand, to keep pace with new technologies or to consolidate unfunded debt. Essentially, bonds are a promise from the company to pay back principal or a loan, plus a fixed percentage of interest. Unlike savings certificates, most bonds pay regular interest over the term of the security.

As explained earlier, although corporate bonds can be classified in a number of ways, one of the most common is according to how they are backed. Based on this classification, some of the major types of corporate bonds are:

- Mortgage bonds

- Collateral trust bonds

- Equipment trust bonds

- Income bonds

- Guaranteed bonds

- Debentures

- Junk bonds

Let's briefly look at each of these types of bonds.

Mortgage Bonds

Mortgage bonds are issued by corporations and are secured by specific, fixed assets of the corporation, such as real estate. In other words, mortgage bonds are backed by *mortgages* on certain specific properties owned by the issuing corporations. Since such assets are considered to be excellent collateral, mortgage bonds are one of the safest corporate bonds. Such mortgages are much like those securing home loans, and they may be first, second or third mortgages (or liens) against the properties.

Generally, a large corporation mortgages only a portion of its property as security for any single bond issue. Detailed descriptions and identifications of the mortgaged property, as well as all other details pertinent to the particular bond issue, are spelled out completely and formally in the bond indenture, generally held by a trustee.

Mortgage bonds may be issued as closed-end or open-end. A *closed-ended* issue means that any additional bonds issued on the same property will have a *junior claim* on the assets—a type of bond issue not having first right to assets in the event of default. *Open-ended* issues can be followed by additional bonds of the same class at a later date. All such open-ended issues would have equal claim against the property in case of default.

Collateral Trust Bonds

A *collateral trust bond* is a type of bond that is secured by securities held in trust as a guarantee of redemption to the bondholders. The trustee may be a commercial bank or other independent agency, and such bond issues may specify that full redemption will occur if the trust-held securities decline to or below the total issue's value.

The collateral on these bonds may be in stock of a subsidiary corporation. Since the market value of the pledged securities may fluctuate, issuing companies are required to back the collateral trust bonds with securities that exceed the bonds' face value by 25 to 33 percent.

Equipment Trust Bonds

Major transportation firms—railroads, trucking companies and airlines—commonly issue *equipment trust bonds*. These bonds are often backed by newly purchased equipment. Since equipment is relatively easy to liquidate, equipment trust bonds are considered quite safe and offer low yields.

Income Bonds

The most speculative bonds are called *income bonds*. They are normally issued when the issuing company would otherwise become bankrupt. Income bonds are exchanged with other outstanding bonds on the condition that interest will accrue and be payable only if earned. Bondholders of outstanding issues must authorize the exchange. As with common stock, the corporation's board of directors declares whether or not an interest payment will be made. That decision, however, is dictated by provisions of the trust, which spells out the terms of a bond contract, including the appointment of a trustee, terms and conditions of repayment, rate of interest and maturity date and priority of claims.

Because of the risk that no interest will be paid, income bonds *offer* higher interest rates. Some income bonds are backed by mortgaged property. Others are functionally debentures—long-term bonds that are unsecured and backed only by the good faith and reputation of the issuing corporation.

Guaranteed Bonds

Guaranteed bonds are issued by one organization, and backed by a second firm's promise to repay in the event of bankruptcy. Their interest and/or maturity payments are often guaranteed by a company with shared resources or equipment, such as a parent company. The good faith and credit of the guarantor backs the bonds. These bonds may be guaranteed for principal only, for interest only, or for both.

Debentures

A *debenture* is a bond secured not by assets, but solely by the issuing organization's *promise* to pay the stated interest and to repay the principal, according to the schedule specified in the bond. It is comparable to an unsecured note. The credit of the issuing organization generally provides the only security of a debenture.

Debentures usually are issued by either the very strongest or the weakest organizations. Virtually all government bonds are debentures, and they are considered to be among the safest bonds (especially those issued by the U.S. government) by virtue of the government's power to tax. Also, large corporations that enjoy extremely high levels of credit and anticipated future earnings often issue debentures and find ready markets for them.

On the other hand, corporations that already have covered much of their properties with mortgages, so that additional mortgage-secured issues would be considered relatively weak and not too salable, sometimes move to the issuance of debentures to obtain additional capital.

Because more risk is involved in debentures than in many other securities, they command a higher interest rate. If the issuing company declares bankruptcy, claims on the assets by debentures are subordinate to all other types of bonds.

Junk Bonds

A *junk bond* is a low-rated debt security issued by a company. Junk bonds are often debentures backed only by a company's assets; however, if a company does go bankrupt, bondholders are paid out of the company's assets before stockholders.

■ U.S. GOVERNMENT SECURITIES

Billions of dollars are needed every year to keep the federal government going. Since taxes alone cannot finance the entire budget, the federal government and its agencies, such as the Federal Home Loan Banks, issue *debt securities*. The largest issuer of bonds—and the world's largest debtor—is the U.S. Treasury. Unlike corporate bond issuers, there is little chance the government will default on its obligations. Government securities are backed by the full faith and credit of the U.S. government—its taxing power. Although government agencies' securities are not backed by the taxing power of the federal government, it is very unlikely that the government would ever permit securities issued by one of its agencies to default.

There are two main benefits to government securities. First, they are considered very safe. As already mentioned, the financial security of the federal government and its agencies is ultimately backed by the collective income of one of the most productive nations on earth. And, secondly, income from most of these securities is exempt from state and local taxes, although it is subject to federal income tax. It is this combination of safety with some tax relief plus the ease of buying and selling these securities that makes them a major part of institutional portfolios as well as individual investment strategies.

Marketable Government Securities

Three principal types of bonds and securities are issued by the federal government. These so-called *marketable securities* are those issues that are bought and sold quickly in the open market and include:

- Treasury bills

- Treasury notes

- Treasury bonds

Let's briefly look at each of these marketable securities.

Treasury Bills

Treasury bills or *T-bills* are short-term securities that mature in a year or less and are auctioned by the Treasury in denominations of $10,000 to $1 million. They are in *book-entry* form, which means the Treasury keeps the names of owners on record, and never issues an actual certificate. T-bills do not pay periodic interest but are sold below face value (i.e., at a discount). Their return is the difference between the discounted purchase price and the amount received at maturity. The Treasury redeems the T-bills upon maturity at par value. The discount is treated as interest and is taxed at the federal level as interest income instead of capital gains.

Treasury Notes

In addition to T-bills, the government issues *Treasury notes*—highly liquid, intermediate-term, interest-bearing securities. They are issued in denominations of $1,000 to $1 million and mature in one to 10 years. Notes are currently issued in registered or book-entry form and pay interest semiannually.

Treasury Bonds

Treasury bonds are long-term debt instruments, issued in both book-entry and registered form. They have maturities ranging from 10 to 30 years and are issued in denominations of $1,000 to $1 million. Interest is paid on Treasury bonds every six months, but the government retains the right to call or redeem some issues before maturity.

Treasury bills, notes and bonds can be purchased directly from the 12 Federal Reserve banks or one of their branches, banks or brokers. Because of their decreased risk, these securities offer lower interest returns than corporate bonds.

Nonmarketable Securities

The government issues U.S. Savings Bonds as a way for small investors to preserve their capital while earning some interest. Of the 12 series of U.S. Savings Bonds that have been issued in the past, only two types—Series EE and HH—are currently issued. These *nonmarketable U.S. Treasury securities* differ from other issues because they cannot be used as loan collateral nor can they be sold on the secondary market. Those investors who have a low tolerance for risk and want to be certain that their principal is safe may be interested in purchasing U.S. Savings Bonds.

Series EE Bonds

Series EE bonds are discount bonds that do not pay current income but are issued at discounted prices, in this case equal to *half* the face value of the bond. For example, a $50 denomination is issued at $25. If held until maturity, the investor receives the face value ($50) plus variable interest. These bonds may be purchased at a bank or through automatic payroll deduction.

Series HH Bonds

Similar in nature to Series EE bonds, *Series HH bonds* function as an interest-bearing security. They are nonmarketable and nontransferable, and mature in 10 years. Unlike Series EE bonds, these bonds pay interest semiannually. They are available only when traded in exchange for Series E and EE bonds. Investors cannot buy them with cash.

Government Agencies Empowered to Issue Securities

The government agencies empowered to issue securities reflect a wide range of banking, housing and foreign aid interests. Each has enough income and equity to back bond issues of various sizes and maturities. Some agencies issue *mortgage-backed bonds*, a debt secured by a pool of mortgages. Others issue bonds that, while not direct liabilities of the U.S. government, are usually considered *moral obligations* of the government and, therefore, it is unlikely that the government would permit these issues to default. The five most prominent agencies are:

1. the Government National Mortgage Association;

2. the Federal Home Loan Mortgage Corporation;

3. the Federal National Mortgage Association;

4. the Federal Farm Credit Banks; and

5. the Federal Home Loan Banks.

Government National Mortgage Association (GNMA)

The *Government National Mortgage Association (GNMA or Ginnie Mae)* is a government-owned corporation that buys mortgages from private sources and guarantees payments to investors who subsequently purchase securities in the mortgage pool bonds offered by the association. It was originally part of the Department of Housing and Urban Development (HUD).

Ginnie Mae securities consist of mortgages insured by the Federal Housing Administration (FHA) and Veterans Administration (VA) and are backed by the full faith and credit of the U.S. government. Investors purchase *mortgage pass-through* certificates, available in minimum denominations of $25,000, which give them a part interest in a mortgage pool of single-family homes. These certificates, often referred to as *Ginnie Maes*, are the most popular type of GNMA security. The monthly earnings of each investor are "passed through" from the homeowner to a bank, then through to the investor in a GNMA program. If a homeowner is late in making mortgage payments, Ginnie Mae ensures that the investor is paid on time.

Federal Home Loan Mortgage Corporation (FHLMC)

The *Federal Home Loan Mortgage Corporation (FHLMC)*, often called *Freddie Mac*, buys existing home mortgages and resells them to the general investing public. It is the second largest pass-through mortgage issuer. Freddie Macs are backed

---

ILL. 7.5 ■ *Advantages and Disadvantages of U.S. Treasuries*

Advantages

- Principal and interest guaranteed against default
- May be sold through a broker before maturity without loss because interest accrues daily until the date of sale
- Highly liquid
- Exempt from state and local income taxes

Disadvantages

- Competitive bidding on Treasuries may be too complex for average investor
- Generally pay about the same interest as a bank certificate of deposit (CD); however, CD interest is fully taxable

---

by FHA, VA and privately guaranteed mortgages and carry the general guarantee of the FHLMC. These securities yield slightly more than Ginnie Maes because they are not backed by the U.S. government.

Federal National Mortgage Association (FNMA)

The *Federal National Mortgage Association (FNMA)*, often called *Fannie Mae*, is a publicly held corporation that provides mortgage capital when credit is tight. In addition to conventional mortgages, Fannie Mae purchases residential mortgages from agencies like the VA, the FHA and the Farmers Home Administration. Fannie Mae issues short-term discount notes and debentures.

Fannie Mae discount notes prices begin at $5,000. The debentures begin at a $10,000 minimum. They offer maturities of 3 to 25 years. As explained earlier, debenture is not backed by fixed assets, but by the full faith and credit of the issuer.

Mortgage-backed securities are secure investments but offer no inflation protection. In addition, there is no special tax treatment for mortgage securities. Interest income and any capital gains are taxed at ordinary levels.

Federal Farm Credit Banks

The *Federal Farm Credit Banks*, an agency supervised by the Farm Credit System (FCS), issues discount notes and bonds, generally for maturities under a year. They are issued in book-entry form only, with longer-term issues in $1,000 denominations and shorter-term issues priced at $5,000. These bonds are exempt from state and local income taxes but are subject to federal income tax.

Federal Home Loan Banks

The *Federal Home Loan Banks* supports the nation's savings and loan institutions, which in turn provide credit for residential mortgages. Home Loan Bank obligations are backed by mortgages, cash and other bank assets. They are issued as short-term discount notes, interest-bearing notes and bonds. Interest on notes is payable on maturity; interest on bonds is payable every six months.

■ MUNICIPAL BONDS

A *municipal security* (or a *muni*) is a loan to a state, city or district entity, that bears a promise to repay the principal amount plus an agreed rate of interest over the term of the bond. In the ranking of investments by safety of principal, municipal securities are considered second only to U.S. government and U.S. government agency securities. The degree of safety, of course, varies from issue to issue and from municipality to municipality. Much of the safety of any municipal issue is based on the viability of the issuing municipality and the community in general.

The funds that municipal bond issues raise may be used to finance the construction or improvement of public works such as schools, highways and water treatment facilities. Although these bonds often pay lower rates than other bonds, they are generally exempt from federal income taxes, which can make these bonds appealing to investors in high tax brackets.

Municipal bonds generally are issued in $5,000 denominations and are usually traded in units of at least $25,000. After the initial sale of the bonds through the underwriting broker, the bonds may resell at par, at a premium above par or at a discount. Municipal bonds usually pay a fixed rate of interest at specified dates until maturity.

When municipal securities are issued, their primary distribution is through an underwriting broker. Brokerage firms may also decide to *make a market* for the bonds in the secondary market. In other words, these firms will advertise and offer munis as part of their inventory.

Tax Benefits

The interest paid by most municipal securities is exempt from federal income taxation. Because the federal government does not tax the interest from debt obligations of municipalities, municipalities reciprocate by not taxing the interest from federal debt securities. This *doctrine of reciprocal immunity* was established by the Supreme Court in a decision handed down in 1895. To qualify for the exemption from federal taxation, the municipal security must be issued to fund government (public rather than private) activities.

In many cases, interest from municipal bonds is also exempt from state taxation if (1) the bonds are issued by a municipality in that state and (2) the bonds are sold to an investor who lives in that state. Some states also exempt from taxation bonds issued by a territory of the United States.

This tax-advantaged status of municipal bonds allows municipalities to raise money at a lower cost than corporations: municipalities are able to offer tax-exempt bonds at lower interest rates than offered by similar taxable bonds. Because municipal rates are generally lower than corporate rates, municipal securities are most attractive to investors in high tax brackets. However, investors should always carefully calculate a bond's overall yield, including tax savings, before choosing it for their portfolio.

Issuers

The three primary entities entitled to issue municipal debt securities are

1. state governments;

2. territorial possessions of the United States (Puerto Rico, the Virgin Islands, Guam); and

3. legally constituted taxing authorities, which include county and city governments and the agencies they create.

Types of Municipal Bonds

Municipal bonds are issued for a variety of purposes, but they generally fall into one of two general categories: general obligation bonds or revenue bonds.

General Obligation Bonds

A *general obligation (GO) bond* is a type of municipal security that is backed by the full faith and credit of the taxing power of the issuer. General obligation bondholders have a legal claim to the revenues received by a municipal government for payment of the principal and interest due them. The proceeds from the sale of these bonds are used to finance projects that don't produce income (e.g., bridges, highways, prisons). They are generally not used to finance operating expenses or maintenance of existing properties.

General obligation bonds are backed by taxes. State-issued debt securities are backed by income taxes, license fees and sales taxes. Cities, town and counties issue debt securities backed by property taxes, license fees, fines and all other sources of revenue to the municipality. School, road and park districts may also issue municipal bonds that are backed by property taxes.

Revenue Bonds

A *revenue bond* is a common type of municipal issue and can be used to finance any municipal function that generates income. In contrast to the interest and principal payments of GOs, which are payable from general or real estate taxes, the interest and principal payments of revenue bonds are payable to bondholders only from the specific earnings of revenue-producing facilities such as utilities (water, sewer, electric), housing, transportation (airports, toll roads), education (college dorms, student loans), health (hospitals, retirement centers) or industrial facilities (industrial development, pollution control).

Like corporate bonds, revenue bonds are rated according to the potential of a facility to generate money to service the bond debt. In recent years, municipalities have tended to issue more revenue bonds and fewer GOs. Because revenue bonds are not repaid from taxes, they are not subject to statutory debt limits the way GOs are. Revenue bonds are meant to be self-supporting, but if the facility they finance does not make enough money to repay the debt, bondholders, not taxpayers, bear the risk.

Next, we'll look at zero-coupon bonds—a type of bond that possesses unusual characteristics that distinguish it from many other types of bonds.

■ ZERO-COUPON BONDS

Zero-coupon bonds or *zeros* are bonds that pay no interest, but are sold at deep discounts from face value. The bonds are issued both by corporations and the U.S. government and are particularly appealing to investors who want capital appreciation rather than current income. Investors who think interest rates are at or near their peak can lock in current interest rates until the bonds mature. Unlike other bonds whose interest could not be reinvested at yields as high as when the bonds were purchased (if interest rates were declining), these bonds accrue interest as if it were paid every six months and reinvested at the yield quoted when purchased.

When zeros mature, the investor receives the interest in a lump-sum payment. The *return on investment* is the difference between the price paid initially and the amount received at maturity. With a zero-coupon bond, the investor knows ahead of time exactly how much money will be received when the bond is due.

Types of Zero-Coupon Bonds

There are basically four types of zero-coupon bonds.

1. *Corporate zeros* are issued by large corporations. These zeros, limited in number, are long-term investments that require an investor's faith in the corporation and its credit worthiness.

2. *Treasury zeros (strips)* are packaged and sold by large brokerage and investment houses. These houses buy huge lots of long-term U.S. Treasury bonds, strip off the semiannual interest coupons and sell the coupons, which come due twice a year during the life of the bond. The buyer is guaranteed $1,000 upon the bond's maturity. Principal and interest are guaranteed by the U.S. government.

3. *Tax-exempt zeros* are issued by municipalities, states and other agencies. Like other municipal bonds, their interest is exempt from federal income tax and from state and local income tax in the issuing community. Also like other tax-exempt bonds, these zeros pay a lower rate.

4. *Zero-coupon CDs* are similar to zero-coupon bonds. They are obligations of large banks and, like bank deposits, are insured up to $100,000 by the FDIC.

Advantages of Zeros

Investors in zero-coupon bonds do not purchase them as income investments, but rather, see them as a means of locking in an acceptable rate of interest for the life of the bond. Therefore, zero-coupon bonds may be a good investment for those who know they will need a certain sum of money at a certain time in the future or for those who are able to hold bonds until maturity. These bonds are relatively safe investments and offer no *reinvestment risk* (also known as *interest rate risk*) to the investor. Investors know exactly how much they must invest now to get a certain amount of money at a certain point in the future. Reinvestment of interest payments is done automatically.

Zero-coupon bonds pay yearly interest, but the interest is not received yearly. Instead, the investor receives it in one lump-sum payment when the bond matures.

Disadvantages of Zeros

Although the return on investment seems appealing, there is a problem: The IRS insists that the investor pay taxes on the yearly interest, even though it is not received until the maturity of the bond. As the bond becomes more valuable over the years, the amount due the IRS for taxes will increase. Although the investor must declare the interest, he or she will receive no cash income from the bond to pay that tax.

Another disadvantage of an investment in zeros is that they are more subject to *market risk* (also known as *price risk*) than are interest-paying debt obligations. You will recall that market risk is the risk that the price of the investment will fluctuate during its life (due to changes in market conditions, interest rates, investor sentiment and so on). Zero-coupon bond prices tend to be extremely volatile because of their deep discount and low (zero) interest rate. If interest rates rise, the value of zeros falls even more than the value of regular bonds because the investor has no cash from interest payments, he or she cannot take a zero's interest and reinvest it at a higher rate elsewhere.

■ INVESTMENT STRATEGIES

As stated earlier, the primary investment objective that bonds support is income with relative safety. Investors can meet that objective through bond investing with a variety of strategies. Some of the more common are outlined below.

Buying short-term bonds enables bondholders to hold their investment until maturity, thus locking in a fixed, predictable return and relative stability of principal. Many bond buyers attempt to reduce the risks by only investing in high-grade bonds of stable companies.

Others lessen risk by diversifying—investing in several different corporations or buying bond funds or bond trusts (discussed in more detail in later chapters).

In periods of declining interest rates, long-term bonds not only provide fixed income, but will increase in market value. The downside of locking in long-term high rates is that the issuing firm may call in those debt securities before maturity.

Many investors earmark bond maturity proceeds to specific needs—a house purchase, balloon mortgage payment, travel or a child's education. Matching the maturities to their budget can save bondholders from a crisis position that would require them to sell their bonds in a below-par market. Bonds also operate well in retirement strategies. For most people, retirement means reduced income and, therefore, a lower tax bracket. Investors may want to buy bonds that pay interest at staggered intervals during retirement to provide funds in addition to Social Security. The increased income from bonds enables retirees to maintain their lifestyle after retirement, and, since they are usually in a lower tax bracket, they pay less of that income to the IRS.

■ SUMMARY

Corporations, the U.S. government and its agencies as well as state and local governments issue bonds and other securities to finance their ongoing activities. Investors purchase bonds for three reasons: interest income, possible increase in value and repayment at maturity. Some are relatively short term, and some are long term. Still others have no maturity date, but continue until liquidated or withdrawn at the will of the investor.

In the next chapter, we'll look at a number of vehicles that offer investors the opportunity to own shares of interests in investment pools. In other words, investors are able to participate in investment asset portfolios that are generally much larger (and often more diversified) than they could own individually.

■ CHAPTER 7 QUESTIONS FOR REVIEW

1. Bonds that are backed only by the good credit of the organization issuing them are called

   A. zero-coupons
   B. debentures
   C. municipal bonds
   D. nonmarketable securities

2. The interest rate stated on the face of a bond is called its

   A. nominal yield
   B. current yield
   C. yield to maturity
   D. yield to call

3. A callable bond

   A. is payable to anyone presenting it
   B. pays higher returns than a noncallable bond
   C. is subject to claims of the company's creditors
   D. may be retired by the issuer before its stated maturity date

4. All of the following entities may issue municipal debt securities EXCEPT

    A. state governments
    B. corporations headquartered in the United States
    C. territorial possessions of the United States
    D. city governments

5. In which market are almost all U.S. government bonds traded?

    A. Exchange markets
    B. Third market
    C. Over-the-counter market
    D. Fourth market

8
Investment Company Products

T here are a number of vehicles that offer investors the opportunity to own shares or interests in *investment pools*, that is, to participate in investment portfolios that generally are much larger (and often are much more diversified) than the investors could own individually. The major kinds of such vehicles are offered by investment companies. These companies, and the shares or interests they offer to investors, are the subjects of this chapter.

Investment company shares have become increasingly popular in the last few years, giving many individual investors the opportunity to participate in large, diversified portfolios of securities professionally selected and managed. Among the topics covered in this chapter are face-amount certificate companies, unit investment trusts, closed-end management investment companies and open-end management investment companies (mutual funds).

■ ■ ■ ■ ■

■ INVESTMENT COMPANIES IN GENERAL

A good means of access to equity and debt markets for most investors is through an *investment company* that operates in a way that fits the investor's strategy. An investment company is in the business of pooling investors' money and investing in securities for them. The management of an investment company attempts to invest and manage funds for people more effectively than the individual investors could themselves (given the limited time, knowledge of various securities markets and resources that most investors have). Investment companies operate and invest those pooled funds as a single large account jointly owned by every shareholder in the company.

Throughout the past several decades, investment company shares (especially mutual fund shares) have become increasingly popular as investment options among investors at virtually all financial levels—particularly among individuals in the vast middle-income and moderate-means bracket. Investment companies have experienced tremendous growth during this period, and their shares currently enjoy a relatively high degree of popularity.

169

The purpose of an investment company is to invest the pooled capital of many individual investors in a large, diversified portfolio of securities that will fulfill certain objectives, such as preservation of capital, current income or growth. These securities are selected, supervised, administered and managed through professional facilities provided (or arranged for) by the investment company. Each investment company *share* generally represents a proportionate, fractional, ownership interest in the company's entire (but indivisible) portfolio of assets.

Definition

An *investment company* is either a corporation or a trust through which investors pool their funds to obtain diversification and management of their investments. When an investor purchases a share of an investment company, he or she not only buys an ownership interest in the company's diversified portfolio of assets, but also in effect, and for certain fees, hires the company to select and supervise (and often to manage and handle completely) those asset investments.

The investment company shareholder's overall profit or loss is based on the earnings and capital increases (or losses) the investment company realizes on its underlying securities. It is in the same proportion that his or her shares bear to the total outstanding shares of the company. In other words, if the certificate holder has 5 percent of the total outstanding shares of the company, his or her portion of the company's net earnings (or losses) is 5 percent.

Neither the investor nor the investment company has anything to do with the control, management or other operations of the organizations in whose securities the company invests. It is this complete absence of financial or management responsibility that distinguishes the investment company certificate from other financial instruments and from the securities in which the company itself invests.

Brief History

Investment trusts (as these investment vehicles were called prior to 1940) began in Europe. During the last half of the 1920s, investment trusts became popular in the United States. They expanded rapidly in both number and size, and as their underlying investments (primarily common stocks) climbed at fantastic rates, so did the asset values of their shares. Investors appeared to become rich almost overnight. With the market crash in 1929, however, the asset values of the investment trusts fell with the market prices of their underlying securities. Many of the trusts paid off their investors at a few cents on the dollar, if at all. Most shareholders lost heavily. As a result, the popularity of investment trusts fell to a low ebb following the crash, and generally remained there throughout the Great Depression of the 1930s.

Because of the disastrous experience of investment trust shareholders following the crash, the federal government authorized the Securities and Exchange Commission (SEC) to make a thorough investigation of this field and to submit its recommendations to Congress. In addition to developing extensive statistics, the SEC found that many investors knew little or nothing about the investment company shares they owned or about the objectives or practices of the companies issuing those shares. Most companies made very limited, if any, information available to investors, since there were virtually no disclosure requirements in effect at that time.

The SEC also found considerable evidence of poor or unscrupulous management and misrepresentation among the investment companies, and in some instances, outright fraud. Lack of disclosure requirements, regulations and regulatory authority obviously provided a fertile field for the development of those faults.

Investment Company Act of 1940

Based on the SEC report and recommendations, Congress enacted the *Investment Company Act of 1940*, and empowered the SEC to administer and enforce the Act, thereby establishing federal regulation and supervision of investment companies. The primary purpose of the Act was (and continues to be) to regulate investment companies to ensure that they adhere to special rules and regulations and to keep investors fully informed about investment company operations.

In administering and enforcing the Act, the SEC deals principally with full and accurate disclosure, and with the prevention of fraud, misrepresentation and unscrupulous management, but only in a general way with the investment policies, of investment companies. Moreover, the SEC neither approves nor disapproves—nor offers any opinion on the investment merits of—the underlying assets in which the investment company invests or the shares that it offers to investors.

The SEC requires that investors be provided with a *prospectus* that contains all information pertaining to a new offering, including management, description of securities, legal and financial disclosures and use of proceeds. In addition to considerable detail about the company and its officers, the prospectus must state the company's fundamental investment policies—these policies cannot be changed without shareholder approval. This is especially significant from the standpoint of investors in management company shares, as will become apparent in our subsequent discussions of the various classes of companies.

With the advent of federal regulation and supervision in 1940, investor interest in investment company shares again started to rise, and generally has continued to rise to date. But probably of greater significance, increased investor interest has been due to the return, with few exceptions, of almost universally rising trends in our economy, security prices and individual affluence, plus increased and more effective sales efforts by or on behalf of investment companies. In addition, the entry of many life insurance companies into the mutual fund field, the advent and growth of real estate investment trusts (REITs) (discussed in Chapter 9) and the near-meteoric rise in money market funds, all within the last decade or two, have contributed to the increase in total pooled fund assets to hundreds of billions of dollars (many times what their assets were at the inception of the 1940 Act).

Aside from any time savings and the convenience involved, the primary appeal of investment company shares, as compared with direct investments in stocks, bonds and/or other assets, lies in the assumption that the shares afford a more favorable combination of profitability and safety—by virtue of the professional management and broader diversification of the securities represented by the shares.

■ CLASSIFICATION OF INVESTMENT COMPANIES

The Investment Company Act of 1940 classifies *investment companies* as any business whose purpose is to invest, reinvest, own, hold or trade securities. These investment companies manage diversified portfolios of various types of securities in accordance with certain specified investment objectives, which must be stated in their registration statements and prospectuses.

Diversified or Nondiversified

A management company is registered with the SEC as either a diversified or a nondiversified company, depending on whether it meets certain standards established by the Act. It is a *diversified* company under the Act if it:

1. has at least 75 percent of its assets invested in securities issued by other companies or government entities;

2. has no more than 5 percent of its assets invested in any single corporation; and

3. holds no more than 10 percent of the voting securities of any single corporation.

A company that does not meet these qualifications is a *nondiversified* company under the Act.

Primarily because of the more favorable corporate income tax treatment accorded diversified investment companies (although the diversification requirements of the Internal Revenue Code are somewhat less strict than those of the Act), most management companies are registered with the SEC as diversified companies under the Act.

The Investment Company Act of 1940 (including its subsequent amendments) specifically exempts from regulation certain types of companies that would otherwise fall within the Act's definition of an investment company. These exemptions include such organizations as banks, insurance companies, savings banks, companies whose principal business or purpose is other than investing in securities, companies having no more than 100 security holders and not offering or planning to offer their securities to the public, certain companies that are subject to state or federal regulation under statutes other than the Act and so on.

All nonexempt organizations falling within the definition of the Act, that is, virtually all true investment companies, are required to register with the SEC, are subject to regulation under the Act and are known as *regulated investment companies*. These are divided into three major classes: (1) face-amount certificate plan companies; (2) unit investment trusts; and (3) management companies—either closed-end or open-end investment companies (called *mutual funds*). A *closed-end* management or investment company is one that issues a fixed number of shares that may be traded in the secondary market, but which are not redeemed by the company itself. On the other hand, an *open-end* company sells shares to investors whenever they desire to buy and will redeem those shares upon request. Of the three major classes, management companies are by far the most numerous and exceed all others in total number of shareholders and total assets.

First, let's look at the three classes of investment companies and then we'll discuss mutual funds, the most popular of the investment pools, in more detail.

■ FACE-AMOUNT CERTIFICATE PLAN

Face-amount certificate plans constitute a small portion of the total investment company product currently outstanding and being purchased. They issue certificates that represent *debts* to the holders, thus differing from the shares of ownership typically issued by other types of investments companies.

Nature of the Plan

The face-amount certificate plan is a method by which an investor may make regular, periodic purchases of investment company shares. Special arrangements are offered to investors to encourage and facilitate their regular and continuing purchases. In short, these arrangements are installment payment plans for purchasing mutual fund shares. A plan generally calls for the investment of a given dollar amount each month, quarter or other stated time interval, over a specified number of years—the amount, interval and number of years being selected in light of the investor's circumstances and financial objectives. The plan guarantees specified redemption values (according to schedule or provision) payable on surrender of the certificate any time prior to or at its maturity.

Organization and Operation

Under such a plan, the investor receives a *face-amount certificate*—a contract under which the company is bound to pay a fixed sum (the face amount of the certificate) at maturity to the purchaser, provided he or she has made the required initial lump-sum payment or series of installment payments. If the holder surrenders the certificate prior to the maturity date, he or she is paid a specified surrender value (according to a table or provisions in the certificate) based on the amount actually paid in and the length of time the certificate has run. In addition to the guaranteed maturity value or prematurity surrender value, the holder may receive value that is not guaranteed. Thus, face-amount certificates offer a systematic savings method and a higher degree of safety, but generally a lower rate of return than expected from most other equity securities.

Because of the fixed amounts promised at maturity or earlier surrender, the face-amount certificate company naturally sets these guaranteed values on the conservative side of the investment results it actually expects to realize—for the sake of safety. Thus, the guaranteed certificate values are below the results that normally would be expected on a comparable investment in a contractual accumulation plan. However, in addition to the guaranteed values, as noted earlier, additional discretionary amounts generally are credited to the certificate periodically in amounts determined by the company's directors, based on the company's actual investment experience. Although not guaranteed, any such additional credits that are declared, of course, enhance the value and yield of the certificate.

Although no sales costs are deducted from the holder's payments into the plan, the sales costs must come from somewhere. Actually, they are deducted from the earnings of the underlying portfolio, before the discretionary interest credits (all or part, depending upon the provisions of the certificate) are declared periodically by the company's board. Clearly, since these sales costs are not taken from payments into the certificates, they must be recouped from investment earnings before net earnings can be credited to the certificates. The costs are legitimate and justifiable expenses, but investors should not overlook them when making evaluations as to what certificates to buy, hold or sell.

■ UNIT INVESTMENT TRUSTS

A *unit investment trust* is an investment company organized under a trust indenture. A UIT does not have a board of directors, does not employ investment advisers and does not actively manage its own portfolios (trade securities). A UIT functions as a holding company for its investors. UIT managers typically purchase other investment company shares or government and municipal bonds. They then sell redeemable shares, also known as *units* or *shares of beneficial interest*, in this portfolio of securities. Each share is an undivided interest in the underlying portfolio. Because UITs are not managed, when any securities in the portfolio are liquidated, the proceeds must be distributed.

A UIT may be fixed or nonfixed. A fixed UIT typically purchases a portfolio of bonds and terminates when the bonds in the portfolio mature. A nonfixed UIT purchases shares of an underlying mutual fund. Under the act of 1940, the trustees of both fixed and nonfixed UITs must maintain secondary markets in the units, thus guaranteeing a measure of liquidity to shareholders. Changes in the underlying securities of unit trusts seldom are made and usually are permissible only under specified contingencies. Earnings are distributed periodically, and proceeds are returned as each bond matures.

To assemble a trust, the sponsor of the UIT takes a large position in a group of securities, primarily bonds. For example, a municipal bond UIT might contain 27 new issues worth $75 million. Once established, the securities in the UIT are fixed and held by a trustee (usually a bank) until maturity. Unlike mutual funds, no one "manages" the UIT portfolio holdings once they are selected. Most sponsors never sell off any bonds from their unit trusts, not even issues on the brink of default. Nor do they add other securities to the original portfolio. As a result, the return, or yield, is fixed and predictable.

ILL. 8.1 ■ *Unit Investment Trusts*

Advantages

- Investors lock in high yield for the long term in a diversified, professionally selected portfolio
- Provide steady, fixed income
- Annual management fee usually is lower than that of a mutual fund

Disadvantages

- Portfolio is not actively managed
- Sales charges are high and cut into the yield
- Minimum investment requirement may be higher than some mutual funds

The UIT provides income for a set period of time—for example, 3, 10 or 30 years. At the end of the specified period, the trust liquidates. In the case of bond funds, the trust guarantees that the unit holders will get back their principal at maturity. Thus, the UIT provides long-term investors the same fixed, guaranteed return they get from investing in single bonds. But, by investing in a UIT, rather than individual bonds, investors spread their risks through diversification. Furthermore, the initial minimum investment is considerably less than needed to buy several bonds (often as low as $1,000); however, it may be higher than investment in some mutual funds.

Most of these trusts are set up to terminate at the end of a definite period (e.g., 20 years). At that time, the trustee must sell the underlying securities and distribute the net proceeds to certificate holders. At any time during the life of the trust, the certificate holder may redeem his or her shares, that is, receive the proportionate number of shares of the trust's underlying securities (or security) or the equivalent value in cash (less certain costs and fees) from the trustee in exchange for the shares.

■ MANAGEMENT INVESTMENT COMPANIES

Investment companies, brokerage firms and some financial institutions offer their customers the opportunity to invest through affiliations with *management investment* companies. The investor buys shares in a particular *fund*, not the investment company itself. The aggregate money invested in the fund is then used to trade in a variety of stocks, bonds or a combination of both. As noted earlier, there are two types of management companies: open-end companies and closed-end companies.

Open-End vs. Closed-End Companies

Open-end companies issue *redeemable securities*, that is, securities that give holders a right to obtain from the company their proportionate share of the company's net assets or the cash equivalent. The price of each share is calculated at least once each day, based on the current market value of the fund's investment portfolio minus the fund's operating expenses. Dividing that figure by the number of shares outstanding gives the *net asset value (NAV)* per share of stock in a particular mutual fund. Almost all open-end companies offer and sell new shares of their own stock on a continuous basis, hence the name, "open-end." Open-end shares normally are bought from and redeemed by the company through its principal underwriter.

It is often less risky for an individual to invest in a mutual fund than to invest in stock on his or her own. Professional managers study the market and make investment decisions based on each mutual fund's stated investment objectives, which are outlined in the fund's prospectus. In addition, mutual funds offer more diversification than most individuals could achieve on their own.

A *closed-end company* is one that issues a fixed number of shares. These shares are listed and traded in the secondary market and are not generally redeemed by the management company itself. Closed-end funds serve the primary function of pooling shareholders' monies for investment purposes. They offer the same benefits as mutual funds: professional management, stated investment objectives, diversification and cost efficiency.

However, closed-end companies neither redeem outstanding securities nor engage in the continuous sale of new securities, hence the name, "closed-end." They operate with relatively fixed supplies of capital, and their shares normally are bought and sold on securities exchanges or the over-the-counter market, the same as shares of common stock.

Therefore, the basic difference between open-end and closed-end companies is in the form of capital structure. Closed-end funds generally raise money from shareholders only once, in underwritings sponsored by the brokerage firm. Unlike mutual funds, closed-end funds do not stand ready to redeem their shares at net asset value. Instead, shareholders who wish to sell their shares must do so by trading them on a national exchange or over-the-counter at a price determined by the market. Now, let's look at each of these in more detail.

■ CLOSED-END MANAGEMENT COMPANIES

Closed-end companies are less complex, and, from the standpoint of number of companies, number of shareholders and total assets, they are the lesser of the two classes of management companies by a substantial margin. Nonetheless, there are some very sizable companies within this class. Their shares are popular with many investors and frequently are found in estates of almost all sizes.

Nature of Closed-End Companies

A closed-end company is virtually identical in basic nature and structure to the commercial or industrial corporation, except that its business happens to be investing in marketable securities. It operates on a relatively fixed amount of capital that it obtains primarily from an initial issue and sale of a relatively fixed number of shares of its own stock to investors who become its proportionate fractional owners—its shareholders. This initial issue of shares normally is sold by the same methods used to distribute new issues of common stock.

Once the initial issue is sold, the company generally no longer offers its shares for sale nor does it typically repurchase or redeem its own shares. After the initial sale, its shares normally may be obtained or disposed of only by trading between investors—purchased or sold on an exchange or in the over-the-counter market, the same as shares of stock of other corporations.

Use of Capital

Like most other corporations, the closed-end company's principal purpose is to invest and manage its capital so as to maximize income or capital growth for its shareholders. About the only difference is the form of assets in which capital is invested. Instead of investing directly in land, plant, equipment, labor or inventory of its own (except to the very minor extent necessary), the typical investment company invests indirectly in these income and capital-growth producing factors of other organizations through ownership of their securities. Thus, the closed-end company's principal assets generally are the stocks or bonds of other corporations, governments or units of governments.

The company derives its earnings primarily from the dividends, interest or capital gains realized on those securities and its capital growth (or decline) from the appreciation (or depreciation) in total market value of all its securities holdings. These earnings, from which the company deducts its various fees and expenses, are the source of distributions paid to the closed-end investment company shareholders. The value of any one shareholder's ownership interest at any given time, at least for all practical purposes, is the amount for which he or she could sell the investment company shares on the open market at that moment (their *market value*), just as in the case of the common stock of other corporations.

Organization and Operation

The closed-end company has a board of directors, officers, executives and supplementary personnel to handle the functions and details that are common to any corporate business. In addition, because of the complex and volatile nature of its assets, the company employs securities analysts, advisers, managers and other securities specialists to aid in its constant effort to maintain the best possible portfolio of securities at all times, in keeping with its stated objectives. Fulfilling its stated objectives involves continuous management and supervision of its securities holdings: selecting, investing, eliminating and reinvesting. The company also handles all administrative and accounting details, collects investment income from dividends, interest or capital gains on its holdings and pays its salaries and other expenses. From its net earnings, it makes its own distributions (when and as declared by its directors) to its shareholders.

Characteristics of Closed-End Shares

As stated, closed-end investment company shares are virtually identical in almost every respect to shares of common stock of other corporations. Each share represents a unit of proportionate fractional ownership interest in the company.

Distributions

Holders of investment company shares actually receive two types of income distributions from the company: *dividends* and *capital gains*.

Dividends are paid from the net investment income of the company, that is, from net earnings realized by the company from dividends and interest on its securities holdings after deducting its expenses. Such dividends normally are declared and distributed quarterly. They are taxable to the shareholder the same as are any dividends paid by a corporation in another line of business. Of course, if the dividends arise from tax-exempt income (e.g., from municipal bond interest), they pass through to the shareholder on a tax-exempt basis.

Capital gains, on the other hand, are paid from net gains realized by the company on sales or exchanges of its portfolio securities. When available, capital gains distributions normally are declared annually. They are considered a return of capital that should be reinvested if the capital investment is to remain intact.

Reinvestment Option

A number of closed-end companies provide (at the shareholder's option) automatic reinvestment of capital gains, and sometimes of dividends, by automatically *selling* the shareholder equivalent additional company shares at net asset value or at the market offering price, depending on the company. Some companies actually declare capital gains distributions in shares, requiring action by shareholders to obtain cash.

For such purposes, a company may issue new shares, or may use previously issued shares that it has reacquired. In any event, whether paid in cash or reinvested, such distributions of either dividends or capital gains are considered to have been received immediately by the shareholders for income tax purposes.

Performance of Closed-End Shares

Both the income distribution and price performance patterns of closed-end shares are almost identical to those of common stocks because:

1. closed-end shares are closely akin to common stock;

2. the company's assets consist almost entirely of securities (chiefly common stock in most instances) of other organizations; and

3. its earnings are derived from those securities.

Consequently, the evaluation of these shares (for purposes of acquiring, holding or disposing of them as investment assets) should involve virtually the same considerations as the evaluation of stocks.

Closed-end shares, of course, provide the advantages of (1) broader diversification than most investors could obtain through direct purchases of individual stocks and (2) professional selection, supervision and administration of the underlying securities. On the other hand, the costs of providing these advantages must be recouped from earnings before the company makes distributions to shareholders.

■ OPEN-END INVESTMENT COMPANIES

Open-end companies (commonly called *mutual funds*) are by far the larger, as well as the more active and complex, of the two classes of management investment companies today. Most of these companies came into being after 1929, gaining a degree of popularity in the 1940s. But, in line with the general trend of our economy, these funds have been growing at an increasingly rapid rate since World War II. In the last 20 years there has been tremendous growth in both the number of mutual funds offered and the assets invested.

Why the movement of investor funds into mutual funds? Part of the answer lies in declining interest rates that may shake dollars out of bank instruments and into the higher yields of bond funds. Still, yield is secondary to some investors. Many choose to invest in mutual funds because of the array of choices in the marketplace. With more than 5,000 different mutual funds clamoring for investment dollars, there is a wide variety of new funds from which to choose—limited only by a port-folio manager's imagination.

Nature of Open-End Companies

An open-end, or mutual fund, company is set up to issue an unlimited number of shares. Investors actually buy from and sell back to the mutual fund itself. When investors buy into an open-ended mutual fund, the fund issues new shares of stock. The only restraint on the number of new shares issued is investor demand; techni-cally, there is no limit on the number of shares that may be issued. When a mutual fund investor wants to sell his or her shares, the company then buys them back. Consequently, there is no selling or buying among investors.

Like closed-end companies, most open-end companies have basically simple capi-tal structures. However, unlike the closed-end company, mutual funds have an ever-changing amount of capital with which to work. The continuous sales of new shares bring in new capital, while the continuous redemptions or buy-backs of previously issued shares are a drain on capital. When new sales exceed redemptions, the com-pany has net additional capital to invest. But when redemptions exceed new sales, there is a net reduction of capital, that is, the company must pay out the difference either from its cash assets, if sufficient, or by liquidating some of its securities holdings.

Once a mutual fund defines its objective, the portfolio is invested to match it. The objective must be clearly stated in the mutual fund's prospectus and can be changed only by a majority vote of the fund's outstanding shares. Typically, a mutual fund's portfolio will include 50 or more different stocks, bonds or options. Some mutual funds are limited to specific aspects of the world economy, such as international funds, which invest in foreign stock. Some mutual funds, called index funds, invest in securities to mirror a market index, such as the Standard & Poor's 500.

Use of Capital

The principal purpose of a mutual fund, like the closed-end company, is to maxi-mize income or growth (according to its stated objectives) for the benefit of its shareholders. In either type of company, assets are invested almost exclusively in the securities (chiefly common stocks) of other organizations. These securities are continuously managed and supervised to maintain the best portfolio possible.

Complexities are added in the case of a mutual fund, however, due to the ever-changing amount of capital it has to work with and its potential need for quick cash in the event that redemptions should exceed new sales at any future point in time. Selection of securities, for example, is involved in the investment and reinvestment not only of original capital but also of subsequent net additions to capital from new sales in excess of redemptions. Moreover, the mutual fund must select securities for liquidation from its own portfolio when redemptions exceed new sales.

Organization and Operation

The typical mutual fund is organized like most publicly owned corporations with a CEO, a team of officers and a board of directors, all in place to serve the interests of the investors. The four key players are described below.

1. The *board of directors* concerns itself with investment objectives, long-term strategy, portfolio funding, cash flow matters, accounting and business administration duties.

2. The board contracts with an outside *investment adviser* (portfolio manager) to invest the company's assets, implement investment strategy and manage the day-to-day trading of the portfolio. The fund's investment adviser may be an individual or an investment advisory company.

3. As a means of safeguarding investors' assets, the Investment Company Act of 1940 requires each investment company to place its securities in the custody of a bank (with assets of at least $500,000) or a stock exchange member firm. The *custodian* handles the clerical and safekeeping functions involved in issuing and redeeming mutual fund shares and holding the fund's portfolio.

4. The *underwriter* (often called the *sponsor* or *distributor*) markets fund shares, prepares sales literature and, in return, receives a percentage of the sales charge paid by the client. The underwriter's compensation is part of the sales load paid by the customer when shares are purchased. Sales fees are not part of the fund's expenses.

Characteristics of Open-End Shares

Open-end shares are similar to closed-end shares in almost every respect. Both represent fractional ownership in the diversified securities portfolios of their respective companies. Dividend and capital gains distributions are made to shareholders of both types of management companies in the same form and on virtually the same basis, generally with the option of automatic reinvestment in company shares. Federal income tax treatment is also the same as discussed earlier with respect to closed-end shares.

From the standpoint of the investor, the primary differences from closed-end shares are the way mutual fund shares are purchased and sold, and the costs of owning mutual fund shares.

Purchase and Sale

Mutual funds are purchased from and sold to (that is, redeemed by) the company:

- directly;

- through its principal underwriter; or

- through dealers working under arrangements with the company's principal underwriter.

ILL. 8.2 ■ *Classification of Investment Companies*

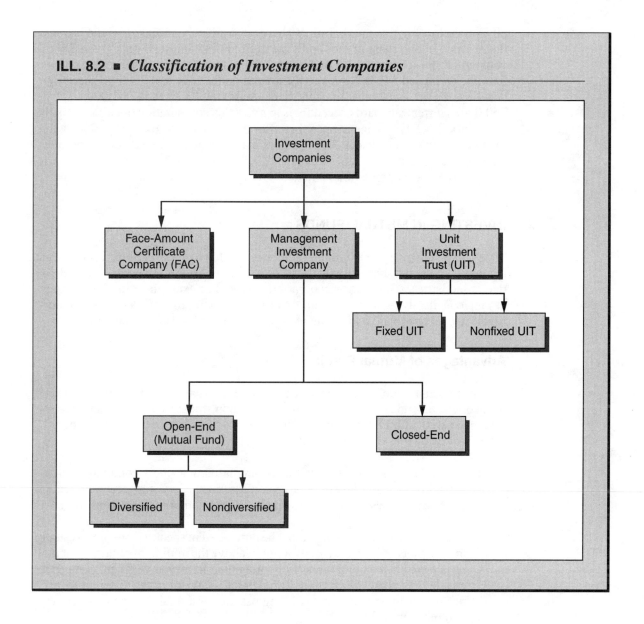

Mutual fund shares are subject to *continuous issue*, that is, the fund management company issues new shares to new fund investors. Thus, the shares are not traded between individuals, but may be *purchased through securities dealers* or *directly from the investment company.* The fund may charge a sales charge (or *load*) for the purchase or offer shares without a sales charge on a no-load basis. The sales charge compensates agents who sell or promote the fund. Fund management costs are paid from a percentage of the portfolio assets. Fund sales charges vary from a high of 8½ percent to less than 3 percent for a low load fund.

Mutual fund share prices are not subject to supply and demand. Rather, shares are priced according to what the underlying securities of the fund portfolio are worth. This price is stated as net asset value. The net asset value (NAV) per share is computed by dividing the fund's net assets (that is, the current market value of all its securities holdings plus an allowance for all its other assets, less an allowance for all its liabilities) by the number of its shares that are outstanding. It is the pro rata dollar value of one share of the fund's portfolio. For example, if on a given day the value of all the securities held by the ABC Fund (adjusted for other assets and its liabilities) equaled $10 million and if the fund on that day had 750,000 shares outstanding, the net asset value of each share would be $13.33 ($10,000,000 ÷ 750,000). Current standard procedure is to make this computation once each day the New York Stock Exchange is open, but after the close of the Exchange. This value then is used in pricing shares for all orders placed between the last prior computation and the current computation. Any subsequent orders received are held for pricing until the new computation is made.

■ INVESTING IN MUTUAL FUNDS

Today, there are over 5,000 mutual funds from which to choose. Some funds invest in stocks, some in bonds, some in both. Other mutual funds are geared toward particular industries, securities or geographic region. For example, a fund may invest in precious metals such as gold bullion or trade only mining stocks. While many funds take a conservative investment approach, some funds are speculative.

Advantages of Mutual Funds

The income and price performances of mutual fund shares are much the same as those of closed-end shares and as those of common stocks that usually serve as the principal assets of both types of management companies. Many investors cite at least five advantages of mutual funds over stock.

1. *Diversification.* Unlike stock that is purchased in a single company, mutual funds invest in a variety of securities, affording the investor greater protection from large losses; even if one security loses, another may perform well.

2. *Flexibility.* Unlike stock that must be purchased in specified amounts (usually in round lots of a hundred), any amount above the minimum requirement may be invested in a mutual fund. By pooling their money, investment companies enable their shareholders to hold fractional shares of many different securities—something that is virtually impossible for a small investor to achieve without a mutual fund.

3. *Professional management.* Fund managers (not a broker or the investor) decide what assets will be held or traded in the portfolio. They have access to more information than the average investor, including corporate annual reports and up-to-date information about a company's stock. In addition to buying and selling securities, fund managers provide status reports and other administration.

4. *Automatic reinvestment or payment.* Stock dividends are paid directly to the brokerage firm or investor; many mutual funds have automatic reinvestment options or, on request, will forward dividends to the investor in cash.

5. *Easy access to money.* When stock is sold, the investor usually waits five business days before the money can be released. Some mutual funds allow investors to write checks against money in the fund.

ILL. 8.3 ■ *Comparison of Stock and Mutual Funds as Investments*

	Stocks	Mutual Funds
What investor buys	Shares of a single company, usually in round lots of 100	Shares in the fund, which is a collection of securities
What it costs	Cost is determined by number of shares purchased and price	Any amount above the minimum investment can be purchased
Who controls the portfolio	Investor and broker determine when to buy or sell stock	Fund managers decide which assets are held and when to trade them. The investor decides when to buy or sell his or her shares in the fund
How dividends are received	Paid directly to stockholder or to brokerage firm	Reinvested in fund to buy more shares or paid to investor in cash
How liquid	After stock sale, investor waits five business days before money can be released	Money can be quickly transferred—often it is available at the end of the business day

Each investor should evaluate whether mutual funds are a better choice than purchasing individual stocks on the stock market. Moreover, whether or not funds collectively do better than the market, the investor may move his or her money from one fund to another—to counter business cycles—just as with other securities. Thus, a large portion of the responsibility for the overall results realized from investments in shares of managed investment funds remains with the investor.

Realizing a Return

Investors profit from mutual fund investments in three primary ways: through growth, through dividends or through capital gains distribution. *Growth*, as previously stated, results from the appreciation in value of the underlying assets in a mutual fund's portfolio. The gain is reflected in a rise in the NAV of fund shares, and investors profit when they redeem their shares.

The net investment income from stock dividends or bond interest on securities held in the fund's portfolio is passed through to shareholders as *dividends*. Dividends are most often paid quarterly through the fund's custodian. Investors often have a choice of reinvesting the funds, otherwise checks are sent to the investor.

If a fund realizes capital gains through the sale of securities, these profits may be distributed too. A capital gain is profit resulting from the sale of an asset and is distinguished from other types of profit for tax purposes. These profits are further distinguished as short-term and long-term capital gains. The profit (or loss) from the sale of an asset held for six months or less is *short-term*; all other gains are *long-term*. Short-term gains may be passed on to shareholders in the form of dividends or reinvested. Long-term gains are distributed no more than once a year to shareholders as a capital gains distribution.

Risks of Investing in Mutual Funds

There are risks associated with mutual funds. Mutual fund investors undertake a *financial* or *credit risk* of the principal investment. Funds are forbidden, by law, from guaranteeing the safety of the principal or a predicted rate of return. Some experts feel that placing all of one's investment funds in one fund—especially equity securities—is a gamble. Finally, investors must assume many of the same risks inherent in owning the underlying security. For example, bond funds are subject to the same interest rate risk as the underlying bonds.

Fund Performance

Some funds perform better than others given certain economic or political climates while others perform consistently, regardless of changes in the economy. Therefore, before investing in any mutual fund, the investor should consider the one-year, five-year and 10-year performances of the fund.

Mutual fund indexes, such as *Lipper Indexes*, provide information on the aggregate performance of a variety of groups of mutual funds over the past week. For example, the performance of growth funds, gold funds and international funds are evaluated. In addition to daily group indexes, financial newspapers also publish individual mutual fund ratings. However, the investor should remember that past performance does not guarantee a fund's future success or failure.

In addition to indexes, investors may consult a number of sources for information and guidance in choosing a fund. These sources include a broker, a financial planner, business magazines or specialized investment newsletters. For example, mutual fund investors may find *The Mutual Fund Encyclopedia* invaluable for identifying investment opportunities and analyzing a fund in depth. Each report includes analysis of a fund's risks and returns, performance history and portfolio compositions, plus insights into the fund manager's investment strategies. Many of these sources can provide investors with toll-free numbers to call for more information. In all cases, a fund must provide the potential investor with a prospectus before accepting any investment.

Prospectus

A fund must issue a prospectus that provides relevant information to potential investors before accepting their initial investment. The prospectus provides complete disclosure of information about the fund. To assist the investor, the table of contents on the cover of the prospectus outlines the relevant information, including the following:

- *Date*—a prospectus must be updated at least every 16 months.

- *Minimum investments*—initial investments (usually between $250-$1,000) and future minimum investments are specified.

- *Objective*—the objective of the fund (growth, income, etc.) is stated to help the investor determine whether it will meet the investor's own goals.

- *Performance*—a description of how the fund has performed in the past. (Note: this does not guarantee that the fund will continue to perform this way in the future.)

- *Risk*—a description of the level of risk inherent in the fund's objectives.

- *Features*—an outline of how the fund operates, how trades are made, whether and how dividends are reinvested, etc.

- *Fees*—indications of sales charge (*front-loaded* or *back-loaded*); its schedule of any *break points* or scale reductions in sales charges as assets increase; management fees; fees for withdrawing money and any additional fees.

Reading Mutual Fund Quotations

The daily performance of mutual funds is measured directly from the performance of stocks and bonds held in the fund. Under the heading of "Mutual Funds," the financial pages of daily newspapers and financial papers list the previous trading day's purchase and redemption prices per share for the various closed-end and open-end companies. The listing normally carries the name of the fund, the net asset value (the dollar value of one share of the fund's stock), the NAV change (the difference between today's net asset value quote and that of the previous day) and any load (the commission). If there is no commission, the *offer price* contains a NL entry, standing for "No Load" or no commission charged. The prices for the funds are given in dollars and cents.

From the latest published quotations, an investor can determine:

- approximately what his or her purchase or redemption price would be in a current share transaction;

- the immediate past trend in the share's redemption value; and

- the approximate sales charge per share (the difference between the NAV and the public offering price).

■ COSTS OF OWNING MUTUAL FUND SHARES

The ownership of mutual fund shares involves costs that differ (at least in appearance and mechanics, if not in fact) from the costs of owning closed-end shares. These costs are based on the fund's costs of doing business and providing its services. They may be divided (according to the stage of share ownership in which they occur) into purchase costs, holding costs and redemption costs.

ILL. 8.4 ■ *Reading Mutual Fund Quotations*

	NAV	Offer Price	NAV Chg.	Total Return YTD
First American CIA:				
AstAll p	10.51	NL	−0.04	NA
Balanced p	10.77	NL	−0.01	NA
EqIdxA p	10.71	NL	−0.05	NA
FxdInc p	10.90	NL	−0.02	NA
GovBd	9.32	NL	−0.01	NA
Intinc	9.91	NL	−0.02	NA
Ltdinc	9.97	NL	. . .	NA
MunBd	10.53	NL	−0.01	NA
MfgSec	10.19	NL	−0.01	NA
ReqEq	12.54	NL	+0.02	NA
SpecE p	16.21	NL	. . .	NA

1. The *sponsoring company's name* is listed first. Its funds appear below in alphabetical order:

    * A *p* after the fund name means the fund charges a fee for marketing and distribution costs.
    * An *r* after the fund name means the fund charges a fee (back-end load) to redeem shares for cash.

2. *NAV* means *net asset value*—the dollar value of one share of the fund's stock.

3. The offer price includes net asset value plus any commission or *load* that buyers pay.

    * When *NL*, standing for *No-Load,* appears, no commission is charged.

4. *NAV change*—the difference between today's net asset value and that of the previous day.

Purchase Costs

Mutual fund shares usually are purchased in dollar amounts—not by number of shares. For example, an investor normally would buy "$100,000 of ABC Fund shares"—rather than "200 shares" of ABC Fund. The number of whole and fractional shares purchased is determined by dividing the dollar amount invested by the public offering price per share. The public offering price typically includes a sales charge of 0 percent to 8½ percent (except no-load funds, which make no sales charge). Thus, a "$1,000 worth" purchase is reduced by, say, an 8 percent sales charge, or $80. That leaves $920 available for the purchase of fund shares at their net asset value. This purchase cost of owning shares is defined specifically in the fund's prospectus.

There is another purchase cost—the broker's *commission*—that the fund must pay out of the $920 before the remainder is invested in securities.

Holding Costs

While an investor holds mutual fund shares, he or she incurs certain *continuous costs* that normally are deducted from the fund's investment income before distributions of the remainder of that income are made to the investor. These costs include advisory or management fees, which usually run to about .5 percent of fund assets each year, and the operating costs of the fund, both of which were discussed previously.

Also, in its constant effort to maintain the best possible investment portfolio, the fund continuously is buying and selling portfolio securities. Each of these transactions normally is handled through a broker and calls for the regular broker's commission. These brokers' commissions, of course, represent costs to the investor while he or she is holding the shares.

Redemption Costs

When an investor redeems his or her shares, he or she normally receives an amount equal to the current NAV times the number of shares redeemed. The *redemption price* is the NAV next calculated after the investment company receives the redemption request (known as *forward pricing*). For example, if a request to redeem shares were received by the fund today, that redemption request would be held until the fund next calculates the NAV per share. If the request were received after today's calculation had been made, the redemption would occur at the next calculation. (Forward pricing applies to the purchase of fund shares as well.) The fund may charge the investor a redemption fee, which is usually ½ of 1 percent to 2 percent of the NAV.

It should be emphasized that the foregoing costs of owning mutual fund shares are legitimate business costs. These costs are entirely apart from any gains or losses experienced as a result of increases or decreases in the aggregate market value of the fund's portfolio securities. Such costs merely lessen the gains or increase the losses that the investor would realize if these costs were not involved in the ownership of shares. During a rising economy, increases in net capital to invest (that is, new share sales in excess of redemptions) and increases in market values of portfolio securities normally more than offset the costs of owning shares, resulting in net gains to shareholders.

■ INVESTMENT BY OBJECTIVES

Investment pools come in an extraordinary variety, with a diversity of objectives and policies. How does an investor choose among these options? As with other investments, the investor begins by outlining the investment goals he or she hopes to achieve, based on his or her own risk tolerance. For example, a conservative investor might be interested in preservation of capital with moderate income while a more speculative investor might seek high growth. Then, by studying the stated investment goals in the prospectuses of a number of funds on a comparative basis, it is possible for an investor to choose a fund to satisfy his or her own personal objectives.

Let's look at some of the most common types of mutual funds available.

Growth Funds

The stated investment objectives of a *growth fund* are short-term and long-term capital appreciation. Accordingly, they may invest primarily in growth or speculative stocks, blue chips or various combinations of any or all of these. Although some growth funds may also provide investors with some dividend income, it is usually insignificant.

Growth funds offer the potential for substantial gain over the long term with the safety of diversification. They generally outperform other funds in a rising market but can experience poor performance when the market declines. In addition, the investor must depend on the fund manager's ability to select good stocks.

Aggressive Growth Funds

One of the most volatile of all the types of funds, *aggressive growth funds* often buy stocks with relatively high price/earnings multiples, common stocks with highly erratic price shifts and options. The stated goal of these speculative funds is large profits from capital gains. As with other speculative investments, aggressive growth funds have the potential for tremendous gains—and losses.

Income Funds

Income funds emphasize current income and higher-than-average investment returns. Capital gains may be an incidental objective, which makes these funds conservatively oriented toward preserving principal. Income funds may seek to achieve their objectives by investing in *equity-income* funds—high-yielding stocks, some convertible securities and, occasionally, corporate bonds or government-insured mortgages. They generally offer a relatively high degree of safety of principal as well as above-average income, but usually are not too concerned with achieving growth. In general, equity-income funds are a fairly low-risk way of investing in stocks.

Aggressive Income Funds

Some of these funds may be *aggressive income funds* that attempt to pay the highest possible income. They are much the same as income funds, except that they may attempt to achieve their objective by investing in securities that are not popular, such as securities that are not well known or are thought to have above-average risks or to have a low-to-average growth potential—but which have relatively high dividend payout records.

Balanced Funds

Some investment companies' stated objectives include both current income and long-term capital gains. These funds invest in both stocks and bonds in a conservatively *balanced fund* strategy. They may invest more heavily in common stocks during periods that appear favorable or more heavily in bonds and preferred stocks when the economy appears less favorable, but at all times they maintain some balance between the two classes in their portfolios of investment holdings. Balanced funds generally are considered to follow more conservative policies than common stock funds, and consequently to be less volatile—showing smaller gains in rising markets and less declines in falling markets.

Growth-and-Income Funds

Like balanced funds, *growth-and-income funds* seek both long-term growth and current income by investing in both stocks and bonds. However, unlike balanced funds, growth-and-income funds tend to invest more heavily in equities such as growth-oriented, blue-chip stocks and high-quality income stocks. Because of the emphasis on long-term capital gains, these funds are more risky than balanced funds and, therefore, are suited for investors with more risk tolerance.

Bond Funds

Pooled investment funds that confine their investments to bonds (sometimes specializing in transportation issues or high-grade, medium-grade or low-grade bonds) are called *bond funds*. Some funds of this type invest exclusively in municipal bonds that pay dividends that are excluded from federal income tax. Since those tax-exempt dividends pass through to the fund shareholders in the same way, these funds are primarily for investors seeking tax-exempt income.

Money Market Funds

A type of pooled investment fund that has grown rapidly and to such great size in recent years that it deserves special note is the *money market fund*. These funds invest in short-term, high-grade government and corporate securities, combining a high degree of safety of principal with a reasonably good interest rate—generally much higher than that on typical savings accounts. Thus, they are especially good for people who need a temporary "parking place" for savings or investment funds, or for interest-bearing checking accounts.

Investors earn income by receiving interest on the money the fund lends on a short-term basis (through the purchase of money market securities) to various companies and governmental bodies. Because money market securities are short-term, the rate of interest fluctuates daily, and the investor cannot predict how much interest he or she will earn on any given day. Although it is possible to earn more interest through another investment, money market funds are a relatively safe investment with a steady return.

International Funds

Over the past several years, many investors have chosen *international funds* (which invest in foreign securities) and *global funds* (which combine foreign and U.S. securities). The investment goals of these funds include capital appreciation and dividend income. Because these funds are impacted by the international economy, balance of trade and currency devaluations, the investor should have at least a basic understanding of what these issues are and how they may affect the funds' return. In addition to the same risk inherent in U.S. stocks, for example, foreign stocks hold the added risk of currency fluctuations. If the value of the U.S. dollar falls, other currencies usually rise, giving foreign securities a better return. Of course, if the value of the U.S. dollar rises, foreign securities will provide less return than U.S. securities.

Specialty Funds

Specialty funds are pooled investment funds that have special objectives—objectives normally varying substantially from those of the funds mentioned above—or that have special investment policies or methods, or that invest exclusively in special kinds of assets, industries or geographic areas. Following are typical examples.

- *Sector funds.* Each fund focuses only on a particular industry, such as computer equipment, defense, medical technology or electronics.

- *Option funds.* These are funds that trade in options and sometimes sell options on their own portfolios.

- *Convertible securities funds.* These funds are based on portfolios of convertible stocks and bonds.

- *Venture capital funds.* Such funds rely on high-risk investments in new businesses.

- *REITs.* Discussed in Chapter 9, *real estate investment trusts (REITs)* are specialized pooled investment funds, very much like closed-end management investment companies, which invest in real estate properties or mortgages instead of securities.

The foregoing are examples of the most common, but certainly not the only, pooled investment funds operating today. There undoubtedly are and will be many others, for every new investment idea that becomes popular seems to also become the basis for such a fund.

■ INVESTMENT STRATEGIES

As stated earlier, investors should approach mutual funds with a broad objective such as long-term growth or current income. They can then match their resources and objectives with available funds. It is advisable that the investor have some familiarity with how a fund invests to accomplish its stated objective. That way, when reviewing the securities listed in a fund's prospectus, an investor can decide if the investments are consistent with the fund's objectives. In addition, by studying prospectuses and performance records over time, investors can troubleshoot a bit by paying particular attention to a fund's performance in down markets. In the case of equity funds, this includes *bear market* cycles.

Investors who want income while sustaining a level of growth have two choices with funds: buy a combination fund or invest in two different ones. For example, they could place 60 percent of their capital in an income fund and 40 percent in a growth fund. Capital earmarked for high risk can be placed in a maximum capital gains growth fund or a high-yield bond fund. These funds require more attention than others, but can return high yields under certain conditions.

Those investors who want to shield a portion of their investment income from taxes can do so with municipal bonds funds. The yield may be slightly below corporate bond funds, but may prove more profitable if the investor figures tax-equivalent yield. (*Tax-equivalent yield* indicates what interest rate an investor must earn on a fully taxable investment if the investment is to compete with a municipal bond. It takes into account the individual's tax bracket and the yield to maturity on the two investments.) Investors may also choose money market funds comprised of municipal bonds with short maturities.

A program of dollar-cost averaging—a method of buying shares on a regular basis—can build an investor's equity. Investors merely pay a fixed amount into the fund at regular intervals, regardless of the shares' net asset value. This strategy enables the investor to acquire more shares when a fund is selling at a low price.

Mutual fund investments work well in retirement programs like Individual Retirement Accounts or Keogh accounts. Income and safety would be typical objectives for such accounts. Investors could consider (in order of their relative safety) U.S. government funds, money market mutual funds or corporate bond funds. The long-term nature of the investment permits investors to buy in and then merely sit on the shares until retirement. Also, dividends or distributions of capital can be reinvested and taxed after retirement.

■ SUMMARY

Pooled investment vehicles offer individual investors the opportunity to invest in large, diversified portfolios. Many investors with broad objectives such as long-term growth or current income select mutual funds. They can match their resources and objectives with available funds in that area. In most instances, an astute investor will know how much risk he or she is undertaking by identifying the fund's objective. The key to selecting a good fund is to look at the fund's objectives, the quality of its underlying portfolio and to concentrate on good, steady performers. Whatever the budget, tastes or temperament of the investor, there is a fund that is an approximate fit.

In the next chapter, we'll look at an investment that is closely tied to the American dream—the possibility of owning property or a parcel of land. We'll briefly touch on personal homeownership, but we'll primarily look at the risks and rewards of investing in raw land, trusts REITs, real estate limited partnerships and rental property.

■ CHAPTER 8 QUESTIONS FOR REVIEW

1. All of the following statements regarding an open-end management company are true EXCEPT

   A. it manages a diversified portfolio of securities in accordance with specified objectives that are stated in a prospectus

   B. it issues redeemable securities that give the mutual fund holder a right to share in that company's assets

   C. its mutual fund shares are bought and sold on securities exchanges

   D. its mutual fund shares are bought and sold on a continuous basis

2. Unit investment trusts

   A. seldom change their underlying portfolios

   B. sell redeemable interests in units of specified securities

   C. sometimes have all their assets in a single security

   D. All of the above

3. The net asset value of a mutual fund share is the

   A. difference between today's net asset value quote and that of the previous day

   B. pro rata dollar value of one share in the fund's portfolio

   C. fee paid when the fund is bought or sold

   D. dollar value of one share of stock less the sales charge

4. The primary difference between open-end and closed-end management companies is in the way they

   A. diversify their investments

   B. manage their investment portfolios

   C. raise money from investors

   D. achieve their investment goals

5. Funds that invest in short-term, high-grade government and corporate securities are called

   A. money market funds

   B. global funds

   C. leverage funds

   D. option funds

9
Investing in Real Estate

O wnership of real estate—or of various rights and interests in real estate—is one of the most prevalent financial investments. Much of the reason for this widespread ownership stems from one of the oldest, most fundamental objectives—the almost universal desire to own one's own home, the land that one farms or the ground and buildings used in the operation of one's own business. Because land is a limited resource, many people argue that real estate is as secure and solid as any investment that can be made. Others feel that investing in real estate is speculative, not unlike investing in commodities. In reality, although it can be profitable for experienced investors with large amounts of capital to invest, real estate investments can create problems for the novice with limited funds.

The overall subject of real estate is simply too expansive to be covered in one chapter. Therefore, it is primarily with the investment aspects of various properties that this chapter is concerned. We begin with a definition of real estate and a discussion of it as an income-producing asset. We will then examine the different rights and interests in real estate and the advantages and disadvantages of owning real estate. Finally, the use of real estate as an investment is analyzed.

■ ■ ■ ■ ■

■ DEFINITION OF REAL ESTATE

Real estate is commonly defined as land at, above and below the earth's surface, including all things permanently attached to it, whether natural or artificial. Thus real estate includes the underlying soil and any substances below the earth's surface such as oil and minerals, things attached to the earth's surface by nature, such as trees and water, items erected in a permanent manner on the ground, such as houses and office buildings and the airspace above the land. In addition, real estate includes permanent *improvements* on or to the land, such as streets, sewers and other additions to the land that make it suitable for building. Finally, real estate is *real property*, which means there are certain legal interests, benefits and rights inherent in its ownership. For example, real property ownership permits the landowner to sell all or part of his or her interest in the property. Therefore, a landowner could sell the rights to natural resources lying below the earth's surface.

Items not included in the description above—such as automobiles, furniture, appliances, equipment and other movable goods and articles—generally are considered to be *personal property*, or *chattels*, and not real estate. However, there are some common exceptions. For example, you might think a crop requiring annual cultivation would be real property or real estate; actually, it is personal property, not part of the real estate. A standing tree is part of the real estate but when felled, it becomes personal property. Stoves, refrigerators, store counters and other such movable items normally are considered to be personal property, but when a landlord furnishes these items with real estate leased to a tenant, they are considered to be part of the real estate.

Moreover, articles such as furnaces, water heaters and storm windows, which are personal property before attachment, generally become *fixtures* or part of the real estate when added and permanently attached to the real estate, whether attached by the owner, a tenant or someone else (even if by mistake).

■ RIGHTS AND INTERESTS IN REAL ESTATE

In addition to the physical real estate itself, there are untold numbers of rights and interests (often called *the bundle of rights*) in any given piece of real estate, and every whole or fractional one of those rights and interests belongs to somebody—that is, to an individual, a partnership, an association, a corporation, a government, a unit of government or some other entity.

The whole bundle of rights may belong to one entity, or the bundle may be broken up in virtually any way, with the various rights or groups of rights distributed among any number of entities. It is the possession and exercise of such rights, whether as one, a group or the whole bundle, that provides the basis for the many forms of real estate investment.

Although there are some others, the principal rights and interests in real estate (especially as related to investments) may be divided into three major types, according to how they are held.

1. *Ownership rights*—rights associated with owning real estate;

2. *Leasehold rights*—rights associated with renting or leasing real estate; and

3. *Lien rights*—rights associated with holding a lien against a mortgage on real estate.

Let's look at each of these rights in more detail.

Ownership Rights

To the extent of the real estate he or she holds, and within the limits of the law, the *owner* of real estate has the right to do almost anything that he or she wishes with the property. This includes the right to possess and enjoy it, use it, improve it, lease it, sell it, give it away or pass it on to others at death. It should be noted that the owner of real estate necessarily does not have the whole bundle of rights in the property. Certain rights may be held by others, such as the rights represented by any outstanding leases, liens or easements, with respect to the property. Such rights may have carried over when the property was conveyed to the owner or may have been given up voluntarily or involuntarily during his or her ownership of the property.

Moreover, the nature of improvements, the use or the disposition the owner makes with respect to the property may be limited by building codes, zoning ordinances, anti-nuisance laws or restrictive provisions in the deed conveying ownership to him or her. Except to the extent that any such rights are outstanding or are withheld from the owner, however, he or she generally has full rights in the property. In addition, the owner usually may divide the property and carry over all the aforementioned rights in each of the parts separately.

Leasehold Rights

Leasehold rights in real estate refer to the rights of a tenant who is renting or leasing the property. Subject to payment of rent by the tenant to the landlord, in accordance with their agreement, the tenant (or lessee) has the right of possession of the real estate he or she leases. During the tenancy, the tenant may do almost anything he or she wishes with the property or his or her interest in it, provided that such action is not contrary to the law or to the covenants and implied restrictions of the lease.

One implied restriction applying to all tenants is that a tenant cannot commit *waste*, that is, cannot do anything that will injure or diminish the value of the property interest that will revert back to the landlord once the tenancy is concluded. Normal depreciation (as by time and reasonable wear from proper use) is not considered to be waste since allowance for such depreciation is considered proper in determining the value of a reversionary interest. In other words, the *reversionary value* is the expected worth of a property at the end of the anticipated holding period. Moreover, like the property owner, a tenant is subject to pertinent legal restrictions or limitations with respect to property, such as building codes, zoning ordinances, anti-nuisance laws and so on.

Lien Rights

In general, a *lien* against real estate is a claim against property that has been pledged or mortgaged to secure an obligation. A lien arises because the property owner owes a debt to the holder of the lien. The lien holder has a right to satisfaction of the debt and to obtain such satisfaction from the proceeds of a sale of the property, if the debt has not been satisfied in some other way prior to the sale. If the debt is not otherwise satisfied within a reasonable time, the lien holder generally has the right to *foreclose*, that is, to force the sale of the property to obtain payment of the debt from the sale proceeds. If there is more than one lien against the property, to the extent of the sale proceeds, the liens are satisfied in the order of priority established by state law, normally in the chronological order in which the liens were recorded. In addition, the lien holder generally may transfer the lien (with all the interests and rights it represents) to another. For example, he or she can sell it, give it away or pass it on to heirs by will or by the laws of descent.

As shown in Ill. 9.1, there are basically two types of real estate investments: direct and indirect. *Direct* real estate investments are those in which the investor holds legal title to the property. *Indirect* real estate investments involve a trust, appointed

---

ILL. 9.1 ■ *Types of Real Estate Investments*

Direct	Indirect
• Personal residence	• Real estate syndicates
• Vacation home	• Limited partnerships
• Timeshares	• Real estate investment trusts
• Commercial property	• Real estate mortgage investment conduits
• Raw land	• Participation certificates

---

on behalf of a group of investors, and whose property titles are legally held by the trustee.

■ REAL ESTATE AS AN INVESTMENT

Real estate investments tend to be classified as either direct or indirect investments. A *direct investment* is one in which the investor holds legal title or legal right of ownership to the property. These investments typically include residential property, vacation homes, timeshares (an interval ownership in the use of a vacation home for a limited, preplanned time), raw land and commercial property. In an *indirect investment*, investors appoint a trustee to hold legal title on behalf of all the investors in a group. These investments typically include limited partnerships, real estate investment trusts and mortgage pools.

As noted earlier, much of the direct ownership of real estate stems from the desire to own one's own home, one's own land or the buildings used in the operation of one's own business. Satisfaction of this objective, aside from rent- freedom, a hedge against inflation and certain other considerations, imparts a special *intrinsic* value to property owned for personal use and enjoyment. It is an extra, nonmonetary value that usually is not reflected in the market value of the property and has little or nothing to do with the income-producing value of the property as an investment.

By far, the most significant and universal example of the intrinsic value of direct real estate ownership is *home ownership*. But in addition to the pride, security and satisfaction of owning one's own home, there are a number of financial benefits as well. These benefits include the deductibility of mortgage interest and real estates taxes for federal income tax purposes. Homeowners also may be able to borrow against the *equity* in their homes—the value of the home less the amount still owed on the mortgage. This allows greater flexibility for undertaking other investments.

Home ownership accounts for a large amount of total real estate held and continues to provide an excellent store of value for most people. However, the following discussion will apply more particularly to real estate held for investment purposes rather than as private residences.

Current Income

Many risk-tolerant investors are interested in purchasing or developing real estate for the purpose of increasing their current income or *cash flow*. They often purchase *rental income property*, which could consist of apartment buildings, office buildings, hotels, motels, shopping centers and industrial properties.

Historically, the value of any income-producing property has been measured by the cash flow returns that it generates. To earn an adequate return, the investor attempts to:

- collect rent that is reasonable for the area;

- keep operating expenses (general maintenance, repairs, utilities, taxes and tenant services) reasonably low; and

- spread his or her mortgage payments over a long period of time, which allows the investor to retain more money each month that can, in turn, be invested in other ways.

Appreciation

A second reason to invest in real estate is that the general trend is for land to increase continuously in value. For one thing, there is a *limited supply* of land. Consequently, as with virtually everything that is limited in total amount, land becomes more valuable as more of it is used and less of it is available. At the same time, the *demand* for the limited supply of land is increasing. As the population and number of families grow, more and more people need places to live and work. Moreover, the increasing population and a higher standard of living create an ever-greater demand for food, clothing and other raw materials that directly or indirectly come from the land, and thus increase the demand for it and its value.

Land tends to increase in value, and so do *improvements* on the land. This is especially true if such improvements are designed properly for intended use, are well constructed, are in good condition and are located conveniently. The increasing costs of new construction make existing houses and plants (assuming they meet the above criteria) more desirable, and thus make such improved property more valuable with time, in spite of possible depreciation.

Leverage

An initial real estate investment may also be used to create tremendous wealth. Many investors finance the bulk of a real estate investment with borrowed money. The investor employs *leverage* by making a small down payment, paying a low interest rate and spreading mortgage payments over a long period of time. When the asset is sold, the investor hopes to gain a return that is measured against the actual cash invested in the property. For example, assume an investor purchases a rental property for $200,000, makes a $40,000 down payment and then sells the property five years later for $250,000. In this case, the investor earns a return of 125 percent or $50,000 (less any costs of ownership). The return ($50,000) is compared to the original amount invested ($40,000), not to the original purchase price ($200,000).

In some cases, investors use *pyramiding* to increase their real estate holdings without borrowing additional cash. With pyramiding, the investor uses *equity buildup*—the portion of the mortgage payment directed toward the principal rather than the interest—and *appreciation* in already-owned properties to purchase additional real estate without investing any additional capital. For example, assume an investor purchases a building for $100,000 by making a down payment of $20,000 and taking on an $80,000 mortgage. Over the life of the mortgage, the principal payments on the remaining debt increase the investor's *equity*—the value in the property over and above the investor's mortgage indebtedness. The owner of the real estate reduces the principal balance on the mortgage while the property appreciates, so the *equity buildup* in the property can be used to make other real estate investments. Over time, the investor can hold large numbers of heavily mortgaged property worth millions of dollars.

Although leverage and pyramiding increase potential profits, they also increase risk because *debt service* must be allowed from the investment's cash flow or from additional capital paid in by the investors. In other words, the amount of money needed to meet the periodic payments of principal and interest on a loan or debt (the debt service) must be included in the cost of owning the real estate.

Tax Benefits

Finally, real estate investments have long been popular because of their *tax benefits*. The federal government encourages home ownership by allowing homeowners to deduct real estate taxes and certain other expenses from income. In certain cases, they may also defer or eliminate tax liability on the profit from the sale of a home. For example, homeowners can exclude the first $500,000 of profit (capital gain) on the sale of a home if they are married, and single homeowners can exclude the first $250,000. These homeowners must have lived in the home as their primary residence for two of the last five years, ending on the date of the sale.

Although some of the tax laws now limit the deductibility of losses generated by real estate investments to shelter income, there are still some tax advantages to owning investment property. An investor may recover the cost of an income-producing property that depreciates and loses value over time by taking *depreciation* or *cost recovery* on personal property, improvements and the building itself. This cost recovery is taken periodically over the asset's useful life.

Generally, a certified public accountant or another tax specialist should be consulted for further information about tax benefits.

Disadvantages of Investing in Real Estate

Although real estate is perceived to be a mainstay of value, investment in real estate does have some disadvantages. For example, owning income property can be *time-consuming and expensive*. Even with careful research and an adequate knowledge of real estate, the beginning investor will need expert advice when purchasing and managing property. To make the income property profitable, the investor will have to make informed decisions about how much rent to charge, how to handle tenants' complaints, when to make capital improvements and so on. This may simply be too much for the average investor to handle.

An important point to note here is that real estate, both improved and unimproved, tends to appreciate in value and to show profit when sold at some future date. However, real estate investments may actually *decline in value* for a number of reasons including the following:

1. *General economic conditions.* When inflation increases, there is more money in circulation, which decreases its value and results in an overall increase in wholesale and retail prices. During recessions or depressions, the market values of virtually everything, including real estate, may go down.

2. *Dislocations within the economy.* When an industry slumps, the home values in the area tend to decline. For example, when oil prices fell between 1984 and 1986, major metropolitan areas such as Dallas and Houston were hard hit.

3. *Decline in productive capacity.* Real estate that has been mismanaged, such as farmland that has chemical burnout, may be unable to produce crops and may lose its market value.

4. *Physical damage or deterioration.* The value of real estate declines when the property suffers physical damage or deterioration, such as fire damage or corrosion by salt spray to coastal property.

5. *Depletion.* This is a special kind of cost amortization arising from the reduction in size or quantity of measurable natural resources such as oil, gas, other minerals or timber from the real estate in question.

6. *Obsolescence due to shift in demand.* When updating capital improvements is required to compete, a property's market value has been (and still is being) depreciated by obsolescence. For example, an older hamburger chain's restaurants may look dated and lack the service speed of a Wendy's or a McDonald's restaurant.

7. *Illiquidity.* There are times when real estate is relatively *difficult to liquidate* for its current value, especially if the transaction must be accomplished quickly. Because it is unusual to complete a real estate sale in a day or two, the property owner may have to take a substantial loss to sell a property quickly.

8. *Shifts in the global economy.* Changes in the economic status of other countries also affect the value of real estate in the United States because U.S. values may be hurt (or helped) when economies in other countries stumble or rise. For example, the rise of the deutsche mark is bearish for real estate because it cuts the U.S. inflation rate. Those areas of the United States that expect to experience population growth because of international trade and distribution will prosper.

■ CLASSIFICATION OF REAL ESTATE

All real estate may be classified as either *government owned* (such as land not yet granted, land reclaimed for tax delinquency, roadways and right-of-ways, parks and preserves, schools, military bases and other government land, buildings and installations) or as *privately owned*. Because real estate investments generally are based on the latter, this discussion is limited to privately owned real estate.

Broadly classified, privately owned real estate is either *urban* or *rural*. Each of these classes may be subclassified according to improvements, use, quality, location or special characteristics. Most pieces of real estate may be placed in one or another of the following typical categories.

Urban Property

Real property lying within a town or city, or in the immediate environs of a town or city and having the general characteristics of town or city property, normally is termed *urban real estate*. Obviously, there are several kinds of real property commonly found in this broad urban class.

Unimproved Land

When there is no permanent-type building or structure on a piece of land in an urban area, that property usually is referred to as *unimproved real estate*. Typical examples are vacant lots in otherwise generally developed residential, business or factory areas, and tracts or subdivisions of undeveloped urban or suburban land that are potential sites for residential, commercial or industrial building. Temporary use of such land for garden plots or parking lots, or even erection of temporary buildings on the land to facilitate those activities, does not remove this land from the unimproved category. In fact, much unimproved land is utilized in that manner.

Residential

An urban one-to-four-family dwelling generally is classified as a *residential property*. This includes the house and fixtures, any fences or outbuildings appurtenant to the property, the piece of land upon which the foregoing are erected and any trees or shrubs growing on that land. Typical is the single-family house and lot, but doubles, triplexes and quadruplexes are not uncommon, especially in larger metropolitan areas.

Apartment Buildings

A building employed to provide housing (as contrasted with overnight or short-term lodging) and divided into more than four dwelling units is classified as an *apartment building*. Each dwelling unit (apartment) may consist of one room or a set of several rooms. The real estate generally includes the building and grounds, the fixtures and, as previously mentioned, any stoves or refrigerators provided as part of the apartment by the landlord.

Condominiums

As intended here, the term *condominium* is used two ways: (1) to mean one or more multiple-family dwellings (similar to apartment houses), or a group of single-family dwellings (similar to individual houses), where each dwelling unit is legally considered and treated as an individual piece of real estate, but where ownership of each unit usually also includes a proportionate, undivided ownership interest in the remainder of the building(s), fixtures and grounds and (2) to mean a unit in such a complex.

Commercial Real Estate

Real estate (including the land, buildings, fixtures, etc.) principally employed or designed (or having such potential by virtue of its nature or location) for occupancy by sales and service-type businesses, or by professional and business offices, is classified generally as *commercial real estate*.

Typical examples of commercial real estate are the properties occupied by businesses in the downtown area of a town or city, along thoroughfares leading from the downtown area and in shopping areas in outlying neighborhoods or communities of the town or city. Vacant lots (and other properties convertible to business use) that lie in these areas or that have future business use potential, usually are classed as *unimproved* commercial real estate.

In this category, properties housing retail, wholesale and service stores or shops are most common, but also included are office buildings, hotels and motels, bowling alleys and other commercially operated recreational facilities, restaurants, beauty and barber shops and service stations. More recent developments are the professional office buildings and shopping centers that generally are located in suburban areas or enroute to or from suburban residential areas. A *professional building* for example, may house a host of offices for doctors, dentists and related professions and services. A *shopping center* normally consists of one large piece of commercial real estate that, within a single architectural plan, provides housing for a number of stores and shops supplying most of the basic shopping needs of a relatively large community.

Industrial

Real property used in connection with the manufacturing and warehousing of goods (or having such potential by virtue of its nature or location) generally is classified as *industrial real estate*. Typical examples are factories, plants, foundries, cement and metalworks, coal yards, lumberyards, oil refineries, chemical plants and warehouses. Such businesses generally must be located where transportation and other needed facilities are convenient. Traditionally, this means near railroad tracks or waterways as well as reasonably close to the hub of the city where power, gas and water mains, sewage facilities, fire and police protection and suppliers and consumers are readily accessible. Consequently, industrial property tends to border downtown commercial property on the sides near tracks or waterways.

Unoccupied Slum Housing and Businesses

These include the condemned and deserted tenements and other ancient, run-down dwellings and commercial or industrial properties that are in unusable states of repair—sometimes virtually rubble—and that generally are located in the oldest inner-city sections. Except for tax angles, these properties may have "values" less than zero. Nonetheless, they are often purchased at tax sales on the premise that "anything that cheap can only go up in value."

Rural Property

Real property that is not within an urban area and that does not have the general characteristics of urban property normally is classified as *rural real estate*. There are several subclasses of rural real estate, the most common of which are mentioned here. Some rural properties fall in more than one, or partly in one and partly in another, subclass.

Raw Land

The term *raw land* is used to mean land that is not currently fit for any use, such as desert, badlands or wasteland that is platted and sold. It is sometimes miles from the nearest access road, drinkable water, food or other sign of civilization. People may buy this land on sheer speculation, hoping to realize a profit on some suspected future development.

Farm and Ranch

A farm or ranch is a piece of rural real estate used primarily for agricultural purposes—such as the cultivation of crops, the raising of livestock, the production of milk or eggs or any combination of these. The land and any house, fixtures, outbuildings, structures, fences or trees on the land are all part of the farm or ranch. The typical *farm* is devoted chiefly to the cultivation of such crops as corn, wheat and the like, though this category also includes such specialty farms as livestock feeding lots, dairy farms, poultry farms, orchards, citrus groves, vineyards and berry farms.

Ranches, of course, typically are cattle-raising or sheep-raising operations, sometimes involving thousands of acres per spread. Where irrigation has become available in relatively recent times, however, many ranches now raise some other crops—sugar beets, vegetables, grains and so on. In addition, many ranches have untold oil and mineral resources below their grazing and growing surface land. Some of those resources are being exploited currently, others are reserved by oil and mineral rights, and still others are just there, awaiting whatever happens in the future.

Timberland/Oil or Mineral Land

Land principally covered with timber-producing forests is classified as *timberland*. The standing trees and any improvements on the land are included as part of the real estate. Land substantially valued for the oil or minerals it contains or that lie beneath its surface, whether such oil or minerals are being extracted or merely known (or believed) to exist, is classified as *oil or mineral land*. This does not preclude secondary or collateral use of the land for grazing, farming or recreational purposes, as indicated earlier. Any unextracted oil or minerals in the land, any trees or shrubs growing on the land and any improvements (buildings, fixtures, structures, fences, etc.) thereon are all part of the real estate.

Recreational

Some rural real estate is used for *recreational* purposes, that is, to provide sites for facilities for camping, picnicking, hiking, hunting, fishing, bird-watching, swimming, boating, skiing and skating. In some cases, these recreational sites occupy only a portion, or represent collateral use, of a piece of real estate that otherwise falls into another subclass, such as a farm or a tract of timberland. Or sometimes, the purpose is just plain space—which is popular with some, especially environmentalists.

Timesharing. One of the newer trends in real estate is *timesharing*, which allows investors to buy into a resort complex and vacation there for a limited, preplanned period each year. The investor may purchase one of two types of timeshares: a fee simple or a right to use timeshare. Under a *fee simple (or deeded) timeshare*, the investor receives a part interest in the property and his or her ownership interest is prorated according to the number of weeks purchased. The owner has the right to sell, lease or bequeath his or her interest in the unit. However, under the *right to use* arrangement, the investor has no ownership rights. He or she buys a lease, license or membership for the resort that entitles the investor to use a certain unit for a specific number of years.

The costs of timeshares are relatively fixed and it is possible that the unit will appreciate in value. In fact, many timeshares have been resold at substantial profits. However, financing a timeshare may be difficult and the annual maintenance fees may rise more than originally projected.

ILL. 9.2 ■ *Selecting Real Estate Investments*

Before purchasing property, the investor should carefully weigh the costs, advantages and disadvantages of owning the property. A few of the areas to address are outlined below.

- Assess the investment potential of a property by calculating the total cost of holding the land, including the financing payments, property taxes, insurance and other costs *less* any income that can be derived from holding the property.

- Consider uses to which the land may be put. Avoid land or property that offers no reasonable prospect of being anything more than cheap land.

- Determine whether there are any city, county or state development plans that could enhance the value of the property to be purchased.

- Ask about access to the property: Are there roads or highways? If not, will roads be added, and who will pay for them?

- Have the property appraised for both its current value and its potential future value by an independent real estate appraiser.

- Have all verbal promises put in writing.

- Carefully check the property for vegetation, view, terrain and drainage.

Vacation Homes. Investors may also purchase *vacation homes* in resort areas. These homes provide owners with potential rental income and tax benefits, as well as the use of the residence on a limited basis. When the property is sold, the owner may realize a gain. As with all rental properties, vacation home rentals present some risks. They may be costly to purchase and maintain, difficult to rent and troublesome to sell. In addition, the times when the vacation home is most in demand—summers and Christmas vacation—are usually when the owner would most like to use it.

■ NATURE OF REAL ESTATE INVESTMENTS

To the extent that profit motives are involved, the acquiring, holding, using or disposing of any of the previously discussed rights and interests in real estate is an investment activity. Thus, there generally is an element of investment in homeownership or ownership of property for other personal or business uses. But it is with situations where profits (income or capital gains) are the sole or predominant motives that we are primarily concerned here.

There are untold numbers of ways that the various rights and interests in real estate are used as the basis for investment. Virtually all investments in real estate may be categorized as attempts to realize:

1. *income* resulting from rents from leasing the rights or interests;

2. *appreciation* in the value of the rights or interests; or

3. a combination of income and appreciation.

Several of the typical methods of investing in each of these categories, together with some of the more important factors and considerations involved in each method, are discussed next.

Investing for Income

When *income* is the primary motive for investing in real estate, it is common for the investor to own and manage the property that he or she leases to tenants in return for rent. Traditional income-producing property includes apartment and office buildings, hotels, motels, shopping centers and industrial properties. Because of the variety of rental properties available, it's likely an investor can find one that fits his or her financial needs and risk tolerance.

Typically, the investor must meet his or her mortgage obligation plus certain *operating costs*, including general maintenance of the building, repairs, utilities and taxes. Despite these expenses, rental real estate can provide good current income or cash flow from operations. The investor's *cash flow* is the total amount of money remaining after all expenditures have been paid, including operating costs, taxes and mortgage payments. An investor's available cash may be used for spendable income, to purchase fixed assets, to pay taxes or reduce liabilities. A *negative cash flow* results when the cash flow from rents is less than needed to cover expenses.

Many investors determine a *target rental amount* that they must charge to generate an adequate return on their investment. That is, they will invest in a parcel of real estate only if they believe annual rentals will equal or exceed, say, 10 percent of their investment outlay in the property. In estimating the net rental from any given piece of real estate, there are many considerations.

Gross Rental

Typically, the starting point in estimating the net rental is estimating the *gross rental* that tenants reasonably can be expected to pay for the property. Factors that may affect current and future demand for a property include the type of property (house, apartment, business, farm, etc.), the condition and desirability of the property, the location, the number of potential tenants for the property, the general and local economic conditions and trends and the rate and direction of expansion in the area. For dwelling property, the gross rent usually must be in line with rents for comparable properties in the locality. Generally, comparable property rent is also a factor in determining gross rent for a farm or business property, although the income productivity of the farm or business frequently is another major rent-determining factor.

Charges Against Gross Rent

Once the expected gross rent has been determined, the next step is estimating the costs involved (i.e., the costs that should be charged against gross rent). The difference between gross rent and these costs, of course, is the *estimated net rental*, which represents either an estimated profit or an estimated loss. Unless the estimated net rental for a given property is on the plus side by a substantial margin, an investment in the particular property should be avoided. Most knowledgeable investors would want a favorable margin for error.

The following are among the most common and important (but not necessarily the only) costs that should be considered as charges against gross rent.

- *Maintenance costs.* These include the costs of *upkeep and repairs* required to maintain the property in suitable condition for leasing: needed repairs or replacement of plumbing or electrical fixtures, heating or cooling systems, roof, windows, doors, external painting and interior redecorating. Also included in this cost category are premiums for the property and liability insurance.

- *Management costs.* Some investors personally manage their rental properties; many, however, employ *property managers*. Property managers handle virtually all business aspects of rental property: advertising for and finding tenants, making leases, arranging for necessary repairs and maintenance, paying insurance premiums and taxes, handling any complaints from tenants and collecting rents. In addition to all costs incurred on behalf of the investor, the property manager charges a fee for his or her services.

- *Property taxes.* Among the most significant costs against rental income are the real estate taxes levied on the rental property. Special assessments against rental property, as for streets, walks or sewers, are additional tax costs that sometimes are considered as charges against rent, but more often as costs of improvements (capital investments).

- *Income taxes.* After the foregoing and any other allowable costs or expenses have been deducted, any remaining rental income is subject to usual federal and state *income taxes*. The investor who is attempting to estimate his or her net income from the property should consider these taxes as an additional charge against the expected gross rent and, if rental income is in addition to the investor's other taxable income, it should be considered as top income, that is, as being taxed at the highest rate applicable to his or her income.

Rental Property Risks

Although a rental property can offer substantial income, tax benefits and the chance to earn a profit on the sale of the property, owning rental property creates some special risks for investors. Investors face the risk that operating expenses will exceed rent levels or that unanticipated expenses, such as property tax increases or major building repairs, will be difficult to offset with rent increases. (This is especially true in areas where *rent-control laws* keep rent increases at levels that often lag behind operating expenses.)

When communities are being established or are growing, there is often a need for rental housing. In an effort to profit from the housing boom, developers tend to build more housing than is actually needed. This situation leads to another rental property risk. When the market becomes saturated, rental prices are forced down and the value of rental property decreases.

Another potential risk is that the neighborhood will decline and that tenants will move to other locations. When this happens, the vacancies may be difficult to fill, which means cash flow will suffer and the investor may be unable to meet his or her financial obligations. Finally, since real estate is a fairly illiquid investment, it may be difficult to sell a rental property, even under stable market conditions.

Investing for Property Appreciation

Investors frequently seek out and purchase real property that they believe will *appreciate* substantially in value—much as many investors trade in growth or speculative stocks. Some buy to hold for a relatively short time, expecting very rapid appreciation in value; others hold for a number of years, expecting the appreciation to be more gradual. The goal of these investors, of course, is to convert the appreciation to profit by selling the property at the appropriate time. When investors contemplate holding the property for more than a very short period, they frequently lease the real estate, applying the rent received against taxes and other expenses of owning the property.

Some investors attempt to speed up or give an assist to the appreciation in value of the property they are holding. For example, an investor holding a well- located tract of land may subdivide it into lots, put in streets and utilities and then sell the lots as home sites for substantially more than the original cost of the land plus the subsequent investment in it. Other investors may follow the same general pattern, except that they break up the tract, have it appropriately zoned and grade it to provide sites for industrial plants or other business installations. Still others may buy old or rundown houses, apartments or business buildings—repair, redecorate and otherwise improve the appearance, utility and desirability of the properties—and then attempt to sell the properties for substantially more than they invested.

Sometimes an investor, having in mind a prospective buyer for real estate of a particular kind, will buy such a property himself or herself—then attempt to sell it to the prospective buyer at a profit. However, as we'll discuss later, it is more common for an owner to give a prospective purchaser or lessee the *option* to buy or lease the property at a fixed price within a stated period of time.

Virtually any type of real estate—urban or rural, improved or unimproved, residential, commercial, industrial or farmland—or any type of real property that an investor feels will (or that he or she can make) appreciate substantially in value during the period he or she is willing and able to hold it, may be the basis for an investment.

Valuation Methods

When considering investing in any real property (regardless of kind and whether the objective is to buy, hold or sell that property), an investor is always interested in the *value* of that property. That sounds simple enough, except that there are several ways that property may be valued, as the following list indicates.

- *Market value.* This is the price at which a willing buyer and a willing seller would agree to on a given piece of real estate property.

- *Comparable property value ("comps").* This is the price at which comparable property (same kind, vicinity, age, state of repair, etc.) sold recently. (This is often the way that *market value* is estimated.)

- *Appraised value.* This value is determined by professional real estate appraisers, who analyze market value, comparative property values and trends relative to sales, the market, buyer attitudes and whims, the general economy, availability of mortgage money and a number of other factors that affect the current value of real property.

- *Assessed value.* This is the value of property as officially established, usually by a local government assessor, for tax purposes.

- *Replacement value.* This is the cost of replacing what is being valued. Obviously, this would apply not to the land, but to the things on or in the land (crops or forests growing on the land, buildings constructed on the land, oil or minerals in the land, etc.). This value is commonly used for insurance purposes.

- *Equity value.* This is the current value of the property (usually market value) less any obligations against the property (mortgage, liens, costs of selling, etc.). This value is what the owner would net on the sale of the property— the bottom line of the seller's closing statement—assuming the sale price equaled the market value, all obligations were as expected and the sale took place currently.

- *Book value.* This is the amount of principal paid for the property (down payment and principal payments) *plus* any capital improvements *less* any depreciation taken and less any obligations.

- *Cost basis value.* In general, this is the full purchase price *plus* any capital improvements, *plus* selling expenses, *less* any depreciation taken, less the value of any part of the property previously sold. This method is used almost exclusively to determine the difference (capital gain or capital loss) between the purchase price and the sale price of the property for income tax purposes.

Selection Considerations

Sound investment in real estate for appreciation or capital growth usually requires careful selection of the property. The selection process, in addition to the intuition and whims of the investor, normally involves numerous considerations, some of which are noted below.

The investor should begin by *considering the present condition and trend of the general economy.* As part of this consideration, the investor should weigh the current status and growth rate of population, business or industry; the currently developed (especially the most popular) areas in the locality, and the directional trends of expansion; and any current plans for new or expanded industry in the locality.

Based on the investor's analysis, evaluation and intuition relative to the foregoing, projections should be made into the future—as to *what kinds* of property will be in greatest demand, where such property most ideally will be situated, and *how soon* such demand will materialize.

Armed with these projections, the investor is in a position to seek out properties of the *kind* and in the *location* that should be in greatest demand (and consequently should have appreciated substantially in value) by the *time* he or she wishes to cash in on the investment, and earn a profit.

In making the final selection from such properties that are available, of course, the investor should consider a number of additional factors, such as:

- the amount of investment required and how long it probably will be tied up;

- any work and other expenses involved while the property is being held, and any income-producing uses of the property during this period;

- alternate uses or disposition of the property in event the expected demand does not materialize; and

- the personal convenience, experience and preference of the investor.

Financial Considerations

The various financial considerations involved in real estate investing may be categorized as pertaining to the purchase, the holding and the sale of the property.

The Purchase.   The initial investment in a piece of real estate includes, but generally is not limited to, the price paid for the property. In addition, the buyer typically pays for examination of the abstract and title opinion, a pro rata share of the current year's taxes and insurance on the property, fees and costs involved in obtaining any financing, costs of registering the deed and other pertinent instruments and any other items considered to be part of the purchaser's closing costs. Also, if the property transaction is handled by a real estate broker or dealer, his or her commission or fee may be charged to the purchaser and is a part of the initial investment. (Usually, however, the commission or fee is paid by the seller.)

The Holding Period.   Consideration should be given to how long the property may be held and to what costs may be incurred during this period. While the property is held, the owner generally must pay for state and local real estate taxes; any special assessments (as for street and sewers, etc.); insurance on the property (especially if improved and financed); interest (and usually reduction of principal) on any financing; costs of any repairs or improvements to the property; and so on.

If the property is to be leased to provide some offsetting income while it is held, consideration also should be given to such items as the amount of rent obtainable compared with any additional costs of renting. Also comparative considerations should be given to the *time value* and *opportunity costs* of the money invested, that is, to the interest or other income that reasonably might be realized on the amount invested if that amount were invested in something else during the period in which the property is being held.

The Sale.   With respect to the ultimate sale of the property, consideration should be given to the *estimated net proceeds* that are expected to result from the sale. This is the expected sale price of the property *plus* credits to the seller on closing less the expected costs involved in or resulting from the sale of the property.

On the plus side, in addition to the sale price, the seller generally receives credit for the prepaid portion of any real estate taxes and property insurance premiums as of the date of closing. The buyer usually repays these items. On the minus side, the seller usually must provide a current abstract or title commitment from a title insurance company and, if required, a survey of the real estate; satisfy any liens against the property and pay for correction of any flaws or clouds on the title; pay for the expense of any required inspections and of any needed corrective measures; provide a properly drawn deed; pay any required state excise tax on the transfer of the real estate; and pay the sales commission (generally 6 percent of the sale price of the property) if, as is typical, the seller employs a real estate broker to sell the property.

There may be additional costs that the seller may have to agree to as conditions of sale that the buyer includes in the offer to purchase the property. For example, if the buyer requires financing to make the purchase, the seller may have to agree to pay part of the costs of obtaining that financing, or to provide part or all of the needed financing.

And, finally, if the seller realizes a *capital gain* on the overall investment when the property is sold (the primary objective of this type of investing), it is subject to the usual federal and state taxation. Some special federal income tax rules apply to gain realized exclusively from the sale of a seller's personal residence. In general, such gain is not subject to income or capital gains tax to the extent that, within two years before or after the sale, the sales proceeds are reinvested in another property in which the seller takes up residence. Also, as mentioned at the beginning of this chapter, homeowners can exclude the first $500,000 of profit (capital gain) on the sale of a home if they are married, and single homeowners can exclude the first $250,000. These homeowners must have lived in the home as their primary residence for two of the last five years, ending on the date of the sale.

Real Estate Options

As stated earlier, another method of investing in real estate, which is motivated by the desire to realize a profit on the appreciation in value of real estate, is trading in *real estate options*. It is used primarily when the investor expects a property to appreciate in value very rapidly, and he or she wishes to realize a quick profit on such appreciation without investing a lot of his or her own money.

To illustrate, assume that before such information generally is known, an investor strongly suspects that a company is considering a particular piece of land as the site for a new industrial plant, but the owner of the land is unaware of such consideration by the company. The investor contacts the owner and asks for an option to buy the land any time within, say, the next 12 months at a reasonable, stipulated price—but a price substantially below what the investor believes the company will be willing to pay for the land. In exchange for a consideration (a relatively small investment) from the investor, the owner grants the requested option. The investor then attempts to sell the option to the company (or to any other prospective buyer of the land) for a substantially higher amount than he or she paid. Assuming the investor is successful in selling the option, the difference between what the investor paid for the option and the price the buyer pays represents the rapid appreciation in value of the property—appreciation on which the investor realizes a quick profit for the relatively small investment to obtain the option.

By trading in the option, rather than trading in the real estate itself, the investor not only makes about the same profit without tying up nearly as much money, but he or she also avoids the additional details, expenses and risks of buying, holding and selling the real estate. If the company does not buy the option, the investor always may sell it to someone else—or buy the property—or let the option expire, in which event his or her loss is limited to the consideration paid for the option. Clearly, this type of investing can be based on an expected appreciation in the value or price of real property of virtually any kind, size or location.

■ REAL ESTATE INVESTMENT SYNDICATES

People with only modest amounts of capital may pool their money with other investors and invest in large-scale real estate opportunities such as shopping centers or office complexes. These business ventures, called *real estate investment syndicates*, provide the investors with rental income. However, most of the return on investment is realized when the property is sold.

Real estate investment syndicates can take a number of forms. However, the most common forms are general and limited partnerships, real estate investment trusts (REITs), real estate mortgage investment conduits (REMICs) and collateralized mortgage obligations (CMOs).

Real Estate Partnerships

A *partnership* is a form of business organization consisting of two or more entities—individuals, or companies—who pool their talent and resources to engage in a common enterprise. A partnership can take one of two forms: general or limited. In a *general partnership*, each partner contributes capital to the business in the form of money, assets or service and each shares actively in the control and management of the business. Each act of any partner is attributable to the other partners. Additionally, each partner shares proportionately in the profits of the business. Liability for debts, however, is not limited or proportionate. Each partner is personally liable for the *full* amount of partnership indebtedness. This liability extends not only to each partner's investment in the company, but also to all personal assets.

A *limited partnership* is a form of business organization including both general and limited partners. The *general partners* assume unlimited business liability, while *limited partners* are at risk only to the extent of their contributed capital and committed capital. Limited partners have little or no voice in the management of partnership business and are also called *passive*—or *silent*—*partners* in the venture. The partnership is finite and dissolves upon mutual agreement or upon final sale of invested assets as specified in the original partnership agreement.

Real Estate Investment Trusts (REITs)

A *real estate investment trust (REIT)* is a type of closed-end investment company that invests money, obtained through the sale of shares to investors, in various types of real estate and/or real estate mortgages. For example, REITs are used to finance new shopping centers (particularly the smaller, strip shopping centers), hotels, motels, mini-warehouses and office buildings.

To form a legal REIT, a group of 100 or more members must hold shares in the trust. The REIT shares, called *certificates of beneficial interest*, represent a percentage of equity ownership in the REIT. They are traded publicly and may be listed on national securities exchanges. The REIT's trustees (or directors) must agree to invest *passively* only in real assets on behalf of the shareholders. In other words, a REIT's primary source of income cannot be from profits from the sale of real estate—capital gains or deductions for losses—nor is it allowed to speculate in vacant land for the purpose of reselling it. The REIT's profits can come only through the operation of real estate assets by others through separate management contracts.

For the real estate industry, raising capital through the stock market represents a means to obtain capital that it would ordinarily be denied. For the investor, REITs provide an opportunity for long-term, relatively high-yielding income while protecting the principal from inflation. Most dividends received by investors are subject to tax at regular rates.

The REIT acts as a *conduit* to pass income to shareholders and it does not have to pay taxes itself. To qualify for conduit treatment, the REIT must declare its intention to do so and then meet several obligations under the Internal Revenue Code. Among other obligations concerning structure, sources of income, nature of assets and dividend distribution, obligations include:

- distributing more than 95 percent of its net income to shareholders;

- investing more than 75 percent of its capital in real estate or real estate-related investments;

- issuing transferable shares in a fixed number; and

- limiting investors' liability—meaning that the trustees have the final responsibility for managing the activities of the trust.

Types of REITs

A REIT is formed when the investment company contracts with an underwriter to offer its shares—either publicly or privately. The certificates are initially sold in the primary market and all subsequent sales are through a secondary market. There are three basic types of REITs:

1. *Equity trusts* are shares in the ownership of an assortment of income-producing properties.

2. *Mortgage trusts* are shares in the proceeds of the purchase and sale of real estate mortgages rather than real property.

3. *Combination trusts* invest shareholders' funds in both real estate and mortgage loans.

Investors earn money in REITs through a *pass-through* of income and capital gains. This means that the profits derived from the rental or sale of the REIT to an investor aren't siphoned or taxed at the REIT level, but pass through the REIT to the investor in the form of dividends. This form of distributed earnings is called *single taxation*, because the REIT itself is not taxed but the government gets its share of REIT profits by taxing the investors' dividends.

Risk

Investors in REITs expose themselves to the same types of risks associated with direct real estate investing. The *financial risk* (or risk to the investor's principal) is relatively high in REIT investing. If the property can't return enough to cover mortgage or operating expenses, the shares will decrease in value and the REIT won't distribute any earnings. In addition, the *liquidity risk* can be quite high because in certain market conditions (and with certain properties), real estate cannot be sold.

Real Estate Mortgage Investment Conduits (REMICs)

Investors who are risk-tolerant and have low taxes and high expenses may be interested in mortgage-backed securities. *Real estate mortgage investment conduits (REMICs)* were created by the 1986 Tax Reform Act. A REMIC is formed to hold a fixed pool of mortgages that is divided into *tranches*—or slices. Any prepayments from the underlying mortgages are applied to the first tranch until it is redeemed. Subsequent prepayments are made to additional tranches. In theory, investors choose a tranch that meets their maturity needs and that provides a yield of between 1 and 3 percentage points higher than those earned on mature Treasuries.

Collateralized Mortgage Obligations (CMOs)

An issuer, such as the Government National Mortgage Association (GNMA), puts together a pool of mortgages and then issues pass-through securities in the amount of the total mortgage pool. These mortgage-backed securities are pools of thousands of individual mortgages that have been packaged for sale. A *collateralized mortgage obligation (CMO)* is a type of mortgage-backed bond whose holders are divided into classes based on the length of investment desired.

Investors in CMOs are grouped by the length of time they wish to invest in the CMO. Like REMICs, the CMOs themselves are divided into tranches. Although interest is paid to all the bondholders, *all principal payments* go to the short-term investors first, until that tranch is fully retired. Then, the next class, the intermediate-term investors, becomes the sole recipient of principal until the next tranche is retired, and finally the long-term investors are paid. Actually, nearly all mortgage-backed securities are sold to the public either as CMOs or REMICs—which are simply different ways of packaging mortgages and standard pass-through securities for resale to the investing public.

■ SUMMARY

Investment in real estate has traditionally offered an effective inflation hedge and an above-average rate of return while allowing investors to make use of other people's money through leverage. In addition, there may be some significant tax advantages to owning real estate. However, real estate investments tend to suffer from liquidity problems and may be more sensitive to economic influences and inflation risk than many other investments.

In the next two chapters, we'll look at another category on the risk pyramid—speculative investments—those that offer potentially large profits but are quite risky. These investments include tangibles, collectibles, commodities and financial futures and options.

■ CHAPTER 9 QUESTIONS FOR REVIEW

1. *Real estate* is best defined as land and

    A. all things permanently affixed to it

    B. the air above it

    C. the mineral rights under the soil

    D. the buildings permanently affixed to it

2. Investors purchase rental income property for all of the following reasons EXCEPT

   A. increased cash flow

   B. property appreciation

   C. tax benefits

   D. dislocations within the economy

3. *Leverage* involves the extensive use of

   A. alternative taxes

   B. government subsidies

   C. borrowed money

   D. cost recovery

4. The equity in a property is its current value less

   A. depreciation

   B. physical improvements

   C. mortgage indebtedness

   D. selling costs and depreciation

5. An investment arrangement in which all members share equally in the managerial decisions and profits involved in the real estate venture is called a

   A. limited partnership

   B. general partnership

   C. real estate investment trust

   D. real estate mortgage trust

10

Investing in Tangible Assets

A fter investors have met their liquidity needs, accumulated sufficient funds for future expenditures and are on their way toward achieving their retirement objectives, they may be interested in investing in more speculative ventures. A wide array of investment alternatives is available to investors who have adequate funds to afford losses if investments perform poorly or to those investors who are comfortable with great investment risks. Speculative investments, by most standards, include *tangibles* (such as precious metal and gems, art, coins, stamps and other collectibles), *commodities* (such as grains, livestock and foodstuffs) and *financial futures* (such as foreign currencies). The reason these investments are considered speculative is that compared to other kinds of investments, future value and level of expected returns or earnings are far more uncertain. And there is a more significant risk to losing all or a major portion of the original principal than investments discussed in previous chapters. Speculative investments require specialized knowledge and skill since the risk can be substantial.

In this chapter, we will take a look at speculative investments, beginning with tangibles—what they are, why they are acquired and how they fit an investor's financial objectives. As part of this discussion, we'll also address collectibles as both an investment and a hobby. Then, in Chapter 11, we'll discuss commodities, futures and options, sophisticated investments that make up part of many speculative portfolios.

■ ■ ■ ■ ■

■ WHAT ARE TANGIBLE INVESTMENTS?

In the way of review, the definition this course uses for *investment* includes the objective of financial gain. Unlike a *financial asset* that is a claim on paper evidencing ownership, debt or an option to acquire an interest in an asset, a *tangible investment* is any physical item that has form or substance and can be bought or sold in some market. Examples of tangible investments include *precious metals and gems* (gold, silver and diamonds, for instance), *collectibles* (such as stamps, coins, works of art and antiques) and *natural resources* (such as land and minerals).* One thing these items have in common is their relative scarcity or limited supply.

Tangible assets, also known as *hard assets*, are acquired because they have some perceived *intrinsic value*; they bring pleasure to the owner when they are viewed, held, used or consumed. Hard assets are also acquired for purposes of *financial gain* (or aversion to financial loss). The profit motive in tangible assets—the source of investment return—is tied to *price movements* since these investments don't pay dividends or interest. Profit is realized when an investor is able to sell a tangible at a higher price than he or she paid to acquire it. Thus, any financial gain from most tangible investments comes only at the point of sale.

There are many things that affect the prices of tangibles. Commodities, for example, trade pretty much in a pure auction market. A large supply of the goods coming to market will depress prices. A shortage, either real or imagined, will raise prices. The price levels of substitute materials or political actions will also affect the price of a commodity. The *supply and demand* factors that help to determine the price of tangibles are shown in Ill. 10.1.

■ NATURE OF TANGIBLE INVESTMENTS

For a number of reasons, investing in tangible assets is very different from investing in, say, stocks or bonds. For one thing, there is no formal, national exchange that serves as an arena for buying and selling and disseminating price information. Too, because investors often take actual possession, tangible assets often involve storing, shipping and insurance costs. Finally, investment in tangible assets frequently entails high dealer markup costs. But for many, this type of investment has produced some very attractive returns.

Market for Tangibles

The purchase and sale of tangibles is done in so many ways and in so many places that it is like describing commerce itself. Again, with the exception of certain items, like gold or foreign currencies that can be traded in the *commodities market* (discussed in Chapter 11) or coal and lumber produced by companies whose *stocks* trade on various exchanges, there is no central exchange for the purchase and sale of tangible assets like coins, art, stamps or rare books. Consequently, other types of markets have developed.

Auctions and *auction houses* are frequently the catalysts that move tangibles from seller to buyer and, accordingly, establish prices. Employed since ancient times, an auction is one of the oldest types of exchange methods. It brings together select individuals who are interested in acquiring tangibles. The fair price (to both buyer and seller) is reached by progressive elimination of those not willing to purchase the item at the price being asked.

---

* Because the topic of real estate was covered in detail in Chapter 9, we won't address it again in this chapter. It is mentioned because it is an example of a tangible asset, having substance and form.

ILL. 10.1 ■ *Supply and Demand Factors*

DEMAND

- Money Supply, Distribution

  Tight money increases interest rates, which reduces the present value of future price increases. Money or credit must be available to purchasers.

- Demographics

  An expanding population provides a bigger base of consumers, increasing the demand for goods in general.

- Demand for Final Goods

  Every finished good provides demand for inputs. For example, demand for silver is partly derived from its use in photographic films.

- Government Spending

  With taxes, the government buys tanks, computers, etc. Deficits financed by debt offerings reduce funds available to private borrowers (unless the debt is monetarized by the "Fed").

- Personal Tastes and Preferences

  Popularity changes. Rutabagas may be very nutritious and limited in supply; however, if people don't like the taste, demand stays light.

- Prices of Substitutes

  An increase in the price of natural rubber caused demand to shift to synthetic. Most commodities have substitutes.

SUPPLY

- Weather, Geography

  While weather may affect the psychology of a stock market, it can directly increase or decrease crop production.

- Labor and Productivity

  Machinery, technology, worker education and motivation are key factors in a country's GNP (gross national product).

- Government Supports and Restrictions

  Certain licenses and franchises limit where mining, farming or production can take place. Federal, state and local restrictions exist.

- Foreign Government Policies, International Trade

  No longer can a country escape international effects on trade. The international supplies and demands depend on policy decisions and laws outside U.S. jurisdiction.

- Transportation

  All the commodities on earth are of no value if they aren't where needed. A high percentage of the eastern United States' supply of produce is imported from California, Arizona and Florida.

Dealers, both wholesale and retail, are another way to acquire and sell tangibles. Dealers "make markets" by buying and selling. Depending on the asset, high commission (upon sale) and high markups (upon purchase) are common when working with dealers.

Other tangible markets include flea markets and swap meets, where buyers and sellers informally come together. Some people become investors in tangible assets by lucky finds, discovery or inheritance. In addition, an investor can deal directly with some producers, miners, minters or smelters. Another way to obtain tangible assets is through various governments, which sometimes sell tangible assets that are no longer needed for strategic reserve. For example, the U.S. government stockpiles contain large quantities of copper, aluminum, grains and other tangible resources that are sold to investors.

Finally, as an alternative to investing in tangibles themselves, investors may be able to purchase *common stock* in a company that produces the tangible asset desired. For example, gold mining company stocks trade on various exchanges as do silver, oil and lumber stocks. Some investors prefer to purchase shares of *mutual* funds that invest a portion or all of their portfolios in such stocks. In these cases, the investor obviously does not take possession of the tangible item; instead he or she hopes to benefit from any gains due to the appreciating value of the item and from any dividends the stock may generate.

Expenses

Though all types of investments have some element of expense in acquiring, holding and selling, investments in tangible assets often incur some unique expenses. Acquisition expense can be substantial. For example, the cost of acquiring a piece of artwork could involve *authentication costs* and an *appraiser's fee* in addition to the price of the work (which, if purchased through a dealer, will include the *dealer's markup*).

The costs of holding the investment include *shipping, handling* and *insurance charges*, if the investor takes physical possession of the asset. A safe-deposit box is another expense often incurred in holding tangible wealth. It should be noted, however, that storing assets in a bank vault does not eliminate the need for insurance; FDIC and other government protection does not cover the contents of lock boxes. It may also be necessary to *reappraise* assets periodically, for insurance purposes or otherwise. This is not an inexpensive proposition if the item is unique.

Disposition or sale of tangible assets also involves costs. For instance, if the item is to be sold at auction, the auctioneer or auction house will earn a fee, usually an agreed-upon percentage of the proceeds. In an estate settlement, for example, it is not unusual for 20 to 30 percent of the asset's market value to be wiped away in auctioneer's fees.

Finally, there is the *opportunity cost* of holding the intangible. If assets do not appreciate in value, the investor loses the income or growth that could have been earned on the capital if it had been invested in another way.

Valuation

Because each tangible involves its own unique market value, a generalized discussion of valuation is difficult. However, certain principles do apply. For some tangibles, the value may be influenced by industrial or commercial use. This valuation may place a base under a price that fluctuates above it, at a premium. *Melt-down* or *scrap value* is such a floor mechanism that supports metals. For example, the collectible value of a specific silver dollar may range from $50 to $2,000, depending on its condition. If the coin's collectible value dropped to $0, it would still have some wholesale melt-down value, perhaps $5, for its silver content.

Under extreme market pressures, an individual may decide that the asset has no market value as an investment, and it has no scrap or melt-down value. However, it may be possible to convert the investment to consumption or use. Generally, this "consumption" or "use" value is minimal or, at best, subjectively determined. Assume an investor purchases an 1834 bottle of Chateau Lafite wine for $300 at a private auction. He holds it as its market price climbs to $1,000. However, after the sale, somebody actually drinks some of the vintage and discovers it ages poorly. The market for this wine collapses. Our investor opens his bottle and consumes its contents only to find the most flavorful bouquet and fullness of body that he ever encountered. In monetary terms, the value of that wine was zero, but to its owner, it obviously had intrinsic, (if not market) value and worth.

Taxes

Taking physical ownership of a tangible asset is much like any other purchase of goods. In states having a *sales tax*, the transaction value is taxed. If purchased out-of-state for shipment by the seller to the state where the buyer resides, the seller may not be required to collect sales tax; however, the buyer is obligated to report the transaction and remit the appropriate sales tax to the state in which he or she lives. This is often overlooked by small investors; however, enforcement efforts in this area have increased in recent years.

Jewelry and certain other tangibles are also subject to federal *excise tax*. This, plus the sales tax, will undermine an owner's investment unless the asset actually increases in value. If there is a gain on the subsequent sale of the asset, it is considered income, fully subject to federal and state *income taxes*. Though long-term capital gains are no longer given favorable tax treatment, they still have the effect of deferring the taxation on current gain.

■   WHY PEOPLE INVEST IN TANGIBLES

Many individuals find tangibles, such as gold, silver or artwork, appealing because of their beauty; any investment characteristics are secondary. These collectors tend to purchase tangibles for their direct enjoyment. For example, many people collect coins or stamps simply because they enjoy possessing these items. No one disputes the therapeutic value of such hobbies. Often one is fortunate enough to break even or gain in the process. However, hobby items should be identified for what they are. For purposes of financial product evaluation, the assets generally should not be valued, since only in dire straits would they be sold. This is similar to not evaluating a personal residence as a real estate asset because it typically won't be sold unless an individual plans to move to another residence or must sell because he or she can no longer afford to maintain the residence. Also, the psychological value of tangibles is not subject to objective measurements applied by the financial adviser.

Other investors have no concern for a tangible's aesthetic characteristics. These individuals tend to purchase tangible items for one or more of the following reasons:

- *Inflation hedge.* Acquiring and holding tangible resources offers potential protection against inflation. These will be exchanged later for items actually consumed. Over a long period, tangible assets, particularly gold and silver, tend to increase or decrease in price in the same direction as general prices. During hyper-inflation and currency instability, precious metals and tangibles act as insurance against total loss of wealth. (Even this can be ineffective if governments search out and seize such property.)

- *Current consumption or financial gain.* In this sense "consumption" means enjoyment and may be current consumption or future consumption. For example, a T-bone steak has current value because it can be cooked and eaten. This same steak will have no future value after spoiling. A gold watch has current value because it helps its owner arrive at work on time. It will have future value as long as it performs this function (or can be repaired at less than replacement cost).

  Owners frequently acquire tangibles not for consumption, but to sell or exchange for financial gain in the future. For example, Mr. A has 20 head of young cattle. He feeds them until they are butchered for prime beef. The citizens recognize the fine quality of Mr. A's beef and readily buy it. Mr. A never intended to consume all the beef, but held it for future sale or exchange.

- *Production of other goods or services.* Assume that, in addition to owning cattle, Mr. A also has a barn full of lumber. He is holding this to build a second barn. The second barn will be used in the production (raising) of more steers (beef). Alternatively, he can sell the lumber to a local furniture manufacturer for production of chairs.

- *Perceived value and display of wealth.* Because tangibles can be seen, they serve as an excellent vehicle for displaying wealth. Although it may be considered crass to announce that one is a millionaire, it is perfectly acceptable to drive a luxury car, which advertises that wealth.

- *Portfolio diversification.* Tangibles tend to achieve more efficient portfolio diversification than is possible by holding only intangibles. This is helpful in reducing overall risk without giving up return.

Disadvantages of Tangible Investments

When held in an overall balanced portfolio, tangibles offer the potential for high return. However, as explained earlier, tangibles have several disadvantages that make them unappealing to many investors.

- *High commissions and holding costs.* Depending on the tangible, investors will pay commissions ranging from 1 percent (gold, for example) to 30 percent (an art object, for example) or more on the tangible's purchase or sale, or both. Trading tangibles on a frequent basis tends to enrich only the dealer, even if the price appreciation is substantial.

  An individual might purchase tangible assets as a hobby and for the psychological rewards of collecting. The expectation of profit is secondary or may be nonexistent. In this case, holding costs can be high since tangibles must be stored in safe places to prevent theft or deterioration.

- *A need for specialized knowledge.* Most collectors recognize that acquiring and maintaining a collection—from artwork to baseball cards—requires a great deal of time and skill. Even experienced collectors have been taken in by unscrupulous dealers who overgrade items they sell while undergrading purchases. If collectors are unwilling to gain the knowledge they need to develop a valuable collection, they must rely on experts for advice.

- *No current return.* Unless a tangible appreciates in value, the investor receives no return. Because the prices of most tangibles are quite volatile, most investors would be wise not to hold an excessive proportion of their portfolios in tangibles.

- *Poor resale market.* The investment value of a tangible depends heavily upon the existence of a resale market. If no one wishes to purchase a tangible or the resale value is much lower than the initial cost, the item may have only intrinsic value to the owner. For example, a wealthy individual may purchase a racehorse as an "investment" despite the fact that it is gelded and cannot be used for breeding, that the future purses the horse is expected to win are less than the outlay required to purchase the animal and that the future sale of the animal is not contemplated. However, the intrinsic value of the thrill of owning a racehorse may compensate the owner for the lack of a resale market.

To summarize, a tangible asset's value normally is related to its final use. This is not to say, however, that this value always is determined objectively. Tangible assets often are bought and sold based on emotional factors. For example, perceived rates of future general consumer prices may only partly be tied to increases and decreases in money supply measures. Perceptions of future supplies and demands are judgment factors not easily quantified.

Now, let's look at three major categories of tangibles that are used as investment vehicles: gold and other precious metals, gemstones and collectibles.

■ GOLD AND OTHER PRECIOUS METALS

Certain tangible assets, like gold, silver and platinum are popular investment vehicles that concentrate a great deal of value in a small amount of weight and volume. This section, for purposes of brevity, will focus primarily on gold. In general, similar characteristics apply to silver, platinum and other precious metals.

Gold is, and always has been, held in esteem because of its physical characteristics. It holds its sheen without rusting or deteriorating. It is one of the most malleable metals known—that is, it can be pounded or rolled into thinner-than-paper sheets, drawn into finer-than-hair strands or shaped into intricate designs, without breaking, flaking or puncturing. It is also portable because many thousands of dollars worth of gold occupies little space and can be measured in ounces. Also, dealers can *assay* gold (judge its value) with relatively little difficulty.

Gold is also valuable because people associate it with money. For centuries, gold has been used as money, as a standard for monetary systems and a means for settling international business accounts. Unlike paper money that can by eroded by inflation or the collapse of a government, the value of gold tends to remain fairly constant. Gold is very liquid and can usually be sold quickly at the current market price.

There are a variety of ways to invest in gold, from purchasing gold bullion to speculating in commodities. The most common ways are outlined below.

Coins

Many investors purchase *gold bullion coins* that are minted for special events, such as the Olympics, or for gold investment. For example, the U.S. government sanctioned a series of gold medallions honoring famous Americans. Early *strikes* (or coin mintings) honored Louis Armstrong and Frank Lloyd Wright. These medallions offer the average citizen a way to purchase gold in a recognized form without supporting foreign governments or industries. The medallions are nicely struck pieces and are attractive for display. However, they lack any monetary designation so they are not actually used as "coins" to purchase goods. Their price is based on the value of their gold content.

Popular investments include the American gold eagle and the South African Krugerrand—both of which are readily available but trade at large premiums due to *numismatic* (or coin collector) interest. Other popular gold bullion coins include the Australian golden nugget, the Canadian maple leaf and the Mexican peso.

Gold Bullion

Investors interested in holding a large quantity of gold may purchase *gold bullion*, either as bars or wafers. Bullion comes in a variety of sizes—from less than one ounce to the standard 400-ounce bar, which governments and banks use for international transactions. Each bar is stamped with the *fineness* of the gold and the name and *assayer's* number of the company that created it, such as Credit Suisse. Pure gold has a fineness of 1.000 and an investor looks for bars at least .995 in fineness.

Gold Jewelry

Although purchasing jewelry is a popular way to own gold, it is usually not a good way to invest in gold. The price of jewelry includes the jewelry designer's costs, retail markups and other factors so the cost is substantially higher than the underlying gold value of the piece. In addition, gold jewelry, unlike 24-carat gold bars, is usually a 14-carat or 18-carat blend of gold and other nonprecious metals.

ILL. 10.2 ■ *Bullion Coins*

Coin	Country of Origin	Fineness	Weight in Ounces	Comments
American eagle	United States	0.9167	1, ½, ¼, ¹⁄₁₀	Launched October 1986. Face value $50
maple leaf	Canada	0.9999	1, ½, ¼, ¹⁄₁₀	Launched in 1979. Face value C$50
golden nugget	Australia	0.9999	1, ½, ¼, ¹⁄₁₀	Launched April 1987. Face value Au$100
Britannia	United Kingdom	0.9167	1, ½, ¼, ¹⁄₁₀	Launched October 1987. Face value £100 (highest value of any bullion coin)
gold ecu	Belgium	0.90	½	Successful since its launch; no continuation plans known. Face value 50 ecu
sovereign	United Kingdom	0.9167	0.2354	Produced intermittently; millions trade in the secondary market. Face value £1.00
Krugerrand	South Africa	0.9167	1, ½, ¼, ¹⁄₁₀	Available only in the secondary market; trades at low premiums; importation forbidden

Source: *Encyclopedia of Investments.* Boston, MA: Warren, Gorham & Lamont, Inc., 1990.

Gold Certificates

One of the most convenient and safe ways to own gold is to purchase a *gold certificate* from a banker, dealer or broker. These certificates reflect ownership in a specific quantity of gold that is stored in a bank vault. By purchasing certificates, the investor does not have to be concerned about storing the gold and avoids assay costs, as well as state and local sales taxes that are normally imposed on the sale of coins and bullion. Although the quality and integrity of the issuer should be faultless, some have issued certificates without gold backing.

Gold Stocks and Mutual Funds

Trading in gold (and other precious metals) is done daily on organized exchanges. Many investors purchase publicly traded *stocks* in gold mining companies. Like other stocks, gold mining stocks rise and fall depending on investors' expectations of future profits. For example, an unstable political situation in South Africa impacts gold prices and stocks. If the South African government shuts down gold mines, the shortage of gold causes the price of gold to soar while the price of shares falls because of the lack of gold production in the mines.

Another way to invest in gold mining stocks or gold stocks is through a mutual fund. Like all mutual funds, *precious-metal mutual funds* provide the advantage of a diversified portfolio as well as professional management. Precious-metal mutual fund portfolios typically include a number of South African, North American and Australian shares. These funds pay dividends that are easily reinvested in more shares.

Gold Futures and Options

Investors who are interested in higher-risk, high-return investments may consider investing in gold futures and options. As we'll discuss in more detail in Chapter 11, a *gold future* is a contract to buy or sell agreed-upon quantities of gold at a specified price at a specified future date. For a fraction of the price of owning the gold (say, 5 or 10 percent of the value of the contract), the investor's profit could be many times his or her initial investment. For example, assume an investor buys a contract selling at $400 an ounce that is set for delivery in six months. Each contract represents 100 ounces of gold, so the value of the contract is $40,000 ($400 × 100). According to the exchange rules, the investor must put down 5 percent of the contract, or $2,000. If the price of gold rises to $500 an ounce by the time delivery must be made, the value of the contract rises to $50,000 ($500 × 100). An 80 percent rise in price from $400 to $500 per ounce of gold means a profit of $10,000 (less any commissions and the original $2,000 investment). However, if the price of gold falls, the investor may lose his or her initial investment. In addition to futures, investors may purchase *options* on futures—contracts allowing the buyer to purchase or sell 100 shares of a security.

Both gold futures and options are used for investing in short-term fluctuations in gold prices. They are highly speculative investments and are not for those who are looking for a long-term hedge against inflation or other economic uncertainties.

Strategic Metals

Gold and silver (precious metals) have value mainly as intrinsic metals of beauty, although silver is used heavily in the photographic business and platinum as a catalyst. Other materials have greater industrial and consumer goods applications. One group, referred to as *strategic metals*, is not only very limited in supply but is essential to our defense and key industries. Some of these are located almost completely in foreign countries, a few of which are unstable or unfriendly to the United States. Most of these metals aren't household names (and tend to end in "ium"). Chromium, commonly used in alloys and electroplating, is one that people take for granted but primarily is mined overseas. A full discussion goes beyond the purpose set for this course. However, two basic comments about strategic metals are in order:

1. Strategic metals are highly speculative resources that are not traded readily and frequently demand is by one (or a few) manufacturer(s).

2. Trading in this area is largely a political exercise, trying to gain financial advantage by adversity (shortages) and hostility.

■ GEMSTONES

Gemstones, such as diamonds and the so-called *precious colored stones* (rubies, emeralds and sapphires), are purchased for their beauty and the psychic and aesthetic pleasure they provide. They also serve as viable investments because they provide a source of real wealth as well as a hedge against political and economic uncertainties. Generally, these gemstones can be valued only by experienced personnel at fine retail stores and by dealers, cutters and educated collectors. Investors must understand the determinants of quality.

Diamonds

Diamonds, one of the world's scarcest natural resources, are the most popularly purchased and traded gemstones. Although they are always in great demand, only about 10 percent of the diamonds are of high enough quality to be classed as *investment-grade* stones. Gemologists use universal grading standards to judge the quality of diamonds. The four main criteria are color, cut, clarity and carat weight. These grading standards are universal—they are often used to buy and sell diamonds internationally.

- *Color.* The color of a diamond ranges from white to yellow, with the whitest stones being the most valuable. Perfectly white diamonds are graded "D" and less white stones are graded "E," and so on, through the letter "Z."

- *Cut.* Diamond cutters use various techniques to produce facet angles that enhance the brilliance of a stone. One of the most important features that affects a diamond's value is the perfection of the cut.

- *Clarity.* Most diamonds contain some flaws—a fracture or carbon spot—that affect their value. The clarity grading scale ranges from "flawless," which means that the diamond shows no internal or external flaws or faults when magnified 10 times, to "imperfect," which means the flaws are obvious and may even be seen with the naked eye.

- *Carat.* A diamond's weight is measured in *carats*; one carat is equivalent to 200 milligrams. The price of a diamond usually increases with its weight.

Investment Value of Diamonds

Diamonds have proven to be an effective hedge against inflation and the demand for diamonds is ever present. In a sense, diamonds are fairly liquid assets because they can be sold anywhere in the world—usually at appreciated prices. However, there is no guarantee that the price *will* appreciate and, unlike stocks or bonds, diamonds offer no current interest or dividend income. In addition, the costs of owning investment-grade diamonds are high. The initial investment can be at least $10,000 for the stones, plus the investor must pay for insurance and a safe-deposit box or vault in which to store the diamonds.

ILL. 10.3 ■ *Effect of Color and Flaw Grade on Retail Diamond Pricing: 1-Carat Round Brilliant (1.00+)**

Grade Color	Flaw (Clarity) Grade							
	IF	VVS$_1$	VVS$_2$	VS$_1$	VS$_2$	SI$_1$	SI$_2$	I$_1$
D	$39,000	$26,000	$22,400	$16,800	$14,000	$11,800	$9,400	$6,800
E	27,000	22,000	19,400	15,800	13,400	11,400	9,000	6,400
F	23,000	19,000	16,400	14,400	12,800	10,800	8,600	6,000
G	20,000	16,400	14,400	13,400	11,400	9,600	8,200	5,600
H	17,000	14,400	13,400	11,400	10,400	8,800	7,600	5,400
I	12,000	10,400	10,000	9,400	8,400	7,600	6,800	5,200
J	10,000	9,400	9,000	8,200	7,600	6,800	6,200	4,800
K	9,000	8,000	7,600	7,200	6,800	6,000	5,600	4,400

Note: Observe both the tremendous price fluctuation among stones of the same size owing to differences in the flaw grades and color grades and the disproportionate jumps in cost per carat, depending on size.

* Dollar prices quoted are per carat (using GIA scale for comparison).

Source: *Encyclopedia of Investments.* Boston, MA: Warren, Gorham & Lamong, Inc., 1990.

Precious Colored Stones

Some investors are interested in *precious colored stones* such as rubies, emeralds or sapphires. The rarity and the beauty of these stones are appealing to investors; however, these stones lack the universal appeal of diamonds. Because the shades of color vary more widely in colored stones than in diamonds, it is more difficult to appraise and value these stones. Unlike diamonds, there are no widely accepted grading standards and even experts may disagree on the importance of subtle shadings.

Rubies, the most valued gemstones, primarily come from mines in Burma. The color and clarity of the stone are very important. The deeper the red, the more valuable the stone, and the fewer inclusions (flaws) the better—although no rubies are flawless. Valued gemstones also include green *emeralds*, which come primarily from Colombia, and *sapphires*, blue gemstones found in Sri Lanka, Thailand and Australia.

Investment Value of Colored Stones

The major attraction of precious colored stones is that they are a hedge against inflation and the prospects for appreciation are quite good. For example, in countries where political upheaval is fairly constant, colored stones are often used as a convenient store of wealth.

As investment vehicles, precious stones offer no current income and their erratic prices are highly susceptible to changing market conditions. The initial price of investment-grade precious stones can be quite high; prices usually start at $5,000, but can range from $100 to $24,000 per carat, depending on the type and origin of the stone, its color and inclusions.

Colored stones are also highly illiquid and may be difficult to sell. Not only is future appreciation uncertain, but the value of the stones is reduced by the costs of dealer markups. Gemstones are usually purchased through registered gem dealers whose commissions and dealer markups range from 20 to 100 percent.

■ COLLECTIBLES

The final category of tangibles we'll discuss is *collectibles*, a term that includes a wide variety of items from stamps to rare coins. They are nonfinancial physical assets that are found in limited supply and that provide some aesthetic, psychological or practical value to the owner. Basically, a collectible is a tangible asset that has market value and may serve as a store of value because it is desired by others either for its *rarity*, its *beauty* or its *unique position in history.*

Objects of Rarity

Collectibles that have tangible value primarily because of rarity include antiques, antique firearms, books, foreign goods from troubled or restricted countries and fine wine and brandy. If such items as baubles, buttons, bottles, baseball cards, matchbooks and comic books are included, the list becomes almost endless. Coins and stamps offer the best market for the nonhobbyist investor because fairly objective gradings exist, up-to-date price listings are available and numerous markets are available for the purchase and sale of collectibles.

Objects of Unusual Beauty

In addition to rarity, many collectibles are valued because of their attractiveness. There always will be those individuals who appreciate great works of beauty. A thousand copies of the Mona Lisa will never capture the mysterious beauty of the original. Paintings, lithographs, carvings, statues, vases and other objets d'art always have had financial value. Between 1951 and 1968 the prices of British eighteenth-century and nineteenth-century paintings multiplied more than 10 times; twentieth-century European paintings, 19½ times; and seventeenth-century Italian paintings, 33 times. This was during a period of fairly little price inflation.

This market is specialized. Though some investors acquire artworks strictly for financial appreciation, others value the piece from a current-enjoyment and psychological viewpoint. Museums and governments sometimes buy and sell art treasures for the enjoyment of patrons and citizens. For example, the tiny country of Liechtenstein (a neighbor to Switzerland and Germany) has great art treasures. Occasionally, it sells a piece or two to finance a public project it feels offers greater value to the citizens. The markets for great works of art are generally concentrated in the big cities where international wealth is concentrated.

Objects of Historic Value

The desire to remember or re-create the past partially accounts for the *nostalgia* involved when people collect such things as shreds of clothing from a former president's attire, signatures of famous people or the first issue of a magazine. This reason for valuing items also affects rare items covered earlier, such as coins, stamps and antiques. Signatures and writing samples or legal documents are probably the purest examples of recognized collectibles explained by this phenomenon. One also might recall the good old days by collecting trolley tokens, old paper money or beer cans of discontinued brands. Some of these items, such as comic books and movie memorabilia, have hobbyist followers and surprisingly, organized sales, exchanges and prices.

Market for Collectibles

Unlike financial assets that are traded in formal or informal exchanges, collectibles are bought and sold through networks of dealers and collectors. Buying collectibles involves judgment. Most are traded at auctions, but dealers also are available to help appraise and guarantee authenticity. For this service a buyer pays the broker or dealer a fee or *asked* (retail) price and later is faced with selling at *bid* (wholesale) price. The biggest dangers to holders of collectibles are physical loss, erosion by expense, drop in market price due to changes in taste and the opportunity cost of holding a nonincome-generating asset.

In times of abnormally high inflation, collectibles can provide competitive rates of return as well as a good hedge against inflation. However, investing in collectibles is a long-term activity because prices vary widely and it is unlikely that profits can be made in the short term. A "collectible" has meaning to the investor that differs from the way the term is used by hobbyists, accountants or grammarians. Although some collectibles have appreciated, the resale markets are generally poor and transaction costs tend to be high. For example, artwork is typically subject to a 100 percent dealer markup as well as sales tax.

Despite some drawbacks, finding and investing in collectibles can be an interesting and financially rewarding endeavor. To illustrate, let's look at the major categories of collectibles.

Rare Coins

The study and collection of rare coins is called *numismatics*. Issued by governments as legal tender, rare coins often have collector's value over and above the face value of the coin. A coin's value reacts to forces of supply and demand. Prices established by supply (numismatists and others selling coins) and demand (collectors, dealers and investors wishing to acquire coins) influence dealers' prices across the country. Though the quantity of each type and grade of coin can be estimated, this usually is not known with precision. For instance, the rise in silver bullion prices in the late 1970s raised the price of lower-grade coins above their numismatic value. This resulted in *junk* silver dollars, quarters, halves and dimes being turned over to smelters for refining to sterling ingots. The rush to melt down coins slowed as silver prices collapsed back to more normal levels in 1980.

Determining a Coin's Value

Although most people think the age of the coin determines its value, age alone is not an important determinant of value. At least four other factors—rarity, condition, demand and metallic content—are more important in determining a coin's value.

1. The prime determinant of a coin's value is its *rarity*, which is determined, in part, by the number of specimens of a coin that are known to exist. Generally speaking, the larger the number of coins minted, the more likely it is that a large number survive. The smaller the minting, the fewer the survivors and the more valuable they are likely to be. In some cases, a mistake or misstrike in the minting of a coin can make the coin rare and valuable.

2. The *condition* (or state of wear) of the piece is often more important than the rarity of that type and date of coin. As shown in Ill. 10.4, a numerical grading system has been developed from *"Proof"* (special highly polished coins produced for collectors) to *"junk"* (any coin of low enough value to have little or no numismatic value in the present market). With a few exceptions, the closer to *perfect uncirculated* grade a coin is, the more it is worth.

3. Another important determinant of a coin's value is collector *demand*. For instance, according to *Coin Prices*, there were 1,193,000 of the 1914-D Lincoln cent minted and there are currently thousands of these coins in circulation. However, because many people want to obtain one of each date and mintmark of these Lincoln cents, a 1914-D Lincoln cent commonly lists at $350.

4. Collectors are also concerned with a coin's *metallic content*, especially for coins struck in precious metals. Gold and silver coins will be worth at least the market value of their gold or silver content. The rarer coins will have numismatic value and sell for a premium.

Active Market for Coins

Besides local coin dealers, the market consists of local and national shows. Here dealers, hobbyists and investors can compare the best coins of like type and grades, purchasing interesting or undervalued pieces for themselves or their customers. In addition to local shows, several auctioneers handle numismatic material, often of extremely high value. In recent years coins have become very popular.

Coins are *liquid* to varying degrees, depending on the price a seller will take for them. Dealers often are overstocked with common types and dates and will purchase only additional specimens at discounts to wholesale or meltdown value. Dealers also specialize to varying degrees. For instance, a Canadian coin collection may be difficult to sell to local U.S. dealers. Advertising single coins in trader newspapers may bring a buyer, but slowly. The buyer has a right to expect a return-after-inspection privilege. Thus, even if there is final agreement and the deal is completed, weeks can expire. The prospective buyer will tend to grade the coin low, whereas the seller will try to overlook flaws. Some unscrupulous sellers deal in counterfeit coins or cleaned coins. (Most cleaning, if detected, reduces the value of the coin, but unwary investors mistakenly grade shiny coins above their real condition.)

ILL. 10.4 ■ *Grading System for Coins*

Example	Coin Grades (abbreviated descriptions)
"Proof"	Special coins produced for collectors—highly polished
MS-70	Perfect uncirculated—no bag marks, lines or evidence of handling
MS-65	Choice—uncirculated—fewer bag marks than average
MS-60	Uncirculated—moderate bag marks, brilliant or toned
AU-55	Choice about uncirculated—traces of wear on high points
AU-50	About uncirculated—traces of wear on nearly all high points
EF or XF-45	Choice extra fine—light overall wear on high points, design sharp
EF or XF-40	Extra fine—slightly more wear than above, still sharp design
VF-30	Choice very fine—light, even surface wear, lettering sharp
VF-20	Very fine—as above, moderate wear on high points
F-12	Fine—moderate to considerable wear, lettering all visible
VG-8	Very good—well worn, details nearly smooth but visible
G-4	Good—heavily worn, faintness of details, no center of detail
AG-3	About good—portions of lettering, date worn smooth
"Junk"	Any coin of low enough grade to have little or no numismatic value in the present market. Varies by type and metal content.

An appraisal by a reputable dealer (as evidenced by membership in one or more professional associations) is prudent. Coins, for instance copper, can tarnish or oxidize and lose value. If left in original paper tubes or exposed to the atmosphere, this can happen before the owner realizes what has happened. Safety from theft is a prime consideration and expense of owning coins.

Stamps

The study and collection of stamps (or *philately*) is both a popular hobby and a lucrative investment. A fixed supply exists with demand dependent on hobbyists' enthusiasm, dealers' needs and the perceived trading pattern evolving. Stamps also appreciate free of current income tax (until sold), and are purchased by the investor as a hedge against inflation. Unlike coins, these resources generally cannot be traded as legal tender and have no direct meltdown or scrap value. (They have value as postage, of course, but this is very minimal.) In this sense they are more like an intangible, but are covered here because the objective in purchasing stamps differs from most intangibles.

Stamp dealers are perhaps less numerous than coin dealers, but usually are present even in smaller cities. Postage stamps of low grade often are worth less than the cost of handling, except for pure collector interest. New commemorative issues are printed by the U.S. Postal Service in such quantities that it is unlikely these ever will have philatelic value. Prices are published in *Scott's Standard Postage Stamp Catalog*. As with coins, a dealer may be willing to buy stamps, but usually only at large discount prices.

Antiques

The market for *antiques* includes aged furniture, pottery, porcelain, glass and many other objects. Typically, investors collect antiques as much for the items' aesthetic appeal as for their potential financial gains. In some cases, individuals simply wish to furnish their homes with fine antiques and are willing to pay substantial sums for quality pieces of American, English or French period furniture. However, serious collectors and investors are more likely to store the pieces, rather than subject their investments to the risk of damage from accidents or use.

Investors interested in purchasing antiques are particularly susceptible to fraud. In fact, some dealers specialize in *reproductions* that the uninformed investor may take to be originals. Unless an investor is knowledgeable, the quality, condition, authenticity and historical significance of an antique may be difficult to judge.

Collecting and investing in antiques can be lucrative; however, there is no guarantee that antiques will continue to appreciate after they are purchased. Unlike stocks and bonds, antiques do not yield current income nor are they liquid investments. They are long-term investments that may be difficult to sell at an agreeable price. In general, investment in antiques should be limited to those who wish to become experts in the field and who can afford the sizeable commitment necessary to hold these assets.

Artwork

Buying and selling *artwork* (paintings, prints, posters and sculpture) are similar to acquiring coins, stamps or antiques, only involving more judgment of social trends, tastes and, to some extent, luck. In terms of appreciation, the dealer is probably the most important single influence on what luck is experienced. Because valuation of art is subjective (except perhaps to determine authenticity), more than one appraisal may be prudent. When an estate contains a great number of collectibles, including art, an auctioneer specializing in such items may be hired to oversee the sale. A good auctioneer will advertise in trade and special-interest publications to draw the largest possible number of prospective bidders. The final value can fluctuate widely depending on the inclination of the buyers. Normally, no guarantee of authenticity is acquired at auctions.

Artwork can be damaged, in which case its value is reduced or eliminated. Paintings can fade under bright light. Silver oxidizes (tarnishes) and may need professional cleaning to avoid wear of the artistic carvings or impressions. Insurance is advisable for all collectibles but particularly those of artistic beauty. A small scratch could wipe out much of the value of a painting. Fire destroys canvas and oil almost instantly. Flood water imparts irreversible damage (even partial restoration would be exorbitantly expensive).

Like antiques, artwork is a long-term, fairly illiquid investment. There are holding costs, such as storage and insurance, and sales costs (commission) when the piece is sold. Only investors who can afford to tie up large sums of money for long periods of time can expect to gain from investment in artwork. Of course, there is no guarantee that art produced by a well-known artist with a strong national (or even international) reputation will appreciate.

Rare Books

Rare books—including manuscripts, limited editions and finely bound books—are collected for a number of reasons including their intellectual message, their value as scholarly research and the aesthetic pleasure of owning a copy of a classic work that has been preserved for generations or perhaps even handwritten by the author. A notable work by an important author can command substantial price. For example, although 600 copies of the *First Folio* of Shakespeare's plays were originally published, only 180 copies of this first edition survived. Of these, only about 20 are in their original state. The average selling price of these copies has been in the $300,000–$400,000 range, although one copy sold for $775,000.

Rare books are a highly speculative investment since there are no guarantees that books will appreciate in value. Generally, they are the last commodity to show either a price decrease during a depression or an increase in affluent times. However, changing tastes could render a particular book or author passé in only a short period of time.

Comic Books

The first *comic books* were collections of comic strip reprints and quickly became popular with readers and collectors. Traditionally, comic books feature a number of superheroes—Batman, Superman, Captain America—who defeat various foes or they depict some other interesting character—Donald Duck, Popeye, Richie Rich—who gets into trouble and learns a lesson. Comic books can be bought and sold through dealers or fairs around the country. The comic book's condition and rarity will determine its value.

Baseball Cards and Sports Memorabilia

The game of baseball is the "favorite American pastime" and collecting and trading baseball cards are part of the enjoyment of that sport. Each year a series of cards is issued by a number of companies and distributed either alone or with bubble gum, candy, cookies and cereal. The value of each card is determined by a number of factors, including its scarcity, physical condition and the collector interest in that specific card. The "investors" tend to be youngsters with small allowances, but some older collectors may spend several hundred dollars a year.

In addition to baseball cards, some investors collect uniforms and hats of famous players, statues and limited edition plates, championship pennants, rings and press pins as well as paper items, such as sports magazines and autographed photos. Although they are less popular than baseball cards, football, basketball, hockey and professional wrestling cards are also issued, collected and traded.

There are a number of risks inherent in collecting sports memorabilia. It can be forged or damaged by light, moisture or mishandling, which decreases its value. In addition, although the prices can appreciate substantially over time because of the rarity of some of these sports items, the value of sports memorabilia is strictly determined by public taste. The value of a card or autograph decreases as the player fades into obscurity. Finally, if the memorabilia is traded through a dealer, the investor may receive as little as 25 percent of the current market price for the card.

Movie Memorabilia

Movie-related items from posters to autographs, as well as the actual films themselves, have been popular collectibles for many decades. One of the more popular items is *animation art*, usually in the form of a *cel* (short for *celluloid*) painting on a clear sheet of acetate. Cels, the building blocks of animation, are one-of-a-kind items and are filmed in sequence to create the illusion of motion. Cels are created as production cels used in the actual film or as *limited edition* pieces—created expressly as art and signed and numbered by the artist. As with all collectibles, prices are driven by investor interest, scarcity and condition of the item.

■ SUMMARY

Whether tangible assets appreciate fast enough to conserve purchasing power in an inflationary period depends on selection and timing. The investor casts his or her lot with hobbyists and professional dealers when purchasing at public auctions. The objective of the investor is long-term appreciation in real as well as nominal value. The hobbyist, dealer and consumer are motivated by other objectives. The investor wishing to protect himself or herself from financial setbacks may take possession of hard assets to ride out the storm. The investor who is convinced of depression (accompanied by deflation) would convert all tangible assets into cash and fixed-dollar cash equivalents. This would enable him or her to repurchase variable-dollar value assets at lower prices.

Depending on the time period covered, results of long-term holding of tangible assets have been widely mixed. Many experts have recognized the danger of overly simplistic approaches to investing in a rapidly changing economic environment. In the next chapter, we'll look at more speculative investments—commodities and financial futures.

■ CHAPTER 10 QUESTIONS FOR REVIEW

1. All of the following are tangible assets EXCEPT

   A. minerals

   B. gold bullion

   C. diamonds

   D. grain futures

2. People invest in tangibles for all of the following reasons EXCEPT

   A. current consumption

   B. guaranteed profit

   C. portfolio diversification

   D. inflation hedge

3. Which of the following best defines tangible assets held for investment purposes?

   A. Any item that has some perceived intrinsic value and is held for financial gain

   B. Any physical item that can be seen or touched

   C. Any item that can be collected

   D. Any item that can be sold for a profit

4. The term *collectible* (when used in the investment sense) refers to

   A. precious metals

   B. objects of unusual beauty

   C. objects of rarity

   D. All of the above

5. One of the measures of a diamond's value is its carat, which is its

   A. color

   B. brilliance

   C. weight

   D. flaws

S ome financial experts feel that speculation in *commodities* (including contracts on grains, livestock and foodstuffs), *futures* (including contracts on foreign currencies, commodities and interest rates) and *options* (the right to buy or sell stock and other securities) should never be part of the average investor's portfolio. These ventures can be considered highly speculative; even a small change in the market price can wipe out an investor's original investment. On the other hand, for those investors with the time, special expertise and considerable financial resources needed to correctly predict the commodity or futures market's expectations of interest rates, weather conditions, consumer attitudes and other factors that influence the supply and demand of the underlying commodity, the potential for large gains that this market holds can be very appealing. Investing in commodities, futures and options can be complex. Only investors who are psychologically and financially willing to assume the risks inherent in speculation should consider this market.

In this chapter, we will take a look at some of these speculative investments—commodities, futures and stock options—what they are, why they are acquired and how they fit an investor's financial objectives. We'll begin by discussing commodities and how they are traded.

■ ■ ■ ■ ■

■ WHAT IS A COMMODITY?

A *commodity* is a physical good used in business, in industry and by consumers in everyday life. When people sit down to breakfast in the morning, they are likely to consume a variety of commodities—from bacon to orange juice to the wheat in their toast. Their trip to work depends on even more commodities—the gas and oil in their car, the cotton in their clothes and the coffee they pour when they get there. As we'll see later in this chapter, the route these goods must take on the way into a consumer's life is a highly complex one; sophisticated systems have been put in place over the years to make their delivery as efficient as possible.

The major classes of commodities include:

- grains and oilseeds (corn, oats, barley, soybeans, wheat, rye, rice, etc.);

- livestock and meat (cattle, hogs and pork bellies, turkeys, broilers);

- metals and petroleum (aluminum, copper, gold, platinum, silver, gasoline, crude oil, heating oil, propane);

- food and fiber (cocoa, coffee, cotton, orange juice, sugar, eggs, potatoes, butter);

- wood (lumber, plywood, stud wood); and

- other (rubber, silver and gold coins).

The availability of many commodities is dependent on a number of uncontrollable forces: weather, insects, labor negotiations, political turmoil, changing consumer tastes and price supports. These forces can determine whether a crop will be plentiful or whether precious metals can be mined. Availability impacts commodity prices, which are based on *supply and demand*. When a commodity is abundant, its price may be low; when a commodity is scarce, its price may be high. The supply and demand for many commodities is fairly cyclical. For example, the price of corn is relatively low at harvest when the crop is plentiful. As stores of corn are used, the price begins to rise. The price for other commodities, like gold or silver, is higher in September, when jewelers are preparing for the holiday season.

■ THE CASH MARKET

The *cash market* for commodities is the marketplace with which people are most familiar. When they buy a frozen pizza at the supermarket, they are engaging in a transaction in the cash market—an immediate exchange of an agreed upon amount of money for an agreed-upon quantity of some product. A government bond trader selling 30-year U.S. Treasury bonds to a bank is engaging in a transaction in the cash market. Cash markets can be of any size, range from local to global and are intended to facilitate the trading of the particular commodity on which they are based.

Negotiated Trading

A *cash trade* is a transaction involving the almost immediate exchange of ownership of a commodity or good for an agreed-upon amount of money. Cash trading usually takes the form of an agreement privately negotiated between a buyer and a seller to deliver a specified quantity of a good at a time and delivery point as mutually agreed to by the parties involved in the transaction.

The price for the commodity may be established when the transaction is initiated, or it may not be determined until delivery time, at which point it will be based on the then-current cash, or *spot market* value of the commodity.

How the Cash Market Operates

Commodity cash markets consist of all of the individuals, corporations and business people involved in the production, warehousing, distribution, processing, manufacture and consumption of basic commodities (food stocks and animal feeds, ore, fossil fuels, livestock and so on). It is these basic goods and resources that are the essential raw materials and base products on which the world's economy is built and on which the quality of human life depends.

The creation and evolution of the various commodity cash markets came about in direct response to the need of business and commerce to channel the flow of goods throughout the economy as efficiently as possible. Producers of the various commodities, whether the multitude of domestic and foreign grain farmers or the handful of copper mining corporations that control the supply side of that world market, constantly seek the best (highest) price for what they produce.

Producers attempt to get the highest possible price for their products, and in an effort to get the highest price they may occasionally withhold goods from the market, refusing to harvest crops, or even plowing crops under to artificially lower the supply and thereby support prices. Conversely, buyers attempt to purchase raw goods at the lowest possible price to meet their inventory needs. For example, as automobile sales decline, purchasing agents for electrical wire/motor builders may seek out copper substitutes, thus driving the price of copper downward, which in turn may cause commercial copper mining operations to cut back or even to shut down.

Meanwhile, as sellers and buyers continue to negotiate (each hoping to get the optimum price), those in the middle (such as grain elevators and merchants, importers and exporters, pipeline companies and others involved in distribution) attempt to buy at low prices from producers and sell at higher prices to users within the shortest possible time. Most distributors operate by filling the user's order first (selling), and then buying from a producer as quickly and as cheaply as possible to cover the sale and protect the profit margin on the transaction.

Through such bargaining, the cycle of deal making continues daily across the country and around the world. The marketplace consists of cattle auction grounds and stockyards, grain elevators and corporate offices. In fact, face-to-face negotiations account for only a small percentage of all commodity cash market transactions; the bulk of the business is conducted over the phone or by computer.

Although some cash markets are global in nature, most operate locally. For instance, while foreign currencies and government securities markets serve participants around the world and encompass multibillion-dollar trading volumes, cattle markets are typically local businesses that service a limited number of ready buyers and sellers. Because there are fewer participants, these smaller, local markets offer less liquidity and are much more heavily influenced by local supply and demand.

Forward Contracts

Since the invention of money thousands of years ago, the cash trading system has been the primary means of exchanging money for goods. However, trading cash for needed commodities is not always the most efficient method of transacting business. This inefficiency is due in part to the financial burden of delivering the entire dollar amount immediately upon receipt of the goods or *settlement*, and in part to the expenses associated with the transportation and storage of the often bulky goods until they are needed.

In addition, there are the problems of supply and demand, both of which can be volatile and unpredictable when cash markets are the only means of trading commodities. For example, when there is no method of "locking in" a price for a later purchase or sale, producers, traders, consumers and middlemen face a difficult choice: to trade at today's price and risk losses if the price of the good then falls, or to delay a trade and risk losses if the good's price rises. Because cash markets do not offer guaranteed prices, it is often difficult to establish an equilibrium between supply and demand, and this instability tends to aggravate price volatility.

It is because of such drawbacks that *forward contracts* evolved. Such contracts constitute a direct commitment between one particular buyer and one particular seller. The person selling forward is obligated to make delivery; the person buying forward is obligated to take delivery. A forward contract is nonstandardized in that any terms and provisions contained in it are defined solely by the contract parties, without third-party intervention. This arrangement offers no price protection (*hedge*) to either side of the contract, but does ensure a ready market or supply source, as it almost always results in delivery.

Because forward contracts represent direct obligations between a particular buyer and seller, only the party on one side of the contract can release the party on the other side from contractual commitments. In addition, because there is no third party guaranteeing performance, each party to the contract assumes the responsibility and risks of checking the credit and trustworthiness of the other.

Elements of a Forward Contract

The five components of a typical forward contract, or cash commodity transaction, are:

1. quantity of the commodity;

2. quality of the commodity;

3. time for delivery;

4. place for delivery; and

5. price to be paid at delivery.

The price for the commodity is usually set at the time the parties enter into the forward contract. In some cases, the agreed on price will be the cash market price at the date of delivery. Sometimes, an investor entering into a forward contract may be required to make a cash deposit or put up an agreed-upon amount of money as a margin deposit.

■ COMMODITY FUTURES MARKET

Certain problems with cash and forward transactions, such as lack of price protection and protection against other risks, gave rise to commodity futures trading. Futures trading is nothing new. In fact, futures contracts evolved from forward contracts that were in use in Europe as early as the Middle Ages.

Today, however, *futures trading* is regulated by an exchange and includes not only those who need to buy or sell the actual commodity, but also those who only wish to speculate on the rise or fall of the product's price over time.

The commodities futures industry serves two functions: (1) as a *price-setting marketplace* for business people whose livelihoods depend on how efficiently and economically they are able to buy, sell, serve as distributors for, handle, manage or commercially store bulk commodities and (2) as a *speculative investment market* for risk-oriented retail and institutional customers. Although the cash forward market remains an active market, speculative investments account for more than 50 percent of commodity futures trading.

Futures Trades and Cash Trades

A *futures trade* differs from a cash trade in three major respects:

1. it is not personally negotiated between the buyer and seller originating the trade;

2. the trade is always for a specified grade and amount of a commodity (although the contract specifies a certain grade, another grade may be delivered at a discount or a premium to the agreed upon price); and

3. the commodity must be delivered from the locations and at the times specified by exchange rules.

Actual trading takes place on a designated futures contract exchange, which maintains facilities for continuous trading.

By using futures, buyers and sellers can protect against adverse price changes. This price protection comes in the form of transfer of risk and is known as *hedging*. Hedging is an economic benefit of commodity futures trading. Cash prices are market-determined factors; consequently, producers, distributors and users of commodities cannot usually accurately predict buying or selling prices at later cash settlement dates. Holding goods in inventory for later sale is risky (remember, though, that risk is not necessarily bad). If, for instance, after a buyer acquires goods for inventory market prices rise, the buyer can sell that inventory at a gain. If prices fall, however, the buyer who holds the goods in inventory suffers an economic loss—if he had waited to purchase, the goods would have cost him less.

Hedging or transferring the price risk can be accomplished by taking an appropriate futures position on the goods the buyer will someday want in inventory. For example, if a cattle breeder owns cows (he could also be said to be "long" cows), he could hedge by establishing a short position in cattle futures (to "short" something is to sell it). The futures position acts as a temporary substitute for the transaction the breeder must enter into at a later time in the cash market. In this example, if the price of the cash stock declines, he will suffer a loss; however, the loss will be offset by a corresponding gain in the futures market.

The futures hedger is transferring price risk to the futures speculator. The speculator takes on the risk of changing prices, while the hedger has taken on the risks only of foregone profit. Those individuals trading futures as speculators will try to gather as much information as possible on which to base trading decisions. As speculators and hedgers act on available information, their buying and selling activity is reflected in the commodity's price. If the markets are efficient at processing information, today's futures prices are a reasonably accurate estimate of later cash market prices. This is the second major economic function of futures—the competitive determination of commodity prices for later delivery. Often, futures prices are used by businesses to estimate future cash market prices for long-range planning.

Futures Contracts

Futures contracts are exchange-traded obligations. They are agreements between a buyer and a seller for the purchase and sale of a commodity at an established price and delivery date in the future. Investing in futures is known as a *zero-sum game* because for every investor who gains, there is someone holding another contract who loses. The person who goes *long* (that is, who purchases a futures contract) is obligated to take delivery of the commodity at the agreed-upon future date. The buyer's maximum potential liability is the full value of the contract. The person who goes *short* (or sells a futures contract) has taken on an obligation, too—the seller is obligated to deliver the commodity at the agreed-upon future date. If the seller does not currently own the commodity, his potential liability is unlimited.

A price is agreed upon in advance by the buyer and the seller, and the value of the futures contract varies with the supply and demand for and in the commodity itself. For example, factors such as the weather and its effect on crops will affect corn and wheat futures. At a specific time, a futures contract *obligates* the holder to buy or sell a specific commodity at a stated price by a stated date.

Futures contracts differ from spot contracts in at least four ways:

1. *Futures contracts specify standardized quantities and qualities*. It is not efficient or profitable for businesses to trade one pound or one bushel at a time. Therefore, each futures contract represents a large quantity of the commodity, such as 10,000 bushels of this or 5,000 pounds of that. For example, one contract for wheat represents 5,000 bushels, one contract for gasoline represents 42,000 gallons and one contract for sugar represents 112,000 pounds. (It is because of these large quantities that even a minor change in price can have a significant impact on the value of a single contract.) Each commodity is also graded into categories such as "#2 northern spring wheat" or "#2 hard red wheat."

2. *Futures contracts specify a future month for delivery of the commodity*. The delivery months for each commodity are determined by harvest seasons, volume of trading and other considerations. Each contract trades in specific months over the year ahead. For example, although eggs or gold may be

delivered every month, wheat is usually harvested and delivered in July, September, December, March and May.

3. *Futures contracts are traded on organized commodities exchanges.* Like stock exchanges, commodities exchanges provide a place where their members can make purchases and sales. Commodities are traded on exchanges throughout the world, but the most active markets are the 13 North American exchanges—12 in the United States and 1 in Canada. The Chicago Board of Trade, the largest and oldest commodities exchange, originated the concept of futures markets. Other very active exchanges include the Chicago Mercantile Exchange, the New York Mercantile Exchange and the Commodity Exchange of New York. These exchanges account for 80 percent of the trading volume conducted on North American futures.

4. *Futures contracts can be offset.* Although the holder is obligated to complete the commodities transaction, fewer than 3 percent all of futures contracts result in the *delivery* of the actual commodity. Instead of the product itself, a certificate of ownership called a *warehouse receipt* changes hands. Most contracts are liquidated by another closing transaction before expiration. Futures contracts are standardized, and buyers and sellers benefit from the organizations that act as clearinghouses—liaisons between the buyer and the seller—for the contracts. Because of these clearinghouses, futures positions can easily be offset prior to delivery. In other words, investors close out their original position by buying back a contract they sold, or selling off a contract they bought, netting either a profit or loss. The offsetting transaction must occur in the same commodity, for the same delivery and on the same exchange. For example, investors who bought a futures contract for 5,000 bushels of wheat for delivery in May could close out their position by selling the contract back to another buyer before May. About 98 percent of all futures contracts are offset prior to delivery, and in grain futures, the figure is closer to 100 percent.

■ NATURE OF COMMODITY TRANSACTIONS

Futures contracts can be traced back to biblical times when individuals who produced, owned and/or processed foodstuffs sought a way to protect themselves against adverse price movements. As noted above, today there are 13 North American *commodity futures exchanges*, organizations registered with the *Commodity Futures Trading Commission (CFTC)*, that provide a location (or trading floor) for trading regulated futures contracts.

The term *contract market* is used to refer to that particular exchange designated by the CFTC as the legal location for trading futures contracts for a particular commodity. For example, the Chicago Board of Trade (CBOT or CBT) is the contract market for the soybean complex and T-bonds. The New York Mercantile Exchange (NYME) is the contract market for crude oil. The Chicago Mercantile Exchange (CME) is the contract market for pork bellies and the S&P 500. At the CFTC's discretion, more than one exchange can be designated as a contract market for the various commodities.

Clearinghouse

A *clearinghouse* is an organization that is separate from, but associated with, an exchange (as an example, the CME owns its own clearinghouse). It adds to futures market efficiency by serving as the go-between for the ultimate buyers and sellers of futures contracts. Buyers and sellers of futures contracts rarely have personal contact and do not settle with or deliver directly to each other. Rather, all settlements and deliveries are handled by and through the clearinghouse, making the process much more efficient and less subject to error and disagreement.

Increased Liquidity

A clearinghouse serves to increase the liquidity of the market. It allows investors to establish or offset any futures positions they have taken by buying from or selling to the clearinghouse, rather than having to locate, contact and contract with another buyer or seller directly. Everyone with a position in futures (whether long or short) has a position against a particular clearinghouse rather than directly against another trader. The interchangeability (*fungibility*) of standardized contracts and instruments is a crucial ingredient in the effectiveness of clearinghouses.

Executing Trades

If an investor wishes to take a position in futures, the trade must be executed by a trader who has access to the exchange floor (sometimes the investor is a member and has personal access). The buying customer and the selling customer place orders through their brokerage firms, or *futures commission merchants (FCMs)*. The FCM directs that the trade be executed in the appropriate pit by the *floor broker (FB)*. The FB then confirms the trade to the clearinghouse. If the clearinghouse receives matching confirmations from the floor broker(s) involved in that trade (one on the buy side and one on the sell side), it accepts the position. The buyer has a long position against the clearinghouse's short position, and the seller has a short position against the clearinghouse's long position. In other words, the clearinghouse is the buyer to all sellers and the seller to all buyers.

By stepping between the buyers and sellers, the clearinghouse can act as a guarantor of all outstanding contracts—guaranteeing performance, not delivery. That is, the clearinghouse guarantees that the buyer will receive the monetary value of the position, although it does not guarantee actual physical delivery.

Margin Trading

The procedures involved in a commodity transaction are similar to those of a stock transaction; however, there are two important differences. The risk factor is greater for commodities than for stocks because of wide price fluctuations, and even a small price shift can cause losses. In addition, the margin requirements (explained below) are lower for commodities transactions than for stock transactions. This encourages speculation because the investor doesn't have to put up as much money to secure a futures contract.

All futures transactions are traded on *margin*. This means that the investor has to put down only a fraction of the total cost of the futures contract. Depending on the commodity, the margin requirements range from 2 to 10 percent of the value of the contract. For example, an investor might put down $5,000 to buy a futures contract with an underlying value of $50,000. This *margin deposit* acts as security to cover any loss in the market value of the contract that might result from adverse price movements.

Each commodity has its own margin deposit requirement, expressed in dollars, and it represents the amount of money necessary to initiate a commodities transaction. After the investment is made, the market value of the contract will rise and fall as the price of the commodity goes up or down. Therefore, to assure that the deposit will be sufficient to cover such price swings, the investor is also required to meet a *maintenance margin* requirement, which is the minimum amount that must be in the margin account at all times. At the end of each trading day, the clearinghouse for the exchange calculates the gains or losses on the investor's *position* or stake in the market. If there is a gain, the profit is added to the margin account; if there is a loss, the amount of the loss is deducted from the investor's margin requirements. By trading on margin—by investing only a fraction of the cost of the contract—the investor hopes to profit.

ILL. 11.1 ■ *Understanding Futures Tables*

- *Open* refers to the price at which cotton first sold when the exchange opened in the morning.

- *High*, *low* and *settle* indicate the contract's highest, lowest and closing prices for the day. Viewed together, these figures indicate how volatile the market for that commodity was during the trading day.

- *Change* compares the closing price given here with the previous closing price (listed in the previous day's paper). A plus sign (+) indicates prices ended higher; a minus (−) means prices ended lower.

	Open	High	Low	Settle	Change	Lifetime High	Low	Open Interest
COTTON (CTN)—50,000 lbs.; cents per lb.								
Ja94	69.40	69.50	68.02	68.70	.75	81.40	53.90	3,813

- The *product* is listed alphabetically within its particular grouping.

- The date shows a commodity's *expiration cycle*. Every contract expires during a certain month. *Ja94* indicates January 1994.

- Cotton (CTN) is the *exchange* on which the futures contracts are traded. A list of what each abbreviation means is printed at the bottom of the page each day. Here CTN is the New York Cotton Exchange.

- *Open interest* reflects the previous trading day.

Individual Investor Participation

Investors generally participate in the commodity markets in one of three ways. Individual investors may trade futures by giving their brokers an order to enter into a contract either as a buyer (they *go long*) or a seller (they *go short*), depending on which way the investor believes the market is headed. In addition, individuals may invest in a *commodity pool*—a sort of commodity mutual fund where money is pooled from a large number of investors and invested in commodities by a professional. Finally, some investors give their brokerage firm or money manager written power of attorney to trade for them. These accounts are called *discretionary accounts* or *managed accounts*. In addition to brokerage commissions, the adviser will usually share in any profits earned.

Trading Strategy

Though fundamental factors, such as the supply and demand determinants covered earlier, ultimately will affect long-term prices of commodities, traders employ technical analysis to try to profit from short-term price movements. Basically this involves studying charts of prices and volumes to determine price trends, support levels and so on. Technical charts such as those used by technical traders may give clues to the relative price valuation of a commodity. This can be helpful in deciding the proper time to buy or sell.

Traders in the futures market consist of two classes: hedgers and speculators. *Hedgers* are primarily producers (farmers, mining companies, foresters or oil drillers) or users (bakers, jewelers, paper mills or oil distributors) of commodities. They are interested in using the market to lock in a price that protects them against future changes in the market. *Speculators* do not buy or sell the futures contract to obtain the commodity; they trade futures for the investment potential only. Speculators enhance market liquidity because they are willing to assume greater risk for the chance to make greater profits.

Though commodities trading is associated with risk, it can also be a way for businesses to reduce risk. There are a number of ways for traders to reduce risk, including speculating, spreading and/or hedging. For example, if a cereal company projects that the price of wheat will increase by 30 percent over the next six months, it might purchase a wheat contract today at a specified price to reduce the risk of having to pay higher prices for the needed wheat in six months.

■ FINANCIAL FUTURES

Another segment of the futures market is *financial futures*, a type of futures contract in which the underlying commodity consists of a specified amount of a financial instrument, such as debt securities, foreign currencies or market baskets of common stock. Financial futures are traded on exchanges much like commodity futures.

Foreign Currency Futures

A *foreign currency futures contract* is an agreement between a buyer and a seller that specifies the currency, the quantity of the currency, the delivery date and the price at which the seller must deliver the currency. Foreign currency contracts include the British pound, German deutsche mark, Swiss franc, Japanese yen, Canadian dollar, European Currency Unit (ECU) and others.

Foreign currency contracts are purchased and sold as hedges against exchange rate risk inherent in international trading. When a U.S. company completes a business transaction with a foreign company, both have a substantial risk of loss if the currencies of either country vary after the transaction is completed. For example, assume that a U.S. company agrees to sell a specified amount of automobile parts to a German manufacturer for delivery in six months for three million deutsche marks (DM). At the time of the transaction, the *exchange rate* is two DM to one U.S. dollar. In other words, the contract is worth $1.5 million U.S. dollars.

If the value of the U.S. dollar goes up to three DM (a "strong" dollar) before the transaction is completed, the U.S. company will receive only $1 million instead of the expected $1.5 million, even though nothing has changed in the contract. Conversely, if the exchange rate drops to one DM per U.S. dollar (a "weak" dollar), the U.S. company will receive $3 million. The opposite is true if the transaction is made in U.S. dollars. If the dollar goes up, the Germans will have to pay more deutsche marks; if the dollar goes down, they will have to pay fewer deutsche marks, even though the U.S. company will receive the same $3 million.

Interest Rate Futures

Financial futures are based on the principle that *interest rates*—the cost of credit—can be regarded in the same way as the price of other commodities, and that certain types of organizations, such as banks and thrift institutions, need a means of protecting themselves against volatile interest rates. Traditionally, banks and other savings institutions borrowed short term by securing deposits for 3, 6, 12 months or longer with certificates of deposit while lending long term with mortgage loans with 20-year or 30-year maturities. If the bank charges a fixed rate of 10 percent on its mortgages and pays only 5 percent on its depositors' savings accounts, the institution remains profitable. However, as inflation rises, savers look for alternatives to the low interest rates paid by the bank and the bank's liabilities could soon exceed its assets.

Just as commodities futures can be used by producers to hedge their risks, *interest rate futures* are used by financial institutions to lock in a profitable spread between the institution's assets (deposits) and its liabilities (loans). Interest rate futures contracts are purchased with different maturities to take advantage of fluctuating interest rates. Contracts include Treasury bills, Eurodollars, Treasury notes and Treasury bonds. Interest rate futures trade *inversely* to interest rates. In other words, when interest rates increase, the value of futures decreases. If the financial pages report that T-bond futures have rallied, it means that long-term interest rates have dropped.

Index Futures

Index futures are contracts to buy or sell a portfolio of stocks at a stated price by a certain date. The investor purchases a futures contract written on broad-based measures of stock market performance such as the *S&P 500 Index*, which is made up of 500 stocks listed on the NYSE, AMEX and OTC. In addition to the S&P 500, stock index futures are traded in the *NYSE Composite Index*, *Value Line Composite Index*

ILL. 11.2 ■ *Understanding Financial Futures Tables*

Currency futures are quoted in dollars or cents per unit of the underlying foreign currency (for example, in dollars per British pound or cents per Japanese yen). As shown below, the closing (or settle) prices for one December British pound contract was worth US $95,000 (62,500 pds. × $1.5328 per pound) and a December Japanese yen was US $89,875 (12.5 million yen × .007190 $ per yen).

CURRENCY FUTURES

	Open	High	Low	Settle	Change	Lifetime High	Lifetime Low	Open Interest
JAPANESE YEN (IMM) 12.5 million yen; $ per yen (.00)								
June	.7093	.7100	.7046	.7052	–.0018	.8485	.7046	68,966
Sept	.7162	.7172	.7118	.7123	–.0020	.8580	.7118	4,773
Dec	.7220	.7235	.7182	.7190	–.0023	.8635	.7182	741
Mr90	.7285	.7295	.7264	.7254	–.0026	.8357	.7264	188

Est vol 40,365; vol Mon 43,848; open int 74,668, +1,721.

BRITISH POUND (IMM)—62,500 pds.; $ per pound

	Open	High	Low	Settle	Change	Lifetime High	Lifetime Low	Open Interest
June	1.5782	1.5806	1.5570	1.5608	–.0120	1.8370	1.5570	24,750
Sept	1.5636	1.5660	1.5410	1.5458	–.0124	1.8030	1.5410	1,609
Dec	1.5490	1.5500	1.5250	1.5328	–.0130	1.7450	1.5250	186
June	1.5150	1.5270	1.5090	1.5088	–.0130	1.6950	1.5090	151

and the *Major Market Index*. Each of these indexes is a mathematical indicator that measures the collective performance of specific groups of stock.

Index futures allow investors to participate in the general movements of the entire stock market. For example, investors have the opportunity to purchase a large basket of stocks rather than having to select from over 50,000 individual stocks. Instead of selling individual stocks in expectation of a market decline, investors may elect to sell the entire basket of stocks. When one investor sells an index contract in anticipation of a market drop, an investor who believes the market is going up buys the contract. In every trade there is a winner—and a loser.

Stock index futures are highly leveraged and offer the potential for large profits. However, high leverage also means high risk. And, in addition to the margin deposit requirements that normally run about 10 percent of the value of the contract, brokerage houses require futures traders to have substantial incomes and net worth. Index futures are very volatile and, because the investor is at risk for the entire value of the contract, his or her losses may exceed the initial investment.

■ OPTIONS

An *option* is a contract between two people. The purchaser (also known as the *holder*, *buyer* or *owner*) of the contract has paid money for the *right* to buy or the *right* to sell securities. The seller (or *writer*) of the option contract, on the other hand, has accepted money for taking on an *obligation*. The option seller *must* buy or *must* sell the specified security if asked to do so by the option's buyer. A *stock option contract* (the most familiar option) represents an agreement between two people (a buyer and seller) to buy or sell 100 shares (a *round lot*) of stock.

Option contracts serve a multitude of purposes. They can provide investors and business people with a means to invest for income or capital gain, to speculate on securities, markets, foreign currencies and other instruments, or even to hedge or protect positions in other investments. There are two types of options: *calls* and *puts*.

- A call option is the *right to call* (buy) a security from someone for a specific period of time and at a specific price (the *strike price*). You can buy that right for yourself, or you can sell that right to someone else.

- A put option is the *right to put* (sell) a security to someone for a specific period of time and at a specific price. You can buy that right for yourself, or you can sell that right to someone else. The money the buyer of an option contract pays the seller to take on the obligations in the contract is called the option's *premium*.

■ OPTIONS TRADING

Options on stock (and some other securities) trade on exchange and OTC markets.

Exchange-traded options (also known as *listed options*) have standardized strike prices (that is, the stock price at which the option can be exercised) and bid expiration dates. Options are traded on a number of exchanges, including the:

- American Stock Exchange (AMEX);

- Chicago Board Options Exchange (CBOE);

- New York Stock Exchange (NYSE);

- Pacific Stock Exchange (PSE); and

- Philadelphia Stock Exchange (PHLX).

To qualify for trading on a listed options exchange, the security underlying the option contract must meet minimum listing requirements as specified by that exchange.

Options are traded by brokers on the floors of the option exchanges. These floor brokers buy and sell options the same way they would trade stock—by using hand signals and shouting out their bids or offers in a double-auction market.

The various option exchanges employ market makers and specialists (called *order book officials*, or *OBOs*, on the Pacific and Philadelphia exchanges; OBOs or board brokers on the CBOE; and *specialists* on the NYSE and AMEX) to ensure that the auction process runs smoothly. The board brokers and OBOs keep track of limit orders and maintain orderly markets by trading for their own accounts as market makers.

Each *market maker* on an exchange is responsible for maintaining a fair and orderly market in the options of at least one underlying security. The market maker may hold a position in the option (either long or short) and stands ready to buy or sell the option at any time. The market maker is not required to support a falling market by continuously purchasing the option for his own account.

Broker-dealers often use computerized order routing systems to handle customer option transactions. An order sent through a computerized system will ordinarily be routed from the broker-dealer to the commission-house booth for handling by the exchange member who represents the broker-dealer. The exchange member (the floor broker) will take the order and present it in the trading crowd. If the order is executed, notice of the execution is given back to the commission-house booth, which in turn uses the computerized communication system of the broker-dealer to notify the registered representative and customer.

For some small orders, the routing system may select automatic execution. For quicker action, the system bypasses the commission-house communication booth and floor broker and sends the order directly to the trading post. Each order is executed against an order on the limit order book or a market maker's quote, and the notice of execution is sent directly to the broker-dealer.

The automatic execution system of each exchange has its own criteria, special capabilities and name. The CBOE has the *Order Routing System (ORS)* and *Retail Automatic Execution System (RAES)*. The AMEX has the *Automatic AMEX Options Switch (AUTOAMOS)* system. Each offers its subscribers direct communication to and from the trading post.

Options Clearing Corporation

Created and owned by the exchanges that trade options, the *Options Clearing Corporation* (OCC) is the entity that standardizes option contracts, guarantees performance of the contracts and issues options. The active secondary market in securities options is possible only because of the role of the OCC. The OCC's three-part mission is to standardize options contracts, issue options to buyers and sellers and guarantee performance of the contracts.

On exchange-traded options, the standardized strike prices and expiration months are determined by the OCC. The market itself (that is, interested buyers and sellers) determines the premiums of OCC-issued, standardized options. Options are issued by the OCC without a certificate. The investor's proof of ownership of an option is the trade confirmation and any brokerage account statement received by the customer.

To satisfy the prospectus requirement of the Securities Act of 1940, the OCC publishes an options disclosure document called "The Characteristics and Risks of

Standardized Options." This disclosure document outlines the risks and rewards associated with investing in options. An investor must receive this document from the broker-dealer prior to or at the same time as receiving approval for options trading. The disclosure document must also accompany any options sales literature a client is sent.

Sales literature, according to the options exchanges, does not include material that is strictly educational. A disclosure document does not, for example, have to accompany a letter that explains covered call writing but does not contain specific recommendations. Any educational material, however, must tell the investor where to obtain information on the risks of investing in options.

■ EQUITY OPTIONS

In theory, options can be created on any item with a fluctuating market value, such as securities, houses, cars, gold coins, baseball cards, playoff tickets and comic books. The most familiar options are those issued on common stocks and called *equity options*. Though considered speculative, equity or *stock options* are often used to diversify an investor's portfolio and can serve as the basis for specific investment strategies and trading techniques. A stock option is a contract that gives the holder the *right* to buy or sell a specific security or financial contract on or before a specified expiration date. Many financial instruments have options. However, for purposes of this discussion, we will focus on *stock options*—investment products that are linked to the securities markets, have their own value and are actively traded.

Call Options

As you will recall, a *call option* is a negotiable instrument that gives its holder the right to purchase a specified number (most typically 100) of common stock shares for a specified price on or before a specified date. Calls are usually purchased by investors who believe that the price of the stock will go up. For example, let's say an investor thinks the price of XYZ Common Stock, which is currently trading at $25 a share, will increase over the next few months. She buys a call on that stock, giving her the right to purchase 100 shares of XYZ at $25 per share over the next, say, six months. In five months, the price of XYZ has risen to $35 a share and our investor exercises her purchase option and buys 100 shares for $2,500. Because those shares are now trading at $35, she could sell them and earn a gross profit of $1,000 (less the price of the call option).

Put Options

In contrast to a call option, a *put option* gives the holder the right to *sell* a specified number of stock shares (again, this number is typically 100) at a specified price over a specified period of time. Investors purchase puts when they anticipate the price of a stock will decline. Using the example above, the investor could buy a put option if she thought the price of the $25 XYZ stock was going to go down. Say the stock does, indeed, decline to $15 a share. By buying a put to sell the shares at $25 each, the investor could go to the market, purchase 100 shares of XYZ at $15 a share then exercise her put and sell them for $25 per share to another investor.

Characteristics of Calls and Puts

Calls and puts are not issued by the companies or corporations that issue the underlying stock. Instead, they are issued by the OCC and it is the OCC that stands behind the options. Furthermore, calls and puts are negotiable financial instruments that are actively traded on listed exchanges.

Another unique characteristic of calls and puts is that they do not have to be exercised. The buyer of a call is not obligated to purchase the stock and the buyer of a put is not obligated to sell the stock. In fact, many options simply expire, having been neither traded nor exercised.

There are three other characteristics of these options with which investors should be familiar: the exercise or strike price, the premium and the expiration date.

Exercise or Strike Price

The *exercise* or *strike price* is the price at which the buyer of a call has the right to buy and the buyer of a put has the right to sell the option's underlying shares. This price does not change, regardless of any movement in the actual stock price.

The value (and premium) of the option moves in relation to the price of the underlying stock. When a call has a strike price less than the market price of the underlying stock, it has *intrinsic value*; when it has a strike price greater than the market price of the underlying stock, it has little or no value. By the same token, when a put has a strike price greater than the stock's market price, it has intrinsic value; when its strike price is less than the stock's price, it has little or no value. An option that is "*in-the-money*" is one worth exercising at its strike price relative to the price of the underlying stock; if it is "*out-of-the-money*," it is not worth exercising. If an option is "*at-the-money*," its strike price is the same as the price of the underlying stock. The value of an option—as measured by its premiums—depends on its strike price and the market price of the underlying security.

Premium

The purchase price of an option is known as the *premium*. This is the amount the buyer pays to acquire the call or put. The premium is based on a number of factors, chief of which are (1) the *intrinsic value* of the option and (2) the *time value* of the option. The intrinsic value of the option is calculated by one of the three conditions noted above: the option is either at-the-money (no intrinsic value); in-the-money; or out-of-the-money (no intrinsic value). The option's expiration date will also affect its premium: the longer the time the option has before it expires, the greater its premium.

Expiration Date

Every option has an *expiration date*, which specifies its lifetime. The value of an option diminishes with time. When the expiration date is reached, the option has lost any value. Therefore, timing is critical, since the option owner is holding a wasting asset.

Investing in Stock Options

The holder of a call option or a put option does not have the same advantages or benefits as does a stock owner; for example, he or she is not entitled to any dividends the underlying stock may pay. Furthermore, an option holder owns no property; he or she has only purchased *time*—the right to buy or sell the stock for a certain length of time and has only a limited period of time in which he or she can realize any profit or gain. So what's the attraction of an option?

Although option traders sometimes pursue complex strategies, the basic reason for buying or writing options is to make money on the price movement of the underlying security during the limited life of the option contract. Those who invest in stock options are either bullish or bearish on the underlying stock. *Bullish* indicates optimism that an underlying security or the market is going up. *Bearish* indicates pessimism, the belief that a security or the market is going down.

■ INDEX OPTIONS

Though options on indexes are relatively new to investors, the indexes themselves are not. Indexes that measure the movements of markets or parts of markets have been around for decades. Two primary types of indexes are important here:

- *Broad-based indexes*. Broad-based indexes are all designed to reflect the movement of the market as a whole, but different indexes vary substantially. Some track as few as 20 stocks; others follow the movements of more than

---

ILL. 11.3 ■ *Understanding Options Tables*

An *option* gives an investor the right—but not the obligation—to buy or sell something. Buyers pay a nonrefundable amount in return for *time* to decide whether to conclude the deal. Puts and calls may be traded on a number of investments. There are options on foreign currencies, commodity and financial futures, market indexes and interest rates. A sample of a stock option is shown below.

Option & NY Close		Strike Price Jun	Calls—Last Sep	Dec	Jun	Puts—Last Sep	Dec
BrisMy	40	6⅜	7½	r	r	¼	½
46½	45	1⅜	3¼	s	r	1⅛	1⅝

Put and call quotations contain the name of the company or an abbreviation (in this case *BrisMy* for *Bristol Myers*), with the New York Stock Exchange closing price for the stock appearing below it. The *striking price* is listed next, then the *calls'* closing prices reported, followed by similar quotes for *puts*. The price is quoted per share—even though puts and calls trade in 100-share units. Thus one call or put represents an option on 100 shares. An *s* signifies that no option was listed, while an *r* indicates none were traded on that day.

1,700. Options are available on the S&P 100 Index (ticker symbol OEX), the S&P 500 Index (ticker symbol SPX), the AMEX Major Market Index (ticker symbol XMI) and the *Value Line* Index, among others.

- *Narrow-based indexes*. Narrow-based indexes track the movements of market segments, such as a group of stocks in one industry or a specific type of investment. Narrow-based indexes include the Technology Index and the Gold/Silver Index.

Indexes provide information; they are not, in themselves, investments. Most investors cannot buy (or sell) an actual index to profit from its changing value. Indexes do provide numerical values that are used to track other investments, however, and these values change. An investor can speculate on the direction, degree and timing of that change by purchasing or selling options on that index. Index options make it possible for investors to profit from the swings in the market or to hedge against losses that market movement can cause in individual stock positions.

■ INTEREST RATE OPTIONS

Options on government debt securities are a product of the enormous growth of the federal deficit and wide swings in interest rates. Financed by Treasury bills, notes and bonds, the government's deficit creates a vast market in securities that are sensitive to changes in interest rates. Interest rate options were introduced to allow investors to profit from fluctuations in interest rates (and debt security prices) and to hedge the risks created by those fluctuations. The objectives of investors in interest rate options are similar to those of investors in stock or index options. They hope to profit from changes in the prices of debt securities (caused by fluctuations in interest rates) or to hedge existing portfolios of debt securities against price declines caused by increased interest rates. The securities underlying interest rate options have high values ($100,000 for notes and bonds and $1 million for Treasury bills), and the typical investor tends to be an institution rather than an individual.

Options on debt securities respond to changes in the price of the underlying security just as stock options do. But the values of Treasury bills, notes and bonds move inversely to movements in interest rates. As rates go up, existing debt securities lose value. And as interest rates go down, existing debt securities gain value. A decrease in the interest paid on newly issued bonds will cause the prices of existing bonds that pay higher interest rates to increase. Hence, interest rates have gone down and debt prices have increased.

■ FOREIGN CURRENCY OPTIONS

Any U.S. citizen who has traveled outside the United States has learned about currency exchange in the retail market from the sometimes frustrating experience of translating the value of the U.S. dollar into the currency of another country. Currency exchange in the wholesale market of large banks, international corporations and sophisticated investors is similar in complexity and risk.

Investors trade *foreign currency options (FCOs)* for two reasons: they hope to profit from fluctuating exchange rates, and they want to hedge against the risks arising from fluctuating exchange rates.

Currency Risk

The risk in monetary exchange arises from fluctuations in the exchange rate. On a personal scale, this is a fairly simple matter. If a U.S. citizen goes to Canada, for instance, he may be able to exchange each U.S. dollar for $1.30 Canadian. The next time he travels, his U.S. dollar might buy only $1.20 Canadian or it might buy $1.40 Canadian.

U.S. corporations with contracts to buy or sell goods in a foreign country at a specific time have the same problem as the traveler. The dollars a U.S. wholesaler budgets to buy Swiss watches in six months may not be sufficient if the rate of exchange between U.S. dollars and Swiss francs changes in the meantime.

Characteristics of Foreign Currency Options

The Philadelphia Stock Exchange (PHLX) is set up to facilitate the trading of options on foreign currencies. Underlying each FCO is an arbitrary amount of foreign money as set by the exchange. The strike price of the option is set at a certain amount of U.S. money. Each option contract represents the right to buy or sell the foreign currency for the specified amount of U.S. money. The owner of an FCO, therefore, can lock in a certain exchange rate for a certain time, just as the owner of an equity option can lock in the strike price of an equity option.

A call owner can, for the amount of U.S. money set by the strike price, purchase the amount of foreign currency determined by the contract. It is as if the traveler mentioned above could determine months in advance that each of his U.S. dollars would be worth $1.30 Canadian when the time came to travel.

Underlying Currencies

Options are available on several foreign currencies, including British pounds, Canadian dollars, German marks, French francs, Japanese yen and Swiss francs. Option contract characteristics vary from currency to currency.

Strategies

Investors and speculators trade FCOs for two reasons: to profit from fluctuating exchange rates or to hedge against the risks arising from fluctuating exchange rates. Exchange rates rise and fall because of changes in the values of both currencies involved. The changing value of the foreign currency, then, is not the only problem for investors. The value of U.S. money may be changing as well.

The reverse also occurs. Remember that the instrument underlying the option is foreign currency. Whatever is going on with the U.S. dollar, the investor's strategy is determined by the market price of the foreign money. If the dollar is weakening, the deutsche mark could be growing stronger; an investor would be bullish on the mark. To avoid confusion, it helps to concentrate on the underlying instrument, the foreign currency. Remember that the investor has the right to buy or sell the foreign currency, not the U.S. dollar. When an investor expects the value of the underlying instrument to increase, he uses bullish strategies to profit from that increase. That means buying calls or selling puts on the currency. And when an investor expects the value of the currency to drop, he sells calls or buys puts on the currency. Investors can use a variety of other strategies (including *spreads*, which entail buying a call and a put or selling a call and a put) to speculate on the rise and fall of exchange rates.

Hedge Strategies

The need to hedge currency exchange is a major reason for the existence of options on currencies. Companies that do business with firms overseas make commitments to spend or receive a given amount of foreign currency weeks or months in the future. Unfortunately, they cannot know precisely what the exchange value of that currency will be. Therefore, when they purchase or sell foreign money on the spot market (the market where commodities are sold for cash and delivered immediately), they may take a beating if its value in U.S. dollars changes. Options on foreign currency provide a way to lessen that risk.

■ SUMMARY

The number and types of available commodities, futures and options have grown as potential areas of profit have been identified. This variety has been made possible to a large extent by the freedom to trade these products. The trading markets have grown as well to accommodate the vast number of products and transactions. The securities and futures markets today are global, computerized and in operation around the clock.

Leveraged investment vehicles, such as stock options and futures, offer speculators the opportunity for returns that are relatively large compared with the amount of money they have committed. Speculators can benefit substantially from a small change in the value of a contract. Under adverse conditions, however, such leverage can lead to losses in excess of the money invested.

■ CHAPTER 11 QUESTIONS FOR REVIEW

1. A call is in-the-money when the market price of the underlying stock is

   A. above the strike price

   B. equal to the strike price

   C. below the strike price

   D. equal to the strike price plus or minus the premium

2. Which of the following issues a listed option?

   A. NYSE Composite Index

   B. Options Clearing Corporation

   C. Over-the-counter market

   D. Major Market Index

3. When an investor goes long, he or she

   A. uses borrowed money to finance the purchase of a commodities contract
   B. sells securities, options or futures contracts
   C. buys securities, options or futures contracts
   D. gives the holder of the option the right to exchange it for another security

4. A buyer of a call has the right to buy the underlying shares of a security at a set price called the

   A. premium
   B. time value
   C. ex-rights
   D. exercise price

5. An important economic benefit of commodity futures trading is

   A. speculating
   B. hedging
   C. fungibility
   D. liquidity

12

Evaluation and Management of Financial Products

P revious chapters covered broad categories of financial products. Each investment was described and evaluated using objective criteria based on current facts, market conditions and product offerings. The fundamental methods by which an investor obtains return on investments are important, as is the exposure to various forms of federal, state and local tax. It is the return net of all taxes that contributes to disposable wealth, either for one's own consumption, heirs or charities. It is a basic hypothesis of these chapters that almost nobody consciously contributes more than the minimum required to the government.

In this concluding chapter, we step back from the examination of individual financial products and take a look at some of the factors that go into developing an overall investment plan. We'll focus on how an individual's personal investment goals will affect his or her investment choices and overall investment plan.

■ ■ ■ ■ ■

■ INVESTMENT INFORMATION

Internet resources, books in bookstores, financial pages in local newspapers, programs on television and a number of other sources provide advice on how individuals can accumulate wealth. Yet with all this information, many people seem to have a great deal of difficulty obtaining positive results. People save less in this country than most other developed countries. The average family is burdened with debt. As costs of living rise, most individuals lack the time or inclination to devise financial plans and strategies. For many years, rising tax burdens have continued to erode personal wealth. Too many individuals reach retirement with equity in a home, some cash values in life insurance, a small company pension, a savings account that equals a year's salary or less, government benefits and little else.

The average individual customarily lacks the time to develop a financial plan and strategy as well as to manage available resources. Reading a few articles on investments or financial planning doesn't produce positive results. Before a plan or strategy can be implemented, the work gets heavy at the office, the children come home to visit, the tax filing deadline comes around again or a thousand other demands steal the time that is needed. If a strategy is implemented, results can be affected adversely by the rapid changes that take place in today's environment.

The Role of the Financial Planner

Effective financial planners keep themselves up to date. They are aware of recent changes and pending changes. They read magazines and newspapers and are in constant touch with tax, legal and investment services. They are individuals who keep abreast of events and conditions, both past, current and emerging, that affect their clients' financial resources. A good financial planner keeps clients from wandering off the plan. It takes discipline, and some psychological "hand-holding" to keep a client from selling stocks that have fallen to new market lows. It also takes "statesmanship" to tell the founder of a business that the best thing would be to sell the business. The best strategies often run counter to prevailing market logic.

The financial planner must avoid the trap that many salespersons fall into. There is not a single "right" answer for every investor. Financial planning, to reach its ultimate form, must be *individual oriented*. A family unit is a unique combination of personalities, of moral and ethical viewpoints and, to introduce the first major consideration, personal objectives.

The greatest skills a financial planner should develop are the abilities to understand people and how to communicate. Communication is complicated by the fact that people are complex and often don't want to reveal attitudes, values and characteristics they feel are personal. People are threatened when someone else knows too much about them. Money matters are very personal.

Disclosure and Suitability

An individual's lack of understanding of precisely what benefits and risks an investment entails is usually the result of poor communication. Effective communication will help a financial planner gain the trust and the cooperation necessary to obtain an accurate financial and emotional profile. Financial planners should communicate to their clients that an accurate suitability determination can be accomplished only by evaluating both the client's suitability for an investment and the investment's suitability for the customer.

A suitable investment recommendation matches a client's financial resources and investment objectives with an appropriate product. To makes such recommendations, financial planners must obtain at least the following information about a client:

- financial condition (balance sheet);

- tax status;

- investment objectives;

- risk tolerance; and

- any other information, both financial and nonfinancial needed to make a suitable investment recommendation.

In turn, a financial planner must disclose all material facts about a product. A material fact is one that a person would reasonably require to make an informed investment decision. For example, material facts about a mutual fund include, but are not limited to, its investment objective, portfolio contents, expense ratio, sales charges, past performance, hedging strategies, volatility and risks compared to other investments. The cost of making an investment is a material fact that must be disclosed.

Special consideration must be given to product suitability when a customer wants to invest in products that are speculative, complex or have exposure to significant loss, such as penny stocks, collateralized mortgage obligations or options. In contrast, mutual funds are suitable for a broad range of customers, but fund and customer objectives must be carefully matched.

Financial planners must have a thorough knowledge and understanding of the products they sell. Attempting to sell a product without adequate knowledge and training is unethical because a financial planner is responsible for determining whether the product will meet the customer's investment objectives. Understanding how investments work will help the planner determine that fit and also will help the planner compare the security being recommended to alternative products. Skill and competence are prerequisites to recommending investments.

Financial planners must offer clients an honest and fair explanation of the risks and reward potential of recommended investments. Customer trust must be earned, nurtured and constantly reinforced. The financial planner who remembers this basic rule is the planner who communicates to a client the reason a particular investment is being recommended and how it will serve the client's need. Clients who understand what a particular investment will do for them are more likely to invest, more likely to be satisfied with their investments and more likely to maintain their accounts in good standing.

Each investor is different, with priorities and expectations unique to his or her particular situation. A well-designed investment recommendation begins by helping the customer understand the unique characteristics of the products and how they can be used to suit the customer's personal situation. Preparing and explaining the customer's investor profile is part of the education process, as is making sure the client understands the nature of each type of investment. Though each investor's specific objectives are unique, it is helpful to review some that are common.

■ CREATING AN INVESTMENT PORTFOLIO

As we have seen throughout this text, investment vehicles can be combined to create a portfolio, a collection of investment vehicles assembled to meet a common investment goal. The key to wise investing is to establish a well-balanced portfolio that contains a number and variety of investments selected to meet a particular investor's objectives. For example, a retirement portfolio for the income oriented, conservative investor might contain the following mix: cash and cash equivalents (15 percent), domestic bonds (44 percent), international bonds (10 percent), domestic stock (24 percent) and international stock (7 percent).

As noted, a diversified portfolio should include *income-oriented* investments, such as government and high-quality corporate bonds, and *growth-oriented* investments, such as stocks. Before they select any financial products, however, investors should take into account a number of personal factors. These factors include personal objectives and investment goals, the degree of risk an investor is willing to assume and the amount of money an investor can put into a portfolio. Let's look at each of these factors in more detail.

■ PERSONAL NEEDS AND OBJECTIVES

Earning a return on an investment is not the only need that people satisfy by investing. Many people gain a sense of security from owning certificates of deposit or bonds. Others derive pleasure from owning certain investments such as stamps or coins. Still others gain status from owning expensive assets such as vacation homes or sports cars.

Many experts feel that *need satisfaction* is important in identifying the individual's key objectives. Psychologists tell us that the human first satisfies *physical needs*. The first priority is to generate sufficient funds to provide "necessities" for one's family. After the physical needs of food, clothing and shelter are acquired in sufficient quantities, higher level needs—love, security and status—are approached. Although there is a tendency to approach needs in the sequence covered, this isn't completely true. One individual may need a great deal of safety before he or she tries to find love or friendship. Another may attempt to satisfy "higher order" needs while lower level needs are satisfied only partly or are ignored completely. Some individuals never may realize that higher level needs exist because their efforts are directed almost entirely toward satisfying basic physical and security needs.

The pursuit of personal objectives generally requires money (or time away from financially rewarding work). These goals may be for oneself, members of one's family, a business, a favorite charity or virtually any other person or organization of interest to him or her. Such goals also may vary in countless other ways:

1. Goals may be large or small.

2. They may call for specific amounts or indefinite amounts.

3. Goals may be achieved immediately, on a specific future date, at any future time on demand, at the death of the investor or of someone in whom he or she is interested financially or at some indefinite time in the future.

4. Goals may call for cash in a lump sum or in installments. The installments may be periodic or irregular (as on demand) or of equal or variable amounts. They may continue for a specific period (including for life) or for an indefinite period.

The individual's needs are, as we've covered, personal. Moreover, goals may vary in degree of importance to the investor—from absolute "musts" down to desirable "luxuries." For our purposes, an investor's "musts" are his or her *basic objectives*, and all others are his or her *collateral objectives*. It is, however, helpful for the potential investor to list and prioritize, by degree of importance, his or her objectives. Even though certain needs currently are being satisfied, these also should be covered by the plan (so they can continue to be satisfied). Priority should be given to those basic needs and objectives that would yield the greatest satisfaction. Then, after these have been satisfied, his or her collateral objectives can be addressed.

Social Objectives vs. Personal Greed

If a client's objective is to spend a large proportion of personal wealth on vices, that is a prerogative that generally must be accepted as a given. There need not be an inherent conflict between personal "greed" and social objectives. By investing in special-use property for personal financial gain, the investor merely is responding to tax incentives. These tax incentives, if adverse to the public interest, should be repealed. That type of judgment is not the responsibility of the individual investor; rather it must be addressed by those passing the laws and by the voters.

Projection of Time/Needs

The nearer in time an objective or need is, the more stress it causes. *Procrastination* is the tendency of people to spend money today and to ignore the less immediate (but no less important) needs of the future. A financial plan, to be effective, must recognize future objectives as well as current objectives. Just because it is hard to quantify these distant goals is no reason to ignore them. These include the objectives relating to retirement and death.

Retirement

Retirement is an event most young people hardly consider. By middle age most view retirement as a welcome future opportunity to do what one enjoys, without time constraints. By the time of actual retirement, however, the individual may have deep emotional fears about leaving the security of employment, especially if earlier planning failed and retirement funds are insufficient.

The investor must decide *whether retirement is desired*. If it is not, can the individual physically and mentally work until death? Is a hobby interest able to generate some income? If the individual does want to retire, when? How much additional income is needed, after reduced living expenses, lower taxes, the employer-sponsored pension benefits and Social Security are considered? Though this course is not a retirement planning course, the principles outlined should provide the basis for integrating the retirement plan into the total financial plan.

Death

Death is the conclusion of one's personal financial plan. This event will happen with certainty but may be sooner or later than expected. For example, the individual might die a short time before retirement benefits begin. Death is really not a separate event to be planned for but a *contingency* that must be taken into account in one's overall plans. Death contingencies are those that must be met at the time of death or sometimes thereafter. Some of these needs will be created by death itself (funeral expenses, hospital costs, etc.). Others will arise or continue to exist because someone else lives on (mortgage, college education, etc.).

A major consideration, of course, is that death generally ends the building of an estate—and no one knows how much estate-building time exists before death will come. Whenever it comes, the estate that is already accumulated generally is all there will be to satisfy the death objectives. Whether that estate is adequate is often a moot question.

Investment Goals

Investment goals direct and shape the investment portfolio. As explained, the individual first generalizes about objectives. This is necessary to set the perspective for the planning process. Second, the financial planner jointly discusses the future with the client, in a personal application of general economic, political, tax and social assumptions. This is not an easy task. Just as the framing of a house is far more important than the final application of paint, setting financial strategies is the most important step in achieving a successful financial plans.

Investment goals might include the accumulation of funds for a new home, to provide income during retirement years, to build an estate or simply to speculate. The client will need to address objectives in four critical areas including the following:

1. family, heirs, charity and obligations to others;

2. personal retirement and old age;

3. business commitments and ownership; and

4. death.

Naturally, investors' goals differ considerably, which means a portfolio appropriate for one person probably is not appropriate for another.

It is impossible to measure objectives in static, isolated terms. When the planner asks the individual to outline financial objectives, it is well to remember that the response, in general, is based on past and present conditions. These may or may not provide a solid fundamental basis for the establishment of future objectives in light of anticipated change. The selection of specific financial resource strategies and even the valuation of existing assets to some extent are dependent on the individual's perception of future conditions. As covered, the current market value attempts to *discount* future events by anticipating them and adjusting prices accordingly. The more uncertainty that is built into any forecast and the higher the opportunity costs, the more severe will be this rate of discount. After establishing general objectives, the individual should measure future possible influences as they affect these objectives.

■ DEGREE OF RISK

Once an individual's needs and objectives have been addressed, the next factor he or she must consider is his or her attitude toward risk. As we've learned, a person's attitude toward risk will shape his or her investment choices. By nature, some people are *risk averters*; they are very uncomfortable in risky situations and seek to avoid them whenever possible, or at least expect adequate compensation for undertaking any risk. Others are *risk seekers* who also expect additional return for undertaking additional risk; however, they do not demand as much return as risk averters. Therefore they probably will find more risk acceptable than risk averters would. Most people lie somewhere between the two extremes; they are willing to take some risk at some time to gain higher returns.

Basically, the various sources of risk can be divided into two groups: (1) those associated with the changing conditions of the overall economy and (2) those related to the changing conditions of the issuers of the investment product or security. Almost every investment's possible range of returns is influenced by changes in economic conditions. Many are subject to inflation risk, business cycle risk and interest rate risk. Other investments are particularly subject to management risk, business risk and financial risk—even in very good economic times, some companies go bankrupt.

Investors are often cautioned not to assume more risk than they feel comfortable taking on. The investor must determine how much return he or she should realistically expect to receive for undertaking a certain amount of risk. At the same time, they should understand that to reap larger rewards, they have to take larger risks. That is the *risk/return trade-off*. Investors have to find the comfortable balance of security and risk that works for them.

Investors can achieve this balance by building their investment portfolio in a pyramid fashion, starting with conservative and safe investments at the bottom and then gradually building up, accepting slightly more risk at each level. At the top of the pyramid, investors may have an investment in an oil well or diamonds, but the amount of money they have committed to such high-risk ventures will be small compared to the rest of the portfolio.

To a certain extent, all investment programs are based on the investor's goals and attitude toward risk. If they want to have considerable liquidity, investors should consider Treasury bills or a money market account; if the priority is inflation protection, they may be drawn to stock, real estate or gold; if steady growth over time is important (and they don't expect inflation), they might select common stocks; and, if investors want maximum capital appreciation quickly, they tend to venture into options, aggressive stocks or even futures contracts. In most cases, investors will have several priorities at one time so they will hold a portfolio of several financial products that meet their various investment goals.

■ RISK-REDUCTION STRATEGIES

A number of strategies can help minimize the risks that are inherent in every type of financial product and investment. Of course, no strategy can completely eliminate investment risk from any financial product, but employing the techniques reviewed here will at least improve the odds of long-term financial success. Two of the most common investment risk-reduction strategies used today are diversification and asset allocation.

Diversification

We've all heard the common wisdom advising against putting all our eggs in one basket. That's the idea behind asset diversification. Diversification adds an element of safety to any investment plan by blending investments with different risk characteristics in a way that minimizes the impact of any one risk on the total investment program.

The client might, for example, add a money-market fund to his investment portfolio to balance the market risk posed by his aggressive growth mutual funds, or he might include a fixed-interest account among the stock fund subaccounts of his variable life insurance policy. In either example, a drop in stock prices (market risk) will affect only a portion of the client's investments; the fixed interest accounts, though more sensitive to inflation risk, offer protection against market risk. This long-standing financial strategy can't prevent exposure to investment risk, but it can reduce its impact.

Financial planners like to tell the story of a client who, when asked if his assets were diversified, replied that they certainly were—they were spread among a dozen CDs in five branch locations of his favorite bank. This story is told to illustrate the misconception some people have about the meaning of the term "asset diversification." Though the client may have had a dozen different accounts, each was exposed to virtually the same investment risk. True asset diversification requires investments to be spread among assets that pose different types of investment risk. This client might have achieved a greater sense of diversification had he spread the CDs among several banks, which would have reduced his total exposure to credit risk.

It's worth noting that mutual funds and variable insurance contract subaccounts promote diversification by their very nature. By investing in a variety of different stocks, bonds and so forth, each fund reduces its overall market and capital risk exposure. By the same token, diversification is often the natural consequence of mixing different types of investments into a personal financial portfolio. The combination of different financial products, each with its own inherent form of risk, works to soften the overall portfolio's exposure to any one type of risk.

Vertical and Horizontal Diversification

Diversification can be measured on two scales: vertical and horizontal. Vertical diversification exists when assets are selected for their ability to cover different investment horizons. Horizontal diversification, on the other hand, is achieved through the combination of financial products bearing different risk characteristics, regardless of their intended duration. Vertical diversification is usually accomplished through planning; horizontal diversification may be accomplished through strategic planning, but may also be the consequence of random selections.

Vertical Diversification.   Short-term goals are most commonly met with investments that are quite different from those used to reach long-term goals. A passbook savings account may be ideal for certain goals that are a year or two away, but its exposure to inflation risk makes it unsuitable for long-term goals. Meanwhile, an aggressive growth stock mutual fund may be ideally suited for long-term goals, but would be grossly ill-advised for short-term or emergency fund needs. This vertical diversification occurs naturally by choosing investments that are geared to different time frames.

Horizontal Diversification.   For added security, clients should also diversify horizontally throughout their investment horizons. Whether for short-, medium- or long-term goals, diverting money into at least two different types of assets characterized by different forms of risk ensures an added measure of safety.

Short-term needs might be covered with a checking account (highest inflation risk in return for almost perfect liquidity), a passbook savings account (less inflation rate risk, good liquidity), CDs (higher interest than savings accounts, but less liquidity) and a money-market account. Permanent life insurance (perhaps a variable life insurance policy) is a great way to provide a shield of financial protection while accumulating a cash value (tax deferred, no less) to support long-term goals. Mutual funds, despite their market risk, offer today's average investor the greatest chance to realize above-average returns and combat inflation risk to meet medium- to long-term objectives.

Asset Allocation

Closely related to diversification is asset allocation. While diversification is a general process intended to minimize exposure to investment risk, asset allocation is a strategy that seeks to maximize investment earnings while keeping exposure to investment risk at an acceptable minimum. One is the natural byproduct of the other; diversification occurs naturally through asset allocation.

Asset allocation is the strategy of directing or spreading funds into various investment or asset categories. Doing so helps minimize risk and maximize returns so that, overall, one's portfolio is able to weather all kinds of economic changes. Studies have shown that how investment dollars are spread is far more important to portfolio performance than the selection of individual securities or the timing of their purchase. And this remains true no matter what stage of life an individual might be in. Asset allocation is as critical for those who are already retired as it is for those who are trying to save for retirement.

Asset allocation has three primary goals: to preserve capital, to protect purchasing power and to increase the overall return of one's portfolio. The extent to which one goal takes priority over another or otherwise dominates the asset allocation model depends a great deal on the individual's investment horizon and risk tolerance. Someone who is retired may feel that protecting his or her purchasing power is the number one priority while a younger individual who has many years before retirement would want to focus on increasing his or her return. Therefore, a necessary component of asset allocation requires a bit of client profiling in relation to his or her financial objectives. For example:

- Individuals with long investment horizons seeking to accumulate money for retirement normally choose investments for their *growth* potential.

- Individuals who are already retired want to generate additional current *income* from their assets.

- Individuals who are nearing or at retirement want to *preserve* the capital or assets they've acquired. They seek safety for their savings and tend to navigate toward insured or guaranteed products, such as fixed annuities, money market accounts and CDs.

If asked to define an investment category, most people would not position their goals completely in any one area; most, in fact, would define them as mixed. Just because an individual might have a number of years to retirement does not mean he or she would want to invest all assets into growth vehicles; he or she would probably also desire some safe investments that preserve principal. By the same token, a person who has retired should probably not convert all of his or her growth assets into safe investments. This is where an assessment of the individual's risk tolerance comes into play. What kind of an investor is he or she? Aggressive? Moderate? Conservative? What kind of balance is he or she seeking with regard to risk and return? For these reasons, any asset allocation model must be viewed as a guide, not a foolproof formula. In addition, since savings and investment objectives change over time, as do investment horizons, asset allocations must be reviewed periodically.

Asset Classes

Investment products can be categorized in a number of ways. For purposes of our discussion and because we will present only a very simple asset allocation model, we will use three classes: cash and cash equivalents, stocks and fixed income. Cash and cash equivalents consist of savings and checking accounts, money-market accounts, money-market funds, CDs and T-bills. These investments are all positioned at the base of the risk pyramid and, from a market risk perspective, they are extremely safe investments. They are also characterized by fairly low rates of return.

Stocks include stocks issued by corporations and equity mutual funds. Options for stock investments are many and varied and can be broken down into various classes such as income stocks, growth stocks and aggressive growth stocks. Individually, stocks are subject to various forms and degrees of risk; however, as a whole, they are considered one of the best hedges against inflation.

Fixed income options include bonds, which pay a fixed rate of interest over a specified period of time. Examples include long-term Treasury bonds, municipal bonds, corporate bonds, mortgage-backed securities and mutual funds that invest primarily in bonds.

By allocating assets among different asset classes, individuals can improve their overall return and protect their portfolios from a market downturn in any one asset group. This is because some securities respond well in certain economic climates while others do better under opposite conditions. For example, during periods of expansion or low inflation, stocks tend to perform well. During recessionary periods, fixed income securities and cash equivalents are good performers.

Illustration 12.1 shows a very simple asset allocation model, utilizing the three asset classes defined above, and accounting for differing financial goals and risk thresholds under various economic conditions. This simple model represents a starting point from which a specific allocation mix for a given individual can be developed. Used as a guide, it can help planners review with their clients how their assets are allocated and whether this allocation best fits their specific goals and risk thresholds.

ILL. 12.1 ■ *Sample Asset Allocation Model*

	Cash/Cash Equivalent	Stocks	Fixed Income
Financial Goal			
Growth-oriented individual	20%	60%	20%
Income-oriented individual	20%	30%	50%
Mixed	20%	40%	40%
Risk Threshold			
Aggressive investor	−5%	+10%	−5%
Moderate investor		+5%	−5%
Conservative investor	+5%	−10%	+5%
Market Condition			
High inflation	+10%	−10%	−10%
Modest inflation growth		+5%	−5%
Deflation/recession		−10%	+10%
Bull market	−5%	+10%	−5%
Bear market	+10%	−10%	−5%

STEP 1: Ascertain the client's financial or retirement goals

Is the customer growth-oriented, income-oriented, or both? The following suggest asset mixes for each:

Growth-oriented individual	20%	60%	20%
Income-oriented individual	20%	30%	50%
Mixed	20%	40%	40%

STEP 2: Evaluate the client's risk threshold

Alter the asset mix to suit the client's risk threshold. Those willing to take more risks or who have a number of years to save for retirement may want to increase their holdings in stocks, while more conservative clients may want to increase their holdings in cash or other safe money vehicles or bonds. Using the example of a growth-oriented individual who is a moderate risk-taker, the allocation might be adjusted as follows:

Growth-oriented	20%	60%	20%
Moderate risk-taker	___	+5%	−5%
Adjusted allocation	20%	65%	15%

STEP 3: Determine market conditions

What kind of economic environment is expected for, say, the next year or so? Alter the percentage in the asset groups to reflect any trends. For example, if it is expected to be a period of modest inflation, modest growth and a bull market, the asset mix could be adjusted to take advantage of these positive trends:

Growth-oriented	20%	60%	20%
Moderate risk-taker		+5%	−5%
Modest inflation		+5%	−5%
Bull market	−5%	+10%	−5%
Adjusted allocation	15%	80%	5%

Further adjustments can be made. In fact, it is a good idea to run through various scenarios to see the effects on an asset mix. Advocates of asset allocation recommend that all investors, regardless of their personal investment goals or the current economic scenario, maintain at least 5 percent and no more than 80 percent of their investments in each of the three primary asset groups.

By allocating assets, by mixing savings and investment options, an individual's overall return is improved and the portfolio has some measure of protection when the market is negative for any one asset group. Furthermore, asset allocation creates an integrated, overall savings and investment plan. This plan then becomes the primary focus for periodic review and evaluation, not the individual savings or investment products. As financial goals and horizons change, an individual's asset allocation model should be adjusted.

■ AMOUNT OF MONEY INVESTED

Investors must decide how much money to invest in various financial products. Like objectives, this is a personal decision. Some may wish to invest some amounts on a regular basis; others will invest all of their accumulated wealth at once. Generally speaking, the amount of money that is invested (and how it is invested) often depends on a person's income, number and type of dependents and the investor's age.

Amount and Stability of Income

Generally, the amount of a person's income and accumulated wealth sets the upper limit on how much can be invested. It makes sense to assume that the owner of a successful professional football team might have more money to invest, say, in the stock market than would one of the ticket sellers at the team's stadium.

In addition to size of income, permanence of income is another important investment factor. For example, assume the owner of the football team has made his daughter a vice-president of the corporation. If she will substantially increase her income when she inherits the team in 10 years, it is likely that she can afford to invest a substantial portion of her current income.

Dependents

Investors can arrange their investment programs to take into account the needs of dependents. The financial needs of dependents will change over time and will be determined to a great extent on the degree of their dependency. For example, the amount of money needed to finance a child's college education may be quite different from the amount needed to pay hospital bills and nursing home fees for elderly parents.

Age-Based Investing

What makes sense for beginning investors in their 20s and 30s can be quite different from what is best for people in their 40s, 50s and 60s. The types of financial products these groups invest in often change as they age.

The 20s and 30s

Realistically, this is often a time for spending, not saving. College loans come due and must be paid, a home is usually purchased and furnished and a family is started. Regardless of all these expenses, it is important for people to remember that saving is not a choice, it's a necessity. Many financial planners recommend that people save at least 10 percent of their gross income. They also recommend the creation of an emergency reserve of three to six months' living expenses. The fund should be liquid—money market funds or short-term bond funds (for slightly higher yields). To protect their newly acquired assets, this group also needs life, medical, disability, property and casualty insurance.

As explained in Chapter 2, after they have created a sound financial base, investors are usually prepared to move up the investment pyramid. Most financial advisers

---

ILL. 12.2 ■ *Age-Based Investing*

Financial planners agree that the types of funds individuals invest in should change as they age. Once an emergency fund and *foundation of life insurance* have been established, investors can select financial products based on their investment goals.

Age Group: 20s and 30s

Goals: Establishing a savings plan; saving for a home.

Advisers recommend that investors begin with an emergency fund plus a liquid fund—money market funds or short-term bond funds. People who have a few years before they retire may use some of their savings to invest in small company, growth or income stock funds.

Age Group: 40s and 50s

Goals: Financing retirement; paying for children's education and parents' care.

This "sandwich generation" is in its peak earning years. Advisers suggest that money needed in the near future should be placed in investments with little volatility, such as short-term bond funds. Many investors also choose mutual funds or seek tax-deferred vehicles.

Age Group: 60 and Older

Goals: Maintaining current lifestyle while protecting principal.

These investors must balance three conflicting objectives: income, growth and low volatility. Many advisers recommend eliminating aggressive growth stocks and replacing them with balanced and equity-income funds.

---

agree that investment risk is influenced by the passage of time. Because the future cannot be determined, the further an investment's projections are extended, the more likely they are to be incorrect. This implies greater variation in returns with long-term, rather than short-term, investments.

On the other hand, investors must also consider whether they are more or less likely to achieve an investment goal by holding an asset for a longer or shorter period of time. The answer depends on the type of financial product held. For example, assume that common stock has averaged a yearly return of 10 percent for the past 50 years. If the investor selects an extremely risky common stock in the hope of earning more than that average return, he or she should expect to hold the stock for a number of years.

Individuals who have only three to five years before they intend to use their savings should consider stock mutual funds. The mutual funds selected will depend on the amount of risk with which the investor feels comfortable. Inflation, not market volatility, is the biggest risk for investments at this time of a person's life. Time smooths out interim fluctuations in the stock market. If money is not needed for more than five years, at least part of it should go into *qualified retirement plans* because of tax deductions and deferrals.

As they begin to accumulate more money to invest, this group can begin diversifying—that is, splitting investments among various assets or investing styles, with the idea that if one style is out of favor, the others may earn gains to offset the losses. Generally, stock and mutual fund portfolios should be split among *growth* securities with future earnings growth and *income* securities that will generate current income. Today, it may be wise to add 10 percent to 20 percent in funds that invest abroad.

The 40s and 50s

These people are often called the *sandwich generation*, squeezed by the competing needs to finance their own retirement, pay for their children's education and maybe support their elderly parents. For emergencies, they should keep three months of living expenses on hand—or more, if they lack disability insurance and secure employment. Money needed in the near future for tuition payments or a child's wedding should be put in investments with little volatility, such as short-term bond funds.

Because the 40s and 50s are peak earning years, investing for retirement is paramount and finding a tax-free or tax-deferred vehicle is important. As much as possible should be placed into qualified retirement plans, such as a 401(k). In addition, those who have delayed investing should consider a mutual fund. A first mutual fund purchase should be a solid balanced fund, mixing growth and income.

Diversification is important for those who have built a core investment portfolio. As people get older, it becomes more important not to lose money in down markets. Therefore, to reduce risk while maintaining capital growth, many investors split domestic equity holdings between stock funds that focus on growth or income. Most advisers recommend that investment in stocks be reduced to 60 or 65 percent at this point in life, unless someone has little money set aside. Then equity exposure might go as high as 70 percent.

The 60s and Beyond

After investing for growth in their 20s and 30s, then looking to grow and protect capital in their middle years, 60s-plus investors on the verge of retiring or already there should structure their fund holdings to provide cash flow and preserve wealth. After all, at age 70 people still have a substantial life expectancy.

Retirees must balance three conflicting objectives: income, growth and low volatility. They need income, probably in the form of equity holdings, to cover expenses and inflation. As a rule of thumb, to determine the percentage that investors should have in equities as they age, subtract their ages from 100. For example, a 70-year-old would keep 30 percent of his or her portfolio in stocks, but an 80-year-old person would keep only 20 percent in stocks.

The most common mistake many retirees make today is to invest too conservatively. Investing in CDs and bonds won't protect against purchasing-power erosion. Therefore, many advisors suggest gradually shifting into bonds. Although many people believe they should invest only in municipal bonds, they should be aware that loading up too heavily on tax-free investments could backfire if they collect

Social Security. Half of their Social Security payments becomes taxable when provisional income, which includes tax-exempt income, exceeds $32,000 for couples or $25,000 for single taxpayers. Beginning in 1994, up to 85 percent of payments will be taxed for couples earning more than $44,000 and singles earning more than $34,000 in provisional income.

Managing a Portfolio

Once investors have selected suitable investments that match their investment needs, goals and risk preferences, they cannot just sit back and relax. Investments need to be "managed" for a number of important reasons. Changes in interest rates and other internal and external factors present new situations that require action. As investors get older, for example, they develop different needs and are likely to reduce their tolerance for risk. Therefore, an investor needs to understand *portfolio management* to combine the various types of investment vehicles in a manner consistent with his or her overall disposition toward risk and return.

■ PROJECTION OF FINANCIAL OBJECTIVES

To plan adequately for the future, all financial obligations and cash accumulations, as well as objectives, should be mapped out year-by-year into the future. The year-ahead budget may be very specific. It is advised, however, that longer-term projections of either assets or budget objectives be flexible. This reflects the constant "surprises" emerging in a dynamic or changing society. It also reflects the changing objectives of the individual and family.

It is helpful to begin by listing objectives by when, chronologically, they will occur and approximately how much they will cost in today's dollars. This gives the client a written blueprint that quantifies what lies ahead. Lifetime objectives can be mapped out by when they will need to be funded. Death and disability are contingencies that cannot be mapped out conveniently. Thus, post-retirement death needs are separated. The pre-retirement contingency is taken care of by a family needs analysis, taking into account moral obligations, debts, final expenses including taxes, accumulated savings and a number of related factors.

Meeting Financial Objectives

Financial objectives, if they are to be realized, must be paid for. There are actually three methods used to meet financial objectives.

1. *Cash.* This pay-as-you-go method assumes the financial objectives fit within the capability of some future budget.

2. *Credit.* When it turns out that it is inconvenient, impractical or impossible to purchase something for cash, credit often is used to obtain the goods or services desired. Proper use of credit is a major financial planning topic, about which large portions of books, numerous magazine and newspaper articles and lectures have covered. Indeed, credit is the basis by which the U.S. money supply expands and contracts and most real estate is purchased.

3. *Pre-funding.* A future purchase, as covered, often can be anticipated and funded in advance, either by setting aside one lump sum or by periodic payments into one or more savings vehicles. It is therefore helpful to translate the series of future quantified objectives into *present value.*

Inflation and Taxes

To ignore inflation in the financial blueprint assumes that prices, salary and objectives will be the same tomorrow as today. History provides reasons to believe this will not be so. Likewise, to ignore the impact of taxes assumes that all investment earnings and returns will inure entirely and fully to the investor. The Internal Revenue Code is proof that this will not be so. Thus, the plan—the mapping out of future accumulations and financial objectives—must grapple with both issues.

To reflect the reality of inflation, assets and resources should be projected to increase at rates indicative of dollar price changes. For example, if housing has been increasing at an annual rate of 6 percent—a rate reflecting both a real increase in value and a general rise in housing costs due to inflation—that rate could be used to project the value of one's home in the future. Current or anticipated interest rates should be applied to savings and investments to project their future value. Salary projections should reflect future raises. Then, future objectives should likewise be "inflated" by an assumed cost-of-living fact. For example, if a future objective is funding a child's college education, it is necessary to project what that cost will be when the child turns 18.

Once this is done, the next step is to negate or "wring out" the inflation assumption built into financial assets, returns and wages and to reduce interest rates and returns to *net real rate* by factoring out the loss to income tax during accumulation. This should be done because both inflation and taxes have the effect of reducing returns and purchasing power and a competent investment plan should recognize the *real* increase in purchasing power created by interest or capital gain. Let's look at an example.

Say a $100,000 investment asset earns 8 percent (or $8,000) over the course of one year. If the investor is in a 31 percent tax bracket, only 69 percent of that return (or $5,520) is available. If prices increase 4 percent, the $100,000 effectively has "lost" $4,000 because the $105,520 now must buy $104,000 worth of goods and services to stay equal. The net *real* rate of increase, after taxes and after inflation, is only 1.52 percent (or $1,520). (To further refine this, the $105,520 could be reduced by the tax on the gain, if a sale is projected.)

Basically speaking, this approach adjusts current yield or returns to reflect real rates of increase. This formula is:

$$[\text{Current yield rate} \times (1.00 - \text{Tax on yield})] - \frac{\text{Projected inflation}}{\text{rate over period}} = \frac{\text{Net}}{\text{real rate}}$$

or

$$[.08 \times (1.00 - .31)] - .04 = [.08 \times .69] - .04 = 1.52$$

ILL. 12.3 ■ *Effect of Inflation*

Inflation works like a hybrid. It reduces purchasing power like a tax. It also compounds like interest. To illustrate this point, look at the following example.

- At 0 percent annual inflation rate, prices will be 1 times current levels in 10 years.
- At 4 percent annual inflation rate, prices will be 1.48 times current levels in 10 years.
- At 8 percent annual inflation rate, prices will be 2.15 times current levels in 10 years.
- At 16 percent annual inflation rate, prices will be 4.41 times current levels in 10 years.

The net real rate of 1.52 percent is the expected rate of increase in real terms. Interest earned over that rate is assumed to result from inflation. Adjusting projections for inflation in this manner allows the individual to discuss financial objectives in terms of current dollars. Though periodic adjustments to the plan will be necessary to maintain this relationship, potential "surprises" due to inflation are not as likely. It also emphasizes the need to realize some positive real net rate of return on one's investments.

The disadvantage of this approach is that it ignores the likelihood that financial objectives may increase at varying rates for adjustments to rising prices. Under this method, all financial objectives are discounted to present value by only a single rate, which has been adjusted to remove a single, broad-based rate of inflation. On the other hand, it has the advantage of *equalizing* projected assets and objectives. Any viable plan must avoid basing projected assets on rates containing an inflation factor while measuring needs and objectives in current dollars.

Shortage (Excess)

Once the present value of all future objectives has been derived, it can be compared with current accumulated investments and savings. This brings the two values to an equal position in time—now. The projected objectives already may include a funding assumption. For example, if an objective is to accumulate a projected IRA benefit, which already is budgeted, this should be noted.

When the present value of future objectives exceeds the individual's current financial resources, a *shortage* exists. This is usually the case because very few individuals have more wealth than they need to meet future objectives. The shortage, *if funded by a single sum*, would generate the resources to meet those objectives as they came due.

Few people can set aside the necessary amount all at once. Instead they pre-fund for their future needs. In most instances, retirement savings are funded from the present to the actual date of expected retirement. A *sinking fund payment* table can be used

ILL. 12.4 ■ *Sinking Fund Payment*

	4.00%	5.00%	6.00%	7.00%	8.00%	9.00%	Period (months)
	1.000 000	1.000 000	1.000 000	1.000 000	1.000 000	1.000 000	1
	0.499 168	0.498 960	0.498 753	0.498 545	0.498 338	0.498 132	2
	0.332 224	0.331 948	0.331 672	0.331 396	0.331 120	0.330 845	3
	0.248 753	0.248 442	0.248 132	0.247 823	0.247 513	0.247 205	4
	0.198 671	0.198 340	0.198 009	0.197 680	0.197 351	0.197 022	5
	0.165 283	0.164 938	0.164 595	0.164 252	0.163 910	0.163 568	6
	0.141 434	0.141 081	0.140 728	0.140 376	0.140 025	0.139 674	7
	0.123 548	0.123 188	0.122 828	0.122 470	0.122 112	0.121 755	8
	0.109 637	0.109 272	0.108 907	0.108 543	0.108 180	0.107 819	9
	0.098 509	0.098 139	0.097 770	0.097 402	0.097 036	0.096 671	10
	0.089 404	0.089 030	0.088 659	0.088 288	0.087 919	0.087 550	11
Year 1	0.081 816	0.081 440	0.081 066	0.080 693	0.080 321	0.079 951	12
2	0.040 091	0.039 704	0.039 320	0.038 939	0.038 560	0.038 184	24
3	0.026 190	0.025 804	0.025 421	0.025 043	0.024 669	0.024 299	36
4	0.019 245	0.018 862	0.018 485	0.018 112	0.017 746	0.017 385	48
5	0.015 083	0.014 705	0.014 332	0.013 967	0.013 609	0.013 258	60

to help you determine how much should be invested each month or each year to meet long-term goals (see Ill. 12.4). This table shows the amount to be deposited at the end of each period that grows to $1 in the future.

Let's look at an example. If an investor needs $30,000 in five years when she retires, how much must she save each month to meet her goal? Using the table in Ill. 12.4 and assuming that an investment yields a 5 percent rate of return, our investor will have to save $441.15 a month ($30,000 × 0.014705) for the next five years. However, if an investment yields 9 percent, the investor needs to save only $397.75 a month ($30,000 × 0.013258).

The result gives some measure of how much extra savings an individual should be setting aside to meet the objectives. If this amount is so large as to be unaffordable, either the financial objectives must be reduced, the funding period extended (which may delay retirement) or the inflation-adjusted net interest rate increased to enhance real return. In general, this may mean altering one's posture toward risks.

Rule of 72

Unfortunately, using tables can be confusing and time-consuming. The *Rule of 72* is a quick way to determine how long any amount of money invested at a compound interest basis will take to double. This rule is mathematical shorthand that provides a way to determine how fast an investment is growing. The calculation is simple: just divide the interest rate into 72. If the investor will be receiving 10 percent interest, for example, his or her money will double in 7.2 years ($72 \div 10 = 7.2$). The greater the interest rate, the faster money will double.

■ FORECASTING THE INVESTMENT ENVIRONMENT

Economic projections can begin with fairly simple appraisals. In general, an attempt is being made to measure the individual's financial future in relation to the broader economic and social structure. In limited space, a few examples are helpful.

1. Is salary or earning ability likely to increase? Are career objectives established?

2. Will the *normal* standard of living increase?

3. Are shortages of physical resources or labor inputs likely?

4. Are future business conditions likely to be favorable (i.e., profit margins increase and the rate of return on owners' equity expand)?

5. What demographic changes can be anticipated? Shifts in preferences?

In addition to economic projections, political projections should be made. *Political projections* are almost always a guessing game. However, it has been demonstrated that political activities are a major determinate of both long-term and short-term economic changes. For example:

1. Is the Fed expanding or contracting the money supply? Is the economy in a recession? Are interest rates rising or falling? Is the government (including state and local, plus the federal branches) operating in a deficit or surplus? Based on these items and others, what short-term inflation rate is likely?

2. When is the next major political election? What major fiscal and monetary policy changes are possible in anticipation of the election? As a result of the election? Are there major undercurrents of long-range change in voter sympathy?

3. Will major legislation change the availability of Social Security and other government provided benefits?

Change is inevitable. Those that successfully anticipate change actually can profit from negative events, economic downturns and political changes. Those investment plans that include flexibility and contingency strategies may survive reasonably intact, despite the incorrect forecasts that from time to time are inevitable.

■ COMPARING FINANCIAL PRODUCTS

Throughout this course, we've covered many financial products and, as noted, some do one job better than another. In the chapters covering specific types of products, salient features are covered that should suggest the strategies that are inherent in each resource. However, some are very similar and may be used almost interchangeably in solving objectives.

It is important to remember that the final asset arrangement of any portfolio should maximize the plan's *tax leverage*; the reduction of taxes is a key investment strategy. Since taxes reduce spendable income, the reduction in taxation improves one's position, *assuming everything else is equal*. It rarely is, however. Tax leverage, like any risk factor, usually involves trade-offs. For example, municipal bonds generally are less marketable than many corporate bonds and offer no inflation protection.

When reviewing financial products, each should be evaluated and weighed against risk and reward elements. This may be easier with some types of resources than others. For example, some elements of risk, as applied to a specific asset, may be measured quantitatively, but the majority must be reviewed subjectively.

■ FOLLOW-UP PLANNING

A family's financial plan must be *monitored*. Once a year is probably not too often; it is easy to fall back into old habit patterns. The periodic evaluation should compare the plan's test projection with results to date. If major changes in family objectives occur, the plan must be adjusted or a completely new one drawn up.

In the case of variable annuities, for example, the performance of the selected separate account should be reviewed. The death benefit must be checked against the total financial plan for compatibility and adjusted as needed. The duration of the coverage may need to be altered. A universal or variable life product is one special form of financial plan. The level of premiums must be reviewed periodically for adequacy. Internal Revenue Code limitations must be monitored on a continual basis if the death proceeds are to be sheltered from income taxation.

Investment fads are difficult to anticipate and even harder to ride out to a profit. Popularity, for example, of an industry group of common stocks, means upward momentum but potentially fast pullbacks. Unless someone very skilled monitors such investments constantly, year-to-year comparisons can be devastating. Tax law changes should be reviewed, using either the implicit or an explicit planning procedure. These affect ultimate real disposable income and the risk-balance of a portfolio of financial resources.

Balanced Plan

Some investment advisers and planners strive to develop the ultimate self-correcting, automatic, flexible financial plan. Using hedging techniques and risk offsets, they attempt to build a collection of resources that does well in recession or prosperity. This miraculous plan would have sufficient hard assets to protect it against loss of purchasing power but also would do well if deflation persisted. However, no matter how commendable, a totally self-correcting plan is impossible.

A *balanced plan* should not be confused with a *total financial plan*. The total plan is fluid and dynamic. The total financial plan envelops the special needs of the client's business. It includes integrating retirement plans as provided by government, the employer, an IRA and other sources. Action is required, for example, when the accumulation period changes to the distribution period at retirement or when lifetime assets and retirement income must be diverted to heirs, as a result of the client's death. The financial planner should be there.

A total financial plan *anticipates* future objectives and contingencies. It views the individual's and family's needs through broad cycles. The plan anticipates action steps and lays down specific strategies. Such plans are too complex and unique *to allow to continue* without future assistance and refinement throughout the year.

The financial plan and its underlying assets reflect the individual's personality. It is the family's hopes, dreams and aspirations. The planner helps the family cope with financial fears and helps put together a plan that is acceptable to their risk-bearing ability. It is an exciting, personal, *long-term process* that rewards the life insurance agent, monetarily and emotionally.

■ SUMMARY

In this concluding chapter, the very basic features of a financial plan were presented. The primary purpose of the chapters preceding this was to familiarize the reader with the various forms and types of financial products. At the outset of the course broader financial, economic, political, monetary and fiscal concepts were reviewed quickly. As much as possible, the practical implications of these areas provide the underpinnings for the evaluation of financial products.

The total financial plan evaluates products in terms of risks and costs. Although very important, the risks of loss of principal or market value are only two of a long list of risk factors. Financial *reward* (or avoidance of loss) is the opposite of risk. In general, the higher the risk, the greater the potential reward. A risk trade-off occurs where assuming more risk in one area reduces the risk level in the other. Different individuals have different *risk attitudes*.

Specific strategies must be employed to maximize the effectiveness of the financial plan as measured by real dollars in versus real purchasing power distributed. This is an ongoing, personal process of monitoring, refining and adapting the plan to reflect actual experience, family changes and external factors over time. As a financial professional, you can be of immeasurable assistance in helping your clients achieve their investment goals.

■ CHAPTER 12 QUESTIONS FOR REVIEW

1. All of the following statements about financial planners are correct EXCEPT

   A. they may be affiliated with banks, insurance companies or brokerage firms

   B. they must hold a Certified Financial Planner (CFP) designation to advertise themselves as a financial planner

   C. they must have the ability to communicate effectively with people

   D. they should monitor their clients' portfolios and suggest needed changes

2. According to the text, the conclusion of every financial plan is

   A. retirement

   B. return on investment

   C. death

   D. need satisfaction

3. The amount of money that can be used for investment is determined by the investor's age, number of dependents and

   A. income

   B. risk tolerance

   C. business commitments

   D. basic objectives

4. Using the Rule of 72, how fast will an investment of $1,000 double if it earns 8 percent annually?

   A. 3 years

   B. 6 years

   C. 9 years

   D. 12 years

5. When comparing investments, the investor should remember that, in general, the greater the risk, the

   A. smaller the potential return

   B. more expensive the investment

   C. more likely the investment is to fail

   D. greater the potential return

..... Answer Key to Chapter Review Questions

CHAPTER 1

1. B
2. C
3. D
4. A
5. C

CHAPTER 2

1. D
2. B
3. C
4. C
5. D

CHAPTER 3

1. B
2. A
3. C
4. D
5. A

CHAPTER 4

1. B
2. B
3. A
4. C
5. C

CHAPTER 5

1. D
2. C
3. B
4. A
5. A

CHAPTER 6

1. C
2. A
3. A
4. C
5. D

CHAPTER 7

1. B
2. A
3. D
4. B
5. C

CHAPTER 8

1. C
2. D
3. B
4. C
5. A

CHAPTER 9

1. A
2. D
3. C
4. C
5. B

CHAPTER 10

1. D
2. B
3. A
4. D
5. C

CHAPTER 11

1. A
2. B
3. C
4. D
5. B

CHAPTER 12

1. B
2. C
3. A
4. C
5. D